Oil, the Arab-Israel Dispute, and the Industrial World

Horizons of Crisis

Westview Special Studies on the Middle East

J. C. Hurewitz
Oil, the Arab-Israel Dispute, and the Industrial World: Horizons of Crisis
David E. Long
The Persian Gulf: An Introduction to Its Peoples, Politics, and Economics

This book is the product of a multinational project, sponsored by the Middle East Institute of Columbia University in cooperation with the World Peace Foundation (Boston), the Atlantic Institute for International Affairs (Paris), and the Asia-Pacific Association of Japan (Tokyo). It focuses on the principal unresolved issues of the energy crisis, the Arab-Israel dispute, and their tangled effects that feed back to and feed upon relations with the North Atlantic countries and Japan. Since almost all the papers were originally presented for discussion to three study groups—North American (US and Canada), Western European, and Japanese—it was possible to assess the domestic interests and pressures that inhibit and those that promote cooperation among the major nonsocialist industrial states and to illuminate the linkages between the domestic influences and the national policymaking processes. The book thus provides a uniquely balanced analysis that draws upon national, regional, and international perspectives.

Professor J. C. Hurewitz is the director of the Middle East Institute of Columbia University.

Oil, the Arab-Israel Dispute, and the Industrial World
Horizons of Crisis

edited by J. C. Hurewitz

Routledge
Taylor & Francis Group
LONDON AND NEW YORK

First published 1976 by Westview Press, Inc.

Published 2018 by Routledge
52 Vanderbilt Avenue, New York, NY 10017
2 Park Square, Milton Park, Abingdon, Oxon OX14 4RN

Routledge is an imprint of the Taylor & Francis Group, an informa business

Library of Congress Cataloging in Publication Data

Main entry under title:
Oil, the Arab-Israel Dispute, and the Industrial World: Horizons of Crisis

Project sponsored by the Middle East Institute, and others.
Bibliography: p. 314
Includes index.
1. Petroleum industry and trade—Addresses, essays, lectures.
2. Energy policy—Addresses, essays, lectures. 3. Jewish-Arab relations—Addresses, essays, lectures. 4. Near East—Foreign relations—Addresses, essays, lectures. I. Hurewitz, Jacob Coleman, 1914-.
II. Columbia University. Middle East Institute.
HD9560.6.039 338.2'7'282 76-6470

ISBN 13: 978-0-367-02082-8 (hbk)
ISBN 13: 978-0-367-17069-1 (pbk)

Contents

Preface

One of the most stubborn global problems in the last quarter of the twentieth century, a problem that affects the rich states and the poor, the industrial and the nonindustrial, is the use of energy. The management of the problem entails a great deal more than just the search for new sources of oil, the conversion of other fossil fuels, and the development of new forms of energy. It requires the framing of comprehensive policies on conservation by national governments in cooperation with international agencies, policies that will take into account the ways in which we have become locked into wasteful uses of wasting natural resources. This is particularly true of the industrial states, which are by far the largest energy consumers. In the United States alone, which accounts for one-third of the world's daily energy use, it will probably take the rest of the century to reshape the systems of transportation, the heating and cooling of buildings, and the running of industrial machinery—to mention only the major forms of energy use.

The project, of which this book is the product, was not expressly interested in these aspects of the energy crisis. The technical issues have been the concern of the US Federal Energy Administration and the Energy Research and Development Agency and their counterparts in other countries as well as the International Energy Agency, the OECD, the Common Market, oil companies, academic institutions, and individual scholars. Their work has been used as part of the evidence. The participants in this project considered, primarily, the political economy of the energy crisis.

Most of the growing attention given to the problems under review has focused on the aftermath in the Middle East of the turning point which occurred when the oil issues in the Persian Gulf and North Africa interlocked with the issues that continue to divide the Arab states and Israel. In the judgment of the project's sponsors, the oil-exporting states and their neighbors were as deeply affected by the dramatic changes in the industry after October 1973 as were the major oil-importing or industrial states. It was, therefore, decided to evaluate the causes in the Middle East and their impact on the industrial states as well as the interplay between them.

The project was a multinational one, sponsored in the United States by the Middle East Institute of Columbia University and the World Peace Foundation, in Western Europe by the Atlantic Institute for International Affairs (Paris), and in Japan by the Asia-Pacific Association of Japan (Tokyo). The Middle East, as the sponsors have defined it, embraces the oil states in the Persian Gulf and North Africa and the Arab-Israel zone lying between. In that region, the principal unresolved issues that feed back to and upon relations with the North Atlantic countries and Japan are the energy crisis, the Arab-Israel dispute, and their tangled effects.

Because of the complexity of the issues, the sponsors created study groups in North America, Western Europe, and Japan to evaluate the interaction of the domestic influences and the pertinent foreign policies and policymaking processes. The study-group procedure made it possible to inquire into the domestic interests and pressures that inhibit or frustrate and those that promote cooperation among the major noncommunist industrial states. An attempt was also made to illuminate the linkages between the domestic influences and the national policymaking processes.

The North American Study Group included participants from Canada and the United States. At the first meeting, the study group explored the domestic aspects in the United States and Canada of the Arab-Israel dispute; at the second meeting, the domestic aspects of the energy crisis; and at the third meeting, the international economic and political effects of that crisis. The two other study groups looked into comparable problems from their perspectives. To encourage movement along parallel lines, the three groups exchanged papers and summary minutes of meetings, with some overlapping participation.

Most of the papers in this book were originally prepared for meetings of the study groups and were later revised in the light of the discussion they provoked or put together on the basis of those discussions. The Western European Study Group investigated the responses to the energy crisis and the changing attitudes toward the Arab-Israel dispute on a national basis in selected countries, and the repercussions on Western European economic and military security. While these discussions yielded a great deal of useful information, there is not sufficient room in a book of this length for such detailed analysis. Instead, in chapters somewhat longer than the average, the authors concentrate on domestic trends in selected Western European countries and on related efforts at interstate coordination.

The sponsoring institutions endorse no particular judgments on the issues to which the chapters in this book are addressed. The authors are affiliated here and abroad with universities, research institutes, government agencies, and private business corporations. The stands they take are their own and cannot be said to reflect the positions of their institutional employers. Nor do these views represent any consensus among the study groups or even among the authors themselves, who may on various points contradict one another. Such integration as the book may boast is one of structure and substance but not necessarily of belief.

A symposium of this complexity, which sets out to examine the bewildering worldwide interaction after October 1973 between the highly dynamic conditions in the Middle East and in the non-communist industrial states, has invited continuing difficulties of inquiry, analysis, and balance of treatment and has required the help of many people in many professions in many countries. The members of the three study groups, drawn from scattered callings and too numerous to list by name, served as informed and stimulating respondents to the discussion papers. In the lively exchange of ideas, they helped sharpen the analysis and called attention to errors of fact or interpretation. For their cooperation, the project sponsors are especially grateful.

As coordinator of the venture, I am under particular obligation, for selfless aid at every critical juncture, to my colleagues representing the sponsoring consortium: Alfred O. Hero, Joseph E. Johnson, and Stephen Stamas of the World Peace Foundation; Joseph W. Harned, Jr., Judith D. Trunzo, John W. Tuthill, and Pierre Uri of the Atlantic Institute; and Kazushige Hirasawa, Shoichi Kobayashi, and Mitsuya Okano of the Asia-Pacific Association of Japan. As editor of the book, I have the further pleasure of thanking, besides Messrs. Hero, Hirasawa, and Johnson, the other members of the editorial review committee: Joseph N. Greene, Jr.,

Wolfgang Hager, and Hans Maull as well as Naomi J. Williams, the committee's rapporteur. I am also greatly indebted to Sarah Jackson, as rapporteur of the North American Study Group and a source of constant counsel in the unfolding enterprise.

The multinational project could not have been undertaken without generous gifts in the United States, Europe, and Japan. The Asia-Pacific Association of Japan, the Atlantic Institute, and the World Peace Foundation made direct grants and, together with the Middle East Institute at Columbia University, provided essential services to the study groups and to the preparation of the publication. To the Lilly Endowment for an enabling grant, to the Exxon, Texaco, and Aminoil corporations for helping to cover the costs of individual meetings of the North American Study Group, and to Robert K. Straus for his generosity at the study-group and publication stages of the project, the sponsors are especially beholden. The Western European Study Group acknowledges with gratitude grants in support of its work from Alfried Krupp von Bohlen und Halbach-Stiftung, British Petroleum (London), and Shell (London). The multinational and diversified support insulated the broadly-based assessment against partisan influences.

To Jane Herman, for standardizing the papers for an American publication, and to Judith McQuown, for preparing the index, I am most grateful. For the attentive concern to details in every phase of the enterprise, which helped speed the transformation of individual papers into chapters of a book, I wish to thank Jan Davison and Lenora Procope.

J. C. Hurewitz
Westport, Connecticut
March 1976

Glossary

ACAAR	Action Committee on American Arab Relations
ADL	Anti-Defamation League
AFARCO	Afro-Arab Company for Investment and International Trade
AFESD	Arab Fund for Economic and Social Development
AFLAC	Arab Fund for Loans to African Countries
AIC	Arab Investment Company (Saudi Arabia)
AIPAC	American-Israel Public Affairs Committee
AMF	Arab Monetary Fund
APIC	Arab Petroleum Investment Company
ARAMCO	Arabian American Oil Company
BP	British Petroleum Company
CAPLOT	Canadians Against PLO Terrorism
CFP	Compagnie Française des Pétroles
CIDA	Canadian International Development Agency
CIEC	Conference on International Economic Cooperation
COMECON	Council for Mutual Economic Assistance
DAC	Development Assistance Committee
DC	Democrazia Cristiana party (Italy)
EC	European Community
ECG	Energy Coordinating Group
EDC	Export Development Corporation
EEC	European Economic Community
ELF-ERAP	Marketing trademark and acronym for Entreprise de Recherches et d'Activités Pétrolières

ENI	Ente Nazionale Idrocarburi (Italy)
ERDA	Energy Research and Development Administration (United States)
FDP	Freie Demokratische Partei (West Germany)
GATT	General Agreement on Tariffs and Trade
GNP	Gross National Product
IAEC	International Atomic Energy Commission
IBRD	International Bank for Reconstruction and Development (World Bank)
ICSC	International Commission for Supervision and Control (Vietnam)
IDA	International Development Association (UN)
IEA	International Energy Agency
IFAD	International Fund for Agricultural Development
IFC	International Finance Corporation (UN)
IMF	International Monetary Fund
KFAED	Kuwayt Fund for Arab Economic Development
KFTCIC	Kuwayt Foreign, Trading, Contracting, and Investment Company
LDC	Less developed countries
LLDC	Least developed countries
MITI	Ministry of International Trade and Industry (Japan)
MNC	Multinational corporation
MSA	Most seriously affected
MSP	Minimum safeguard price
NATO	North Atlantic Treaty Organization
NRC	Nuclear Regulatory Commission (US)
OAPEC	Organization of Arab Petroleum Exporting Countries
OAU	Organization of African Unity
OECD	Organization for Economic Cooperation and Development

OPEC	Organization of Petroleum Exporting Countries
PGM	Precision-guided munitions
PLO	Palestine Liberation Organization
SDR	Special drawing rights
SPD	Sozialdemokratische Partei Deutschlands
STABEX	Export Earnings Stabilization Scheme
UAA	United Arab Amirates
UNCTAD	United Nations Council on Trade and Development
UNDOF	United Nations Disengagement Observer Force
UNEF	United Nations Emergency Force
UNESCO	United Nations Educational, Scientific, and Cultural Organization
UNRWA	United Nations Relief and Works Agency (for Palestine Refugees in the Near East)
UNTSO	United Nations Truce Supervision Organization
WHO	World Health Organization

1 The Middle East and the Industrial World

J. C. Hurewitz

The present book examines the interplay between the energy crisis, the Arab-Israel dispute, and the industrial states after the outbreak of the Arab-Israel war on 6 October 1973. The institutionalization of the industrial alliance had proliferated in the postwar years, as the multiplying acronyms—IMF, IBRD, NATO, GATT, EEC, and many others—bear ample witness. A growing number of these institutions were losing vitality by the early 1970s, for they had been called into being in a season of domination by the United States, which took major responsibility for upholding the interests of the industrial world, immodestly labeled by some the First World. The United States had shaped the alliance, among other purposes, to promote the development of a stable system of international relations. The weakening of the industrial alliance contributed to the growing instability of the international system. In a word, the linkage in the October War of the energy crisis and the Arab-Israel dispute did not start the process of institutional decay in the alliance; it accelerated it. Similarly, the linkage, popularly known as the Middle East problem, did not create the tensions among the industrial allies; it exacerbated them.

This symposium thus comes into focus as a study, not of one issue, but of the intersection of three. For analytical purposes, the energy crisis and the Arab-Israel dispute have been decoupled, and the papers about each have been grouped together, so as to give the reader insight into the national responses and the changing national perspectives among the industrial states. The decoupled analysis forms the subject matter of the first two parts of the book. Thereafter, the Middle East problem of popular perception is reconstituted. The chapters of the third part of the book inquire into major effects in the Middle East of the mixing of oil and politics and speculate on likely developments in the coming decade of this still potent mixture. The fourth part considers primary aspects of the evolving patterns of international political economy, as influenced by the energy crisis or its linkage to the Arab-Israel dispute.

The attention to national concerns was deliberate. All too common is the practice of assuming that the Organization for Economic Cooperation and Development (OECD)—shorthand for the industrial alliance or the First World—is a monolith. The variable national responses to the energy crisis underline the diversity of OECD membership. So, too, do the variable national effects of the October War. The industrial states include all the major oil importers. But the United States, Canada, and potentially, Britain are also major producers, and Norway is a net exporter. Nor did the OECD states uniformly experience negative international payments balances as a result of the quadrupling of the price of crude oil in the last quarter of 1973. The US and West Germany showed positive balances in 1974 and 1975, despite the high oil imports.

Analysts have been prone also to contend that the members of the Organization of Petroleum Exporting Countries (OPEC)—which are progressively preempting the title of the Third World—have enjoyed identical benefits from the multiplying oil revenues. In the discussion of the problem of revenue surplus (that is, revenues in excess of a country's capacity for their prudent use), the pertinent literature all too often lumps the OPEC members together, as if their experiences were undifferentiated. Even in the Middle East, where most of the OPEC members are located, distinctions have to be taken into account. At the start of the monumental rise in oil income, Iran, the second-largest oil producer with by far the largest population, had in being an economic infrastructure that constituted a base for potentially solid economic growth at a more rapid pace than in the past. It was also populous enough to entertain realistic expectations for diversifying its economy. By contrast, the economic organization of Saudi Arabia, the largest producer, with only one-eighth Iran's population, was much less developed, so that sound economic growth could only be slower and the limits to variety much narrower. Among the Arab ministates in the Persian Gulf, Saudi Arabia was a superpower. Yet Kuwayt, with less than one-fourth the Saudi population, had by 1973 developed a fiscal infrastructure that enabled it more speedily to integrate part of its swollen revenues into the internal economy and funnel much of the rest into carefully weighed external economic activity.

The energy crisis, in popular usage, has come to have at least five different meanings. For many, it occurred in a specific time frame, starting in mid-October 1973 when the Organization of Arab

Petroleum Exporting Countries (OAPEC), at a meeting in Kuwayt, reduced oil production at once by 5.0 percent and imposed further cuts at intervals, so that by the start of 1974 daily output in those Arab oil states adhering to the plan had diminished by 25 percent. Though vociferous advocates of the cutback policy, Iraq and Libya did not in fact abide by it; they did, however, join the rest of OAPEC in mounting an embargo of oil exports to the United States and the Netherlands. Ever since 1947 when the Palestine problem first appeared on the agenda of a principal United Nations organ, the Arab oil states had been threatening to use oil as a political weapon. But the recurrent threats proved abortive. The earlier failures lulled the leaders of the industrial states into skepticism about the efficacy of the oil weapon. But when it worked in 1973, the industrial governments, instead of pooling information and uniting on action, scrambled, each for its own parochial needs. The scramble produced an immediate fear and an overall immobilism that seemed to place every major importing state in bondage to the major exporters. Those who favor this definition of the energy crisis assume that it ended in mid-March 1974, when OAPEC restored free exports. In this judgment, the crisis derived from the panicked response of the political leaders in the industrial states to the Arab use of the oil weapon and the inferences drawn from the manipulation of the oil industry for political ends having little or nothing to do with oil economics.

According to a second view, related to the first, the energy crisis is one of irrepressible anxiety among the OECD governments, especially in Western Europe and Japan, that springs from a stubborn fear of renewed war and of future embargoes and production cutbacks by the Arab oil states. This fear was still determining, long after March 1974, Western European and Japanese policies on the Arab-Israel dispute as a means of preventing a future resort to the oil weapon. In brief, the politicians appeared to be girding their countries for a recurrence of the last crisis, which was probably unique and nonrepetitive, instead of taking adequate measure of intervening changes.

A third view, this one open-ended, holds that the crisis was already gathering before the October War. As early as 1970, the world oil industry had passed from a buyers' to a sellers' market. Between then and the October War, OPEC and individual members of the organization concluded agreements on price increases and on participation—a euphemism, as seen in the industrial world, for slow-motion nationalization—in upstream operations, that is, in the exploration for and development of oil resources in the OPEC states by outside concessionary companies. In this phase, the public awareness spread among OECD and OPEC members that oil and gas were wasting resources. What loomed as crisis in the OECD looked like opportunity to the OPEC, where the governments and the public were coming to espouse the belief that they had a right to charge whatever the traffic might bear. By such means, they would hope to offset "past exploitation" by the major international oil companies. Moreover, with the added revenues the OPEC members would be able to develop their economies so that, when the natural fossil fuels had run out, their economies would be industrialized and their societies correspondingly raised.

A fourth meaning of the energy crisis, also open-ended, relates wholly to the continuing negotiations between the OECD and the OPEC, which were ostensibly intended to reshape world oil and related energy industries in the common interest. The negotiations on the OECD side, after November 1975, largely became the responsibility of the International Energy Agency (IEA). France cooperated with the IEA without formally joining it. Instead, France saw itself as mediator between the industrial states and the oil-exporting states, and later between the industrial "North" and the nonindustrial "South." The range of the talks, broadened on the insistence of the South to embrace the terms of production and the prices of raw materials no less than those of oil and gas, turned on the creation of a new world economic order.

Finally, there was the crisis of OECD management of the complex of energy problems (the rational development and use of the world's diminishing oil and gas supplies and the search for and development of substitute forms of energy) and the international economic and political side effects of the steep 1973 price rises of crude oil on trade, investment, aid, monetary affairs, and arms transfers. So long as the industrial alliance had preserved its vigor, the US acted as the uncontested crisis manager. But Vietnam, Watergate, a congressional president in search of a public mandate, the reactivated contest between the Congress and the Executive over the distribution of constitutional powers, the continuing disarray of the economy, and above all in matters of energy the growing dependence of the economy on imported oil—all these factors and many more were draining the United States of its capacity to lead the OECD. More than that, there appeared to be no replacement for the leadership role of the United States.

The variety of popular meanings of the energy crisis is reflected in the chapters that follow. The authors were not bound by a strict construction; where pertinent, they evaluated national perceptions in the local idiom. The book thus combines the totality of these interpretations and, taking the chapters together, treats the crisis as open-ended. It accepts OPEC as largely centered in the Middle East and influenced by its Saudi-led Arab bloc. And insofar as the industrial allies have shown ability to cope with the unfolding challenge and to plan for the future, it views the OECD as still largely led by an uncertain and self-indulgent United States, with a strong residual inclination of the Western European states and Japan to fend for themselves.

The political leaders of the industrial states, collectively and severally, were thus still caught in the mid-1970s without agreed comprehensive energy policies or even the plans that should have preceded the policies. Yet in this predicament they were not alone, for no government, not even the communist governments of the Second World, had framed such plans as the basis for policies. But the governments of the Second World had not yet become heavily reliant on oil imports from outside the communist orbit. They thereby escaped the most serious consequences of the dramatic developments of the winter of 1973-74. Still, it should be recorded, their escape, attributable more to the accidents of history and geography than to prudent planning, was no more than temporary.

The communist countries, however, did have a clear set of policy guidelines on the Arab-Israel dispute. They followed the lead of the Soviet Union in supporting the Arab states and the Palestine Arabs in the quarrel with Israel. It was mostly in the extended sense of the politicization of the energy crisis by its linkage to the Arab-Israel contest that the lingering rivalry between the industrial and the communist states was affected. To put it differently, the energy crisis did not grow directly out of the Cold War or the flaws in détente or the continuing strained relations between the superpowers or between the industrial and communist spheres. This explains the absence in the present book of a systematic analysis of the impact of energy problems on the USSR and its communist allies.

Finally, the Middle East oil states, after 1973, were learning the hard lesson that sudden affluence could create as many difficulties as sudden poverty. The institutional creativity of these states faced an instant challenge. They had too few trained economists for the kinds of financial operations thrust upon them. All the Middle East oil states, the ministates in the Persian Gulf among them, had formulated development plans before the fall of 1973. But attempts to speed up the plans overtaxed the transportation facilities and clogged the ports with unloaded ships and, more seriously, overheated the economies, producing immediate inflation. Externally, the oil governments fell under rising pressure to provide foreign aid, particularly to the Fourth World, as the oil-dry nonindustrial states were coming to be known. The attempted use of such aid as a political instrument, they soon realized, could easily boomerang if it were not handled deftly. Yet the trained technicians in the oil states, even in Kuwayt and Iran, were too few to administer elaborate foreign aid programs—to receive applications, to assess them, and to supervise their execution.

To problems such as these, the authors address themselves.

I

National Responses to the Energy Crisis

2 *US International Leadership*

Lawrence Scheinman

The argument developed in this chapter may be summarized as follows: (1) Despite appearances to the contrary, US international energy policy was instituted more for general foreign policy purposes than pursued in its own right, at least until 1975. (2) The lag in framing a comprehensive and coherent national energy policy has impaired the credibility of the United States with its industrial state partners and with the Organization of Petroleum Exporting Countries (OPEC). (3) The design of such a policy aligned with the international energy program of the International Energy Agency (IEA) is a prerequisite to sustained leadership on world energy issues. (4) Even with such a policy, and despite the absence of alternative leadership, it is not certain that the United States will be able to manage the crisis in view of the differences among the industrial states in their policies toward oil and raw materials. (5) These conclusions may be explained by differences in conditions, interests, and purposes in each industrial state which produces different ideas on the direction of the international political and economic order and by the degree to which they can adapt satisfactorily to a changing political-economic world balance.

* * * *

The unfolding Middle East crisis of October 1973 created problems and opportunities for the United States. The problems included an embargo of oil supplies to the United States and the Netherlands and a cutback to other industrial states by the Organization of Arab Petroleum Countries (OAPEC), a series of oil price increases by OPEC; and an uncoordinated bilateral approach to oil-producing countries by West European states and Japan (and the European-Arab dialogue carried on by the European Economic Community, [EEC]) with attempts to barter arms, technology, and aid for guaranteed access to oil supplies at almost any price. These actions threatened to impair American diplomatic initiatives to stabilize the situation in the Middle East. They also widened the gap between Europe (and Japan) and the United States on world economic—though not security—affairs. Already weakened, the political consensus among the North Atlantic states and Japan on the basic political and economic international order declined further.

On the other hand, the energy crisis enabled the United States to capitalize on the concern over the adequacy of supply price of oil to reestablish its influence and leadership in transatlantic relations. The United States recognized the resource crisis as a political opportunity, which it skillfully used to secure the establishment of the IEA as an instrument for mobilizing Western resources and unity.

In 1973, the United States had tried without result, and perhaps less sincerely than it might have, to reach a global agreement on a "new Atlantic Charter." In the months before the October War, as differences intensified over monetary and trade policies and over military offset costs to relieve pressure on balance of payments, European-American relations deteriorated. The Europeans resented the frank political linkage of these economic and monetary issues to security and defense affairs, although not long after most European states appeared ready to acquiesce in a similar linkage of energy to security and defense. Whatever the effects of the oil embargo and ensuing price increases, they also provided an arena in which the United States could seek to recapture its predominant role and fulfill some of the goals it had pursued in the "Year of Europe." Whether this would make it possible to salvage the existing economic and political order was probably less important than the possibility that the United States might again be able to influence the scale and character of impending changes.

In short, as an initial response to the energy crisis, the United States framed political objectives that exceeded the immediate problem of oil shortage or price, that sought to preserve political and economic relationships and institutions among the industrial states, and ensured that the United States would parry the threat to the prevailing balance of power. That response found its most succinct formulation in Secretary of State Henry Kissinger's speech in December 1973 in London which called for comprehensive collaboration in all facets of the energy problem. In the ensuing Washington Energy Conference of February 1974 the participants were asked to create an Energy Coordinating Group (ECG) and to agree upon a consumer action program. The primary objectives were political unity and diplomatic cooperation rather than implementation of concrete material programs that might lock the United States into major commitments and restrict its policy options. As one analyst observed, the "United States sought diplomacy in the energy crisis aimed at interdependence of political objectives and an independence of material resources."[1]

* * * *

The US-sponsored International Energy Agency, established in November 1974 on the initiative of the ECG, seemed to consolidate the interests in energy of the consumer states. The IEA's initial task was the management of the international energy program framed by the ECG. That program consisted of an emergency oil-sharing scheme in the event of an embargo, a long-term cooperative plan to reduce dependence on oil, an oil market information system, and a commitment to promote cooperation with less-developed consumer countries and with petroleum-producing countries. The IEA was the major international pillar of US energy policy, and, at least at the outset, one of its central purposes was to erode the political and economic power of the oil cartel. Whether the IEA actually reflected a genuine consensus or merely represented a concession to American political demands, however, can only be assessed by examining the national interests of the member states.

Most major industrial states belong to the IEA—France being the most notable exception. While political and economic security are interests shared by all consumer states, the relative importance of the two objectives varies widely. The members of the IEA can be distinguished by the scope of their international political interests and responsibilities and by the degree of their energy dependence.

Measured by the first criterion, the United States stands apart from the other IEA members. As the only superpower in the agency, it can least afford to peril its access to such an essential resource as oil and thus curtail its freedom of action. While not directly threatened to that degree in the 1973 crisis, the United States nevertheless recognized the possibility that its position could be jeopardized by a future embargo. Moreover, since the United States was committed to Israel's security and survival, it continued to run the risk of a disruption of supplies by the Arab oil states. US allies were also vulnerable to reduction in supply as a means of pressuring the United States to modify its pro-Israel policies. The IEA emergency oil-sharing scheme was designed to counter this threat. For the United States, however, the need to diminish, if not remove altogether, its vulnerability to an oil embargo was justified by national interest. This has been an issue in the domestic debate on energy policy and underlies Project Independence, the second pillar of US energy policy.

On the other hand, the United States imports about 35 percent of its oil, or less than one-half the average of its IEA partners. Apart from producing some two-thirds of its own crude oil, the United States also has massive reserves of coal and oil shale. With the exception of Great Britain (an IEA member) and Norway (an IEA associate), which were developing oil reserves in the North Sea, and Canada, which is also a producing country, all other IEA members are almost wholly dependent on OPEC imports. Since the OPEC members control most of the oil production capacity for sale in the international market, a strategy of supply diversification does not hold great promise insofar as price levels or security of supply are concerned.

The variation in political interests and domestic resources suggests many potential issues of conflict among the IEA states. Since its inception, the agency has been torn by tensions over strategies for dealing with OPEC and over the individual, and often clashing, policies of member states. The United States has been prone to take a firm stand toward OPEC, while its allies have preferred to support a more cooperative posture. This divergence flows naturally from the differences in political interests and resource capabilities.

The emphasis on cooperation with OPEC weakened the search for reducing or eliminating vulnerability. It was predicated, instead, on a notion of positive interdependence. The OPEC members would, in theory, acquire vested interests in the economic stability of industrial states through long-term investment of revenue surplus in the industrial economies. The industrial states, in turn, would provide an assured market to OPEC countries and technological aid in their industrial development. The energy-poor IEA states were concerned primarily with the stability of the economic marketplace; beyond basic national security interests, they had no major foreign political policy goals or responsibilities, and many even perceived Soviet-American detente as a basis for relaxing their own security concerns. Thus, as long as oil was accessible at a reasonable price, they found this strategy attractive. These states were not averse to considering an indexing system for oil, and they preferred a bilateral context for cooperation if concerted action implied confrontation.

American diplomacy responded to this basically rational position by asserting that the absence of solidarity weakened the efforts of the industrial states to moderate oil-price levels and did not alleviate the problem of the political manipulation of energy supplies. Thus, the Americans argued, a return to "economic conditions as usual," involving increased demand for oil, would increase the vulnerability of oil-importing states to monopoly pricing practices and to supply limitation.

It was on this issue of vulnerability that differences arose between the United States and other industrial states. Reduced vulnerability meant reduced dependence on imported oil and a relatively greater degree of energy self-sufficiency. Self-sufficiency, the United States argued, could not be achieved without high environmental and economic cost. Moreover, development of such costly domestic energy sources—for example, by resort to secondary and tertiary oil recovery procedures, the exploration of the outer continental shelf, and the production of synthetic fuels—served a common interest since increased domestic production would facilitate the proportionate withdrawal of the producing country from the international market and might lead to a decline in price. Eventually those resources would also become available to other consumer states and might be used to enlarge energy stockpiles. However, the few resource-rich states would have to bear the high investments, and equity demanded that those who might benefit from the resulting lower price share the burden.

To guarantee equitable distribution of the investment costs, the United States recommended a minimum safeguard price system which the IEA reluctantly endorsed in principle. The economic justifications of such a system, while far from clear, nevertheless made sense for a country like the United States which is rich in high-cost energy and, for political reasons, is bent on energy independence. By distributing energy costs among industrial states, the safeguard price curtailed the risks of the United States if world oil prices should drop significantly. This, of course, was a principal objective of the proposal, but it was not the only one; a political consideration could be added to the economic one. The minimum safeguard price tied IEA country economies to American foreign policy over which they exercised only a limited influence. Thus, a political objective of the United States, relative invulnerability, was to be paid for by other IEA members, to whom secure access at reasonable prices—an objective, we have noted, that might be achieved also through cooperation—enjoyed higher priority.

* * * *

The concept of a minimum safeguard price was inconsistent with the simultaneous achievement of the two declared US objectives: reduced dependence and lower world oil prices. Reduced dependence appeared attainable only through a combination of conservation measures going beyond voluntary restraint and of protection ensuring that investments in high-cost alternative energy sources would not be jeopardized by a fall in world oil prices. While such measures reduced vulnerability, they were not consistent with lower energy prices. Conversely, successful pursuit of the objective of lower prices entailed the probability of higher reliance on foreign oil if, as was likely, demand expanded in a more favorable oil market.

The ambivalence manifest in American international energy policy was equally evident at the domestic level. The United States has been deprived of a national energy policy, and it lacks the necessary domestic direction and support for firm US leadership of even credible involvement in international energy crisis management. The lack of a national policy might be explained, though not excused, by the historical fact that neither the United States nor any other industrial state had ever framed a comprehensive energy policy or created the attendant institutions. Instead, a segmented system of regulatory agencies and rules were devised to deal with different energy sectors and activities. Only in the nuclear field did the government consistently become involved, from initial research and development to commercial application.

Faced with critical energy problems after 1973, the executive branch of the federal government did create the Federal Energy Administration and the Energy Research and Development Administration (ERDA), while the Congress inspired the formation of the Energy Resources Council with responsibility for coordinating energy policy. The problem of the national energy policy, however, was less a function of interorganizational politics among regulatory agencies and other components of the administrative branch of government than of fundamental differences in doctrine and policy strategy between the president and the Congress. The American inclination to confront OPEC found its domestic parallel in the relations between the executive and the legislature.

Both branches of government agreed on the need to develop a conservation program, but they parted on methods and tactics. These were philosophically-rooted differences which extended beyond the energy crisis to the more general issue of to what extent government should intervene in the marketplace, and reflected higher Congressional sensitivity to short-term constitutency interests than to the requirements for the long-range implications of a changing energy situation. The administration's "free marketeer" position consisted of forcing domestic prices up so as to force consumption down and of relying on market forces and the price mechanism to curtail demand and to stimulate domestic production. This would be achieved through an orderly price decontrol of domestic oil and natural gas to reduce reliance on imports and develop new resources and, thus, simultaneously reach greater self-sufficiency and a more realistic balance between supply and demand. This policy was to be accompanied by more flexible environmental restraints on coal and nuclear power, the stockpiling of oil reserves for an emergency, and the conferring on the president the authority to institute a floor price on imported oil.

The response of the Congress focused on continued government control and intervention in the energy marketplace. The majority contended that the presidential policy would be inflationary and recessionary. It was thought that higher fuel costs would drive consumer prices and wages up and, inescapably, drive consumer purchasing power down. Moreover, government efforts to control inflation through monetary and fiscal policies would retard economic recovery, with the burden falling disproportionately on the poor. Finally, some congressmen also challenged assumptions about the role of the free market forces in enhancing domestic production and took the view that only the oil producers would benefit from the administration's policy.

The legislative and executive branches essentially disagreed over two issues: the appropriate strategy for domestic energy management and the inherent value of the goal of self-sufficiency. A full-scale debate about self-sufficiency had not taken place, and the domestic energy policy fell victim to the requirements of electoral politics. Thus, the compromise agreement reached between the Congress and the administration in November 1975 decreed an immediate lowering of domestic oil prices followed by a phased decontrol over forty months. Although the bill did provide for conservation and for the creation of national oil reserves, thus meeting some of the commitments undertaken by the United States in the International Energy Program, it contradicted the main thrust of the American foreign-policy rhetoric which was aimed at restricting consumption. As the economy recovered, the growing demand for oil would likely have to be met from imports unless another mechanism was found to stimulate alternative high-cost energy production from domestic sources. Paradoxically, this might disqualify the United States from resort to the IEA $25-billion safety net, designed to encourage a country suffering financial disabilities because of oil import costs to adopt serious steps to lessen its dependence on foreign oil. Of course, the safety net was intended as an inducement to other IEA states to join US-led efforts to undermine OPEC rather than as a mechanism to assist the United States. Nonetheless, the United States was not fixing a standard of conduct for other states if reduced dependence remained a central element of its international policy. Did the compromise mean that US international strategy had undergone a fundamental change? Development of a true energy policy involved not only conservation and pricing decisions, but a comprehensive energy policy. While the European Economic Community (EEC) had not achieved a genuine obligatory community energy policy, it did develop a target plan for fuels distributed among oil, coal, nuclear, and hydroelectric sources over a ten-year period. US policy appeared to be approaching the issue through the back door, via development and research programs in a variety of areas without a comprehensive national strategy. Energy policy and its underlying research and development effort seemed to be decoupling.

* * * *

The cost of an indeterminate national policy for international energy management should not be underestimated. Continued ambivalence enlarged the opportunities for consumer states to renew unilateral or collective efforts to satisfy their own immediate needs and objectives. The interests of the IEA states were at best heterogeneous, at worst contradictory, so while those efforts did not dispute or disprove American interests, they could compound the problems of framing concerted IEA policies on energy. The longer the delay in US affirmation of concrete, coherent, and comprehensive energy policies, the greater the probability of the defection of the IEA states. The contentions of the French government, that US bids for energy cooperation and policy coordination were little more than a subterfuge to seize advantage in the resource crisis, would seem all the more persuasive. That this was one element of American policy did not mean it was the only one. Only genuinely cooperative policies—including equitable trade-offs between the United States and its IEA partners like those of the emergency oil-allocation program—would discourage unhappiness over American-led policy coordination. Unfortunately, the domestic legislation necessary for the United States to meet its obligations under IEA (i.e., stockpiling of reserves, oil-sharing authority, and commitment of financial resources) remained in abeyance.

Moreover, there was no evidence that the commitment to international cooperation on research and development had any real substance. The Americans seemed to be following a standard strategy; they selected particular target states (in this case West Germany and Japan) as partners for cooperation on the basis of the technological equivalence between those states and the United States and their "political relevance" to broader US interests. The selection of the Bonn government as a principal partner in research and development seemed to rest on the calculation that if West Germany could be firmly secured, the remaining members of the EEC would fall into line.

Finally, ambivalence raised questions about American reliability. Could the United States really be counted on to meet its obligations? In nuclear fuel supply the United States occupied a position equivalent to that of Saudi Arabia in oil. It remained the principal supplier of nuclear fuels for most reactors in the First World. Several times, recipient states were aroused by unannounced or threatened American action, even though the difficulties could be attributed to a misunderstanding and not a calculated disregard of national commitments. Following implementation of the Energy Reorganization Act of 1974, bringing into being the ERDA—which assimilated the Atomic Energy Commission and the Nuclear Regulatory Commission (NRC)—as the regulatory and licensing agency, shipments of enriched uranium for power reactors in Western Europe were delayed. In keeping with the stipulations of the act, the NRC reviewed the conditions under which radioactive materials were transported. From the European point of view, however, the unilateral decision to suspend shipment without advance consultation raised the question of the reliability of the United States as a source of enriched uranium. The American near-monopoly of enriched uranium and the European effort to step up nuclear power development as an alternative to imported oil converged around this event to produce unnecessary tensions in transatlantic relations. On top of the earlier unilateral American suspension of soybean exports, this delay gave the Europeans pause about the wisdom of reliance on the United States.

A second episode also involved nuclear exports. Senate Bill S. 1439, introduced before the Senate Government Operations Committee in May 1975, was designed to improve physical security in the shipment and safeguard of nuclear materials. Although international safeguards were already fairly well developed, largely by the International Atomic Energy Agency, the Senate bill vested the Nuclear Regulatory Commission with the responsibility for determining which importing countries had adopted physical security and safeguard provisions on nuclear materials comparable to those of the United States. It was not the intent of the bill that was at issue, but that, once more, American policymakers appeared to be taking unilateral steps by investing the United States with the authority to impose and evaluate the conditions under which it would meet its international commitments. Apart from the possibility that such measures might speed up the proliferation of nuclear enrichment facilities and plutonium reprocessing plants elsewhere, it threw into question American reliability as a trading partner and credibility as a government willing and able to live up to its international obligations.

* * * *

The legislative-executive impasse was hardly likely to be broken in an election year, particularly with the country's first Congressional president distracted by an election campaign that began in the spring with contested primaries and could not be delayed until the party convention in mid-summer. Still, it was not implausible to assume that, once a president is sent to the White House with a public mandate, especially if this proved to be a decisive mandate, any policy of the United States that did not flagrantly challenge the major interests of its industrial allies would find support in those allies. The weakness or absence of alternative leadership in the Western world, which had plagued the EEC, need not be expected to continue indefinitely. For the time being, however, there was no question that the preservation of the Western democratic political systems and the grand lines of the world economic order remained the overriding interests. The industrial states could ill afford total alienation from the dominant power in the Western world. Thus, with strong American leadership, the other states might be expected to fall in line; with weak American leadership, they might be inclined to pursue separate policies of accommodation.

This conclusion could be upset if fundamentally incompatible policies were to develop between the United States and its industrial partners on another major issue: the insistent demands of the less developed countries (LDCs) for a more equitable and just international order. The problem was not new, but following the preparatory conference in Paris of OPEC and OECD in April 1975, it underwent a qualitative change.

That meeting failed to reach its intended goal primarily because the oil states were determined to broaden the agenda by the inclusion of raw materials, while the industrial states, chiefly the United States, insisted that oil was a separate issue and should remain so. Although other IEA members shared the American view, it was the United States that polarized producer-consumer interests. The American position seemed to have been shaped largely by concern that an extended agenda would assimilate the oil issue and undermine the very purpose of the IEA, which gave the United States an institutional grip on the energy policies of the industrial states. In any event, the talks revealed mounting cohesion among the LDCs where the OPEC members appeared willing to bring their powerful, new-found influence to bear on behalf of the producers of other raw materials.

Despite the peculiarities of oil production, OPEC could nevertheless serve as an inspiration for other mineral producers. The European states and Japan, collectively, were the largest world importers of oil and raw materials—and in raw materials among the least self-sufficient regions in the world, producing only one-fourth of what they consumed. By contrast, American production and consumption were much more evenly balanced. Thus, American and European-Japanese interests also diverged on issues other than energy. Across a progressively widening range of interests, many of the industrial states might become more amenable to accommodation than the United States. They might increasingly be willing to meet demands for redistribution of wealth and for larger LDC participation in influential international economic institutions.

With fewer multinational corporations and lighter investments overseas, the European countries and Japan had less onerous foreign interests to defend than the Americans. Whatever encumbrance their colonial past imposed, it was insignificant compared to perceived American neocolonialism, public and private. Thus, they were relieved of the burden of ensuring that their foreign policies were not viewed as threatening the political and economic independence of others. Indeed, precisely because of the colonial heritage, countries like Great Britain, France, Belgium, and the Netherlands could claim "natural" historic ties to the LDCs which promote the revision and modernization of economic relations. The European Community, through its associated states, had long pursued accommodative economic relationships with developing states. The Lomé Convention, signed by the EC on 28 February 1975 with forty-six African, Caribbean, and Pacific states, expanded that relationship through an export earnings stabilization scheme (STABEX) covering twenty-two commodities from those countries and ensuring reimbursement in the event that the value of their earnings for export to the Community of the covered commodities fell below specified levels.

The rhetoric of American foreign economic policy by the end of 1975, as reflected in Secretary of State Kissinger's speeches before domestic audiences and the United Nations, implied a shift to a similarly accommodative position. American verbal commitments, however, had still to be transformed into action. The Conference of International Economic Corporations (CIEC) meetings in Paris in December 1975, which established commissions to study energy, development, finance, and raw materials, appeared a first step in that direction. Solid action, however, would have to await the results of the presidential election in 1976. If US policy should then fail to produce concrete programs consistent with the new rhetoric and if the energy crisis should once again grow acute, the vulnerable industrial states might try progressively to decouple themselves from US international economic and political leadership and policies. They might risk sacrificing American security commitments if they were convinced that their primary national economic interests left them no recourse. The probability appears remote; but the possibility ought not to be dismissed.

3 Canada's Quest for Energy Autarky

Ted Greenwood

Until 1973, Canada's energy policy had evolved under the influence of two fundamental policy objectives: the growth of the domestic oil and gas industry was to be encouraged with its viability guaranteed over the long term, and Canadian consumers were to be provided with abundant low-cost energy. Because of the great distances between Canada's major energy reserves and its large population centers, the primary instruments of this policy have been the four large pipeline systems built in the 1950s. The Westcoast Transmission Company's pipeline carries gas within British Columbia; the Trans-Canada Pipeline System carries Alberta gas eastward to Ontario and Montreal; the Trans-Mountain Pipeline carries Alberta oil to British Columbia; and the Interprovincial pipeline carries Alberta and other prairie provinces' oil to Ontario. The National Oil Policy, introduced in 1961, imposed a stable structure on the Canadian oil market. In order to guarantee outlets to western producers, imports were prohibited west of the Ottawa Valley. Quebec and the maritime provinces relied on what was then cheaper imports from Venezuela and the Middle East. By choice and design, therefore, Canada was both a producer and an importer of oil.

The cornerstone of this policy, contributing critically to both objectives, was exportation to the United States. The gas pipelines were connected to American distribution systems, and the oil pipelines cross the border and feed directly into American refineries. Indeed, the promise of exports and their encouragement by Ottawa and the producing provinces were a prerequisite for the formation and cohesion of the transnational consortia that financed and built these very expensive and technically demanding pipelines. At the same time, the greater throughput that exports provided reduced the transportation cost and thereby the ultimate market price to Canadian consumers. Throughout the 1960s the United States was encouraged to buy increasing volumes of Canadian oil. Any gas reserves judged to be in excess to Canada's own needs over a twenty-five-year period could be sold on long-term contracts.

For many years there was little opposition to an energy policy based on exports and heavy usage. Canada was thought to have large reserves of conventional oil and gas and vast untapped potential in the arctic, off the east coast, and in Alberta oil sands. Access to the American market was expected to provide sufficient incentives for industry to guarantee a level of exploration and development, financed largely with American capital, that would assure a continuing supply for Canada. The availability of fairly cheap petroleum products, gas, and electricity (based on hydro, fossil fuels, and, eventually, domestic uranium) would contribute to industrialization and a high standard of living. This permissive attitude toward energy usage resulted in gradually increased levels of exports and one of the highest levels of energy use per capita of any industrial state. As a public issue in the 1960s, energy policy managed to escape the bitterness and rancor over regional disparities and division of authority between Ottawa and the provinces that were so pervasive in Canadian politics. The interests and policies of the producing provinces and of Ottawa were almost coincidental. Energy was abundantly available to everyone. The poorer prairie and maritime provinces and Quebec could even pay a little less than Ontario. Except for Canadian resentment of the American refusal to accept more Canadian gas and particularly oil in an era when excess capacity in Alberta was shut in and occasional disagreements over the price of exported Canadian gas, energy was not a contentious issue between Ottawa and Washington. A fairly stable equilibrium had been established.

That stability began to erode in the early 1970s. Exports of Canadian crude oil had risen steadily in the late 1960s. By 1969 the widening gap between demand and domestic supply in the United States made it impossible for Ottawa to fulfill its obligation to moderate the growth of oil exports. Despite the American imposition in March 1970 of a mandatory import quota for Canadian crude oil supplying the petroleum regions east of the Rocky Mountains, the overall trend continued upward. Canada became a net exporter of oil. By 1973, American demand began straining existing production and transportation facilities resulting, in March of that year, in the imposition of export controls. Exports were thenceforth limited to the surplus remaining after Canadian requirements were met and were placed under the control of the National Energy Board.[1] Traditional expectations about gas exports were also changing. In 1970 the Board refused to license for export the full amount of gas for which applications had been filed. Since then, concern for Canada's own long-term supply has prevented the issuance of any additional natural gas export licenses. In short, in the course of a few years, the increase in American demand for oil and gas, the limitations of Canadian production capability, and altering perceptions about the extent of Canada's resource base began transforming Canadian energy policy from export promotion to export restraint. Still, fundamental change did not occur in the underlying policy objectives, in the official belief that their fulfillment required extensive exports to the United States, or in the willingness to rely heavily on imported oil.

The political environment within Canada was changing, however. A new concern about the quality of the country's physical environment and a resurgent sense of economic strength and nationalism produced a growing desire to reduce the level of economic dependence on the United States and to preserve Canada's resources for Canadians. That close cooperation with the United States produced economic benefits for Canada had been widely accepted as axiomatic. Now it was increasingly called into question. As the American appetite for energy resources grew, the ability of Canada to meet the needs and its willingness to try decreased. Resentment over American ownership of Canadian manufacturing and especially resource industries was growing. Foreign control in the oil and gas sector was about 90 percent, not counting pipelines. As the perception of an energy crisis heightened in the United States in 1972 and 1973 and Americans seemed to be looking north for an increasing share of their future supply, Canada balked. Energy issues became a matter of high politics within Canada and an important symbol of the desire for greater independence from American influence.

In September 1973, a month before the outbreak of war in the Middle East, Canada's energy policy underwent a radical change. In order to dampen domestic inflation but still to reap the benefit of rising world oil prices, a two-tier price structure was introduced for Canadian oil. The domestic price was frozen at about $4.10 per barrel and an export tax of $.40 was imposed on American purchasers. In addition, the government proposed restructuring Canada's oil market. With imported oil now more expensive than domestic supplies, it proposed extending the crude oil pipeline from the Ontario refining center of Sarnia to Montreal and reallocating a portion of the supplies traditionally exported to American refiners to the markets of eastern Canada. The producing provinces, particularly the Progressive Conservative government in Alberta, were severe in their criticism of these pricing policies. They had strongly opposed the previous imposition of export controls but the combination of a frozen domestic price and a federally-collected export tax was intolerable. In a period of rising economic rent in the sale of oil and increasing government intervention in the free market, the latent tensions of regionalism, economic disparities, and federal-provincial conflict were rekindled as driving forces in the determination of energy policy. Severe criticism of the decision to reduce oil exports and of the imposition of an export tax was also heard from the regions of the United States dependent in some way on Canadian oil.

Into this already highly politicized and somewhat emotion-charged environment came the shocks of the rapid rise in world oil prices and the oil production cutbacks that accompanied and followed the Middle East war of October 1973. At the time, Canada was importing about 900,000 barrels per day of crude oil and about 75,000 barrels per day of petroleum products, together accounting for close to half of Canada's consumption. About 25 percent of these imports were coming from Arab states participating in, or who might participate in, the production curtailments. With winter imminent, rumors rampant, and accurate information about Canada's status in the boycott unavailable, anxiety ran high. A rationing plan was developed and held in reserve. An arrangement to ship Alberta crude eastward through the Great Lakes was set up on an emergency basis and maintained as long as ice conditions permitted. Thereafter oil was shipped from the west coast via the Panama Canal. Since production was already at full capacity the result of these emergency arrangements was a decline in exports to the United States.

A combination of a mild winter, production increases by several large producing countries, reallocations by major oil companies, and probably a number of leaks in the boycott rendered the short-term oil supply situation less severe than feared worldwide and in Canada. Nonetheless, the higher prices for imported oil and the demonstration of Arab ability and willingness to manipulate world oil trade for political ends had profound effects on Canada's long-term energy policy. On 6 December 1973 the prime minister stated the objective of achieving Canadian self-sufficiency in oil and oil products by the end of the decade. The following year, this goal was restated in terms of energy autarky. In both formulations the policy instruments were the same: construction of an oil pipeline from Sarnia to Montreal to replace the bulk of imports from the most insecure suppliers; greater production of oil, particularly from the vast deposits in Alberta's oil sands but, depending on the discovery of commercial reserves, also from frontier areas in the north and Atlantic continental shelf; the creation of a national oil company to participate in oil sands development, to carry out exploration and to buy oil directly from exporting countries; expediting the construction of a pipeline to bring arctic gas supplies to market; and increasing reliance on nuclear power for electricity generation. Curiously, the option of strategic storage of oil in the eastern importing areas has hardly been considered in Canada. The government also announced that domestic prices for oil and gas would have to rise gradually to encourage the development of more expensive supplies. The days of cheap energy were over.

The path toward these goals was difficult for Canada. National agreement did not exist concerning their desirability, their feasibility, or the best means for pursuing them. The national consensus on energy policy, already weakening in the early 1970s, was shattered by the actions of OPEC. The most immediate issue was distribution of economic rent. The consuming provinces and Ottawa agreed that Canada's domestic supplies should be used to cushion the economy from inflationary and disruptive effects of the rise in world oil prices being felt in other countries. The oil industry and the provincial governments of Alberta and Saskatchewan felt strongly that the price of domestic oil should be allowed to rise to prevailing world levels although they did not agree on how the additional revenue should be shared. The western provinces viewed the continuing price freeze as an egregious subsidy of industrial Ontario at their expense. No one in Canada doubted that the United States should be asked to pay prevailing world prices, and this was assured by adjustments in the export tax as required. But still there was great disagreement over the formula for distributing the economic rent. The producing provinces felt it was theirs by right as owners of the resource. The eastern provinces wanted it used to subsidize their imports of OPEC oil. The federal government, while willing to return much of it to the producing provinces, felt justified in using these tax receipts to finance income redistribution programs, the cost of which rose with Alberta's oil income.

The $.40 export tax gradually rose to $1.90, $2.20, and then $6.40 as the price of OPEC oil increased and the domestic price for Canadian crude remained frozen. As the stakes increased so did the intensity of the disagreement between regions and governments. Not only oil, but also the price of natural gas became an issue. As the world oil price, and therefore the commodity value, of gas went up, Alberta sought large price increases. Ontario resisted strongly. The former threatened to constrict Ontario's supply and tried to use the higher prices obtainable in the United States as a lever in the domestic market.

Beyond revenue distribution questions, there were also the more fundamental issues of political authority and constitutional rights. Under the British North America Act, the act of the British Parliament under which Canada achieved its independence and which remains the constitutional foundation of the country, each province was awarded ownership of its natural resources, including hydrocarbons. The producing provinces argued that Ottawa's interference in the oil market was usurpation of their power to price their own commodities and confiscation of their revenue. Ottawa countered that it was acting within its rights to administer exports and to regulate interprovincial trade. By an act of Parliament the federal government could, and ultimately did, give itself the power to control domestic prices outside the producing provinces. In response, the provinces took control of the marketing of oil and gas within their borders, enacted for themselves the power to set wellhead prices, and established provincial energy companies to participate in the exploitation of provincial resources. Although frequently argued in legalistic and constitutional terms, the real stakes in these pricing and jurisdictional disputes were the power relationships among provinces and between them and the federal government. It was and remains clear that political, not legal, resolutions were required.

These have been gradually forthcoming. The mechanism has been lengthy and sometimes bitter federal-provincial negotiations and a series of First Ministers meetings. The price of domestic oil was increased to $6.50 per barrel in April 1974, and $8.00 per barrel in July 1975. It rose again in July 1976. The domestic price of gas also rose dramatically as a result of agreements between Alberta and Ottawa and will ultimately reach its commodity value based on the price of oil. Reflecting the higher oil prices in the United States, the price for exported gas has risen even faster. It reached $1.60 per thousand cubic feet in November 1975. Ottawa has left the economic rent from gas exports to be shared at the discretion of the provincial governments between themselves and the industry.

In the distributional conflicts between Ottawa and the producing provinces, the oil and gas industry has seen itself as the major loser. Higher provincial royalty rates and a total restructuring of federal taxation of the industry made operations in Canada unprofitable or at least less profitable than in other places, particularly the United States. This relative non-profitability, the great uncertainty of changing environmental and land-holding regulations, the high cost of exploration in the frontier regions, and the reduced prospects of finding new reserves in traditional areas led to curtailment of new investments, a decline in exploration, and an exodus of some geological crews and drilling rigs. This was certainly not in the interest of either Ottawa or the producing provinces, and ultimately they undertook to improve the situation from industry's perspectives. In an era of extensive worldwide exploration and good prospects for discovering major new hydrocarbon reserves, Canada must compete for capital, equipment, technical skills, and managerial talents with the rest of the world. There has been little evidence to suggest that governments are willing to provide the incentives that private industry claims it needs in order to meet Canada's growing energy needs. The alternative was growing government intervention in the operations of the industry and this was taking place. At the beginning of 1976, after a long delay, the new national oil company, Petro-Canada, came into existence and took over prior federal interests in energy exploration and development and entered into negotiations to purchase some of the holdings of Atlantic Richfield Canada Ltd., Petro-Canada, the Alberta Energy Co. Ltd., the Ontario Energy Corporation, and the Saskatchewan Oil and Gas Corporation, all government-owned corporations, will play an active role in future exploration.

The bearish industry mood toward new exploration and the rather disappointing results from frontier drilling programs have clouded the long-term supply picture for oil and gas. Commercial quantities of oil have yet to be proven in the Mackenzie River Delta region and the high arctic islands. The thirteen trillion cubic feet of gas found in the high arctic at the beginning of the 1975-76 winter drilling season were still insufficient to justify a pipeline; and whether the gas located in the Mackenzie Delta region could support a pipeline independent of Alaskan gas was under debate. In the east coast offshore areas, results have been much worse. Despite some finds at Sable Island off the Nova Scotia coast and others east of Labrador, the level of interest and activity has been waning for several years. In the traditional producing areas of Alberta, British Columbia, and Saskatchewan, results have been mixed. Substantial new gas reserves have been found but no major deposits of oil have been discovered. For the sixth year in succession Canada's oil production in 1975 outpaced additions to reserves. Whether higher wellhead prices will eventually lead to an increase in proven reserves and deliverability, as many economists predict, remains to be seen. In any event new discoveries usually take five to ten years to bring into production.

Expectations of production from oil sand developments were also revised downward. After years of rather scant interest in oil sands production facilities and reported losses by the first commercial plant, the rise in oil prices rekindled industry and government interest in such enterprises. Estimates by the Alberta government and the National Energy Board in 1974 projected a new 100,000-barrel-per-day plant being built every two years or so with production of 400,000 barrels per day by 1985. But inflation and delays have changed all that. The consortia that in 1974 were eagerly vying for places in line to begin construction of mining extraction plants have one by one delayed or canceled their plans. When escalating costs caused Atlantic Richfield to abandon its 30 percent interest in Syncrude, the company now building the second plant, the promise of a massive infusion of federal and provincial funds was required to persuade Imperial Oil, Gulf Canada, and Canada-Cities Service to continue. Field tests of *in situ* recovery technology were going forward in several locations, but the future of commercial scale operations was quite uncertain.

For all these reasons, Canada's efforts to reduce or even to maintain its current level of oil imports until 1980 or 1985 probably cannot rely on additional supplies of oil and gas becoming available. Curtailing exports to the United States will be essential. The 1973 level of oil exports, despite the reduced flow in the last three months of that year, exceeded an average 1.1 million barrels per day. This will not be repeated again in the foreseeable future. Exports averaged about 900,000 barrels per day in 1974 and 707,000 barrels per day in 1975. The average for 1976 was set at about 460,000 barrels per day. These reductions have resulted in substantial shut-in capacity, reminiscent of the 1960s, as Canada endeavors to conserve its shrinking reserves for its own traditional domestic market west of the Ottawa Valley, a large new petrochemical facility under construction in Sarnia, and the new pipeline into Montreal. But this withholding will have limited utility. Given the expected growth of demand, the constraints of efficient production rates from producing wells, and current expectations of supply, self-sufficiency in these markets has been projected by the National Energy Board to end by 1982, even assuming some savings from end use conservation. The new pipeline might thereafter be used to carry oil from east to west.

Exports will continue their decline. Except perhaps for certain types of crude that are produced in excess of Canadian requirements, they are expected to terminate about 1981. In the meantime, traditional American customers are searching for new supplies and the US Federal Energy Administration has established an allocation system. To assist in the transition, Canada has urged American companies to deliver oil to eastern Canada in exchange for additional supplies provided to upper midwest refineries. Such swaps were slow in developing but have begun to occur. The reduction in exports has again made Canada a net importer of oil. Not only will the growth of imports, to be reduced only temporarily when the Sarnia to Montreal pipeline begins operation in late 1976, cause severe balance-of-payments problems, but it will also strain the federal treasury to continue the import subsidy program. This latter fact provides an important incentive for Ottawa to let the domestic oil price move up to world levels.

Producibility of gas has also become a serious problem. Burgeoning domestic demand resulting in part from several years of underpricing relative to oil and in part from the development of a gas-based petrochemical industry in Alberta, production problems in northern British Columbia gas fields, less favorable than anticipated deliverability rates from existing and new reserves, and fewer new discoveries than expected in recent years, have produced an expectation of shortages here too. Taking into account current export commitments but not counting the possibility that arctic gas may become available, the National Energy Board has projected a shortfall of 0.5 trillion cubic feet by 1980, 1 trillion cubic feet by 1985, and 2.5 trillion by 1995. If these estimates are correct, Canada will soon, and at least until Mackenzie Delta gas becomes available, have to decrease gas exports in order to protect domestic markets. However, other analyses suggest that the effect of rising prices will reduce demand and increase supply to the point where shortfalls will not occur until the late 1980s or early 1990s.

In the face of these predicted shortages of oil and gas, attention has turned increasingly to energy conservation, coal, and uranium. Canadian industry and homeowners were not accustomed to conserving energy, but a combination of increasing costs and rising public concern have had a significant impact on demand. Over the long term, however, conservation was a poor substitute for alternative energy sources or new reserves. Although most of Canada's electricity was derived from hydro, the percentage produced by thermal sources, still primarily oil and gas, had been growing. Several large hydro sources were still available and, despite high economic and environmental cost, more were being developed.

Depending on the resolution of the serious environmental problems associated with its mining and burning, coal may gradually be substituted for oil and gas as fuel in many of the country's thermal power plants. This was especially feasible in the west where most of the coal is located and perhaps in the maritimes where significant coal deposits have been mined in the past and new ones have been discovered. The large quantities of coal used by Ontario Hydro and eastern steel mills were imported from the eastern United States. Planning was in progress, however, to begin transporting western coal east by unit train and lake freighter.

Canada has extensive uranium and thorium resources on which to build a domestic nuclear electricity generating industry. It had been a major exporter of uranium and, under new regulations intended to guarantee a thirty-year supply for Canada's needs, will continue to be so. The nuclear issue in general was much less emotionally charged in Canada than in the United States. In fact relatively little significant opposition existed. This was partly because of a different regulatory structure and the public ownership of electric utilities and the nuclear power plant supplier, but partly because of intrinsic differences in reactor design. At the beginning of 1976, five commercial reactors had entered service, ten were under construction, and fifteen to twenty more were planned or under consideration. Unless the public opposition to nuclear power became substantially more powerful politically, the rate of growth would maintain or exceed current levels for the foreseeable future. It would probably be limited by the availability of heavy water facilities. After years of technical difficulties and industry reluctance to enter that arena, federal and provincial governments have begun to act to assure long-term supply. The need was for the domestic market and to support a tightly safeguarded but assertively pursued export policy.

The scale of energy development projects and the requirements for capital were staggering for an economy the size of Canada's. The federal government estimated that by 1985, $110 billion of new capital would be needed for energy development alone. Making available the required level of capital and manpower and managing this scale of investment would be very difficult without severe economic dislocations, including inflationary pressure and shortages of labor and materials.

Besides marshaling the capital, manpower, and technology that will be required to bring to market new energy supplies, Canada's other tasks in the energy sector for the next decade include coming to terms with scarcity of conventional oil and gas, handling the economic drain and political dependency of rising oil imports, and minimizing adverse reaction from the United States as energy exports are reduced. As the price of domestic crude oil and gas gradually rises, relative stability should return to the domestic energy markets. Disagreement and political rancor will continue, however. If shortfalls actually developed in oil or gas availability, the allocation of the shortages would be particularly divisive. Disputes between regions and governments are a pervasive and expected aspect of policymaking on all issues in Canada. Energy policy will be no exception.

National consensus on the underlying assumptions of energy policy was not likely to be achieved. Canadian nationalists remain vocal in their pleas to reduce the interdependence between Canada and the United States. To some extent this sentiment was reflected in official policy on energy and other matters. The Trudeau government has in many instances put Canada's narrow interest, as defined within Canada, ahead of the common interest or any notion of a special relationship between Canada and the United States. The translation of nationalism into official policy was for a time widely attributed in the United States to the need of a minority government to maintain the support of the small leftist New Democratic party. But this was less than the whole truth. Public attitudes and those of federal civil servants have been changing. While by no means going as far as the nationalists would like, even with its majority position in Parliament, the Liberal government has retained the general direction of its policy toward the United States, in the energy areas as in others.

When Canadian interests are not seriously hurt Canada will be willing to make accommodations to the US. Maintaining good relations and avoiding American retaliation for energy price increases or export curtailment must remain important goals of Canadian foreign policy. Ottawa therefore decided to phase out oil and gas exports gradually, giving ample warning of new reductions and offering to cooperate with Washington to reduce the short-term impacts on those areas of the United States that have been heavily dependent on Canadian exports.

Where Canadian interests as perceived by Ottawa can be served by interdependence, its policy has been to foster it. For reasons of economic efficiency, industry and Ontario Hydro have imported large quantities of American coal for thermal and metallurgical purposes. Despite the plans to begin moving Alberta coal eastward by the early 1980s, this dependence on American coal will grow with time. The electricity grid interconnections between Canadian and American utilities have operated to their mutual advantage. In recent years, moreover, Canada has been willing to export increasing quantities of electric power to energy-short American utilities along the border. By 1974, 5.5 percent of Canada-generated electric power was exported. Part of this was derived from American coal imported into Ontario. As Canada's last large economically attractive hydro sources are tapped, additional capacity will continue to be available for export until it is needed at home.

Probably the most significant example of cooperation was the treaty on pipelines carrying hydrocarbons for use in either the United States or Canada across the territory of the other. Although its ratification, if followed by agreements with relevant provinces, would help clear the way for a joint gas pipeline from the arctic, it would by no means guarantee that result. Regulatory review before the National Energy Board and the American Federal Power Commission was in progress and moving slowly. The competition in the United

States between the trans-Alaskan pipeline proposed by El Paso Natural Gas and the joint Canadian-American proposal to use a MacKenzie River Valley route to bring Alaskan and Mackenzie Delta gas to market, and the parallel competition in Canada between the joint project and an all-Canadian proposal of Foothills Pipelines, Ltd., will be fought in economic and nationalistic terms. El Paso and Foothills are strongly emphasizing the all-American and all-Canadian aspects of their projects. It was no accident, for example, that Foothills chose the name Maple Leaf Line for its proposal. In the Canadian decision, the issue of autarky or interdependence was posed starkly. It will be a very significant political choice for the government.

Stimulated by rising world oil prices and a dramatic demonstration in 1973 of the insecurity of Middle East oil supplies, the Canadian government formulated an objective of achieving or moving toward energy autarky. Rather than being closer to realization, however, this policy has become significantly more remote than when it was first enunciated. Canada's interdependence with the United States will continue and perhaps grow. Barring oil and gas discovery rates dramatically different from those that have been found, reliance on imported oil will resume its gradual rise once the impact of the new pipeline to Montreal has been absorbed. In comparison to many other countries, Canada was richly endowed with energy resources, yet it cannot achieve energy autarky in the foreseeable future.

4 *Western Europe: The Politics of Muddling Through*

Wolfgang Hager

Since 1945, Western European energy politics have been inextricably linked with major foreign policy choices. The Coal and Steel Community of 1952 constituted the first step toward the European Community (EC). Far from providing a lasting basis for European unification through pooling the key industrial commodity, coal turned into the most stubbornly declining industry. Carrying the social burden of the decline overtaxed the nascent solidarity of the European Community, and the task fell largely to national governments. The Suez crisis of 1956 once again gave impetus to unification via a common energy policy: the European Atomic Energy Community (Euratom) was conceived as the key to indefinite energy security and to European unity. Since all governments, except the French, started almost from scratch, problems of ex post facto harmonization did not arise. That dream, too, foundered. A year after its inception in 1958, Charles de Gaulle's preference for keeping a national military option made Euratom virtually moribund.

The more fundamental reason for the decline of coal and the failure of nuclear energy, which together led to the great vulnerability of European energy supplies in the seventies, was the switch to oil. The speed with which oil became the main source of energy of Western Europe owed much to US policy. In 1950 the US government, under pressure from the administrators of the Marshall Plan, broke the pricing structure of the oil companies' cartel which had charged Europe (Mexican) Gulf prices for Middle East oil. Much more important, the Eisenhower administration in 1959 decided to introduce mandatory import quotas reserving 90 percent of the market for US domestic production. The enormous oil reserves discovered by the international companies in the Middle East had to be sold in the only major market left in the world: Western Europe. Prices fell in real terms throughout the sixties. Coal and lignite, which in 1957 had satisfied three-quarters of the Community's energy supplies, accounted for less than a quarter by 1970. The development of nuclear energy, unable to compete with cheap oil, was delayed by a decade.

The concern expressed about this development was directed at the dominance of foreign oil companies in Europe's supply, not at dependence on one of the most volatile regions of the world. The trust in the efficacy of the Pax Americana to ensure a considerable stability to economic contractual relations continued absolute at a time when the psychological basis for such trust was being destroyed on the battlefields of Vietnam. Yet national attempts to bypass international oil companies had proved costly and yielded only limited success. In the fifties and sixties, Italy, through the state-owned Ente Nazionale Idrocarburi (ENI), and France, through its 35 percent interest with Compagnie Française des Pétroles (CFP) and the state company, Entreprise de Recherches et d'Activités Pétrolières (ELF-ERAP), sought to break the hold of the international majors over oil supplies. Rich from the monopoly rents derived from Italian gas production, ENI offered terms to the producing countries (i.e., 50 percent participation) which were revolutionary by the standards of the fifties. The stability of the world oil market, however, was not upset since ENI proved singularly unsuccessful in discovering oil. France pursued a double strategy. The CFP became an associate of the majors in the Persian Gulf area, well placed to take advantage of the economic benefits of existing British-American arrangements yet able to wave the tricolor should the diplomatic context require it. ELF-ERAP, like ENI, experimented in novel forms of government-to-government contracts. Heavy reliance on Algeria, including payments for oil well over the going rate, proved a costly failure. The 51 percent share was French-nationalized in 1971. Yet even after the loss, close to 70 percent of French crude was supplied by "national" sources, although the meaning of the term changed with the growth of producer power in the early seventies.

Throughout the postwar years, Italy gave priority to cheap energy as an aid to industrialization. With limited gas reserves in the Po Valley as the only indigenous energy source, reliance on oil was mandatory. From 1960 to 1975 the share of oil expanded from 45 percent to 75 percent of energy consumption, making Italy the most vulnerable country in the European Community. Three effects are worth noting. The stress on cheap oil contributed to the failure of a common Community energy policy, as such a policy would have required some purchase of "domestic" (i.e., German) high-cost coal.

Secondly, the policy entailed price control. While this did not bother the companies in the decades of falling crude prices, it drove the Royal Dutch-Shell Oil Company (Shell) and British Petroleum Company (BP) refineries out of business in 1974, leading to a takeover of their plants by Italian state companies. Thirdly, the cheap oil policy was supported by the encouragement of a substantial export capacity for oil products, much of it located in the Mezzogiorno and largely destined for Eastern Mediterranean markets. The huge new OPEC refinery capacity which was expected by 1980 would pose a deadly danger to an important part of Italy's foreign trade and industrial balance.

The need to reconcile the social imperative to slow the decline of the coal sector with the official free market doctrine, which favored oil, dominated Germany's energy policy in the postwar years. As a result, the government subsidized coal and established coal import quotas while heavily taxing rival oil products to reduce the differential. Even so the share of hard and soft coal in primary energy consumption fell from 75 percent to 34 percent between 1960 and 1973. (While total production was to remain stable thereafter, the proportion of coal was expected to decline to 21 percent in 1978.) The share of imports in total energy supplies rose from 9 percent in 1960 to 55 percent in 1973. More than other major countries, the Federal Republic of Germany left the supply of oil to the international majors. The economics ministry exercised informal control, especially to prevent aggressive pricing and marketing, but perhaps no less effectively than the more elaborate and formal control structure of France and Italy. The reliance on the majors became problematical after the 1973 crisis. The government lacked essential information and an instrument for dealing directly with such governments as Iran which had expressed an interest in bilateral cooperation. In response to these shortcomings, the government created a national integrated company (Veba-Gelsenberg-Deminex).

Great Britain, like Germany, relied heavily on its large coal deposits, but only with the help of subsidies and discriminatory taxes on competing energy sources. Although theoretically British coal could be produced more cheaply than German coal, union resistance to modernization and high wage demands eroded the cost advantage. The miners' strike in February 1974, which forced Great Britain to adopt a three-day working week, showed that coal, though domestically produced, represented a grave threat to Britain's supply security. As for oil, two facts set it apart from all European countries, except the Netherlands. First, two of the seven majors, BP (51 percent state-owned) and Royal Dutch-Shell (Anglo-Dutch) were headquartered in London. De facto, therefore, Great Britain formed part of the otherwise American-dominated network of the world oil market. Secondly, Great Britain, since the mid-sixties, had begun to produce substantial amounts of natural gas in the North Sea. The search for more gas led to the discovery of huge amounts of off-shore oil, enough to sustain an estimated production of 4-6 million barrels per day. Thus Britain expected to achieve energy self-sufficiency in the early eighties.

The Netherlands developed into a key country in the energy supplies of Western Europe. The discovery of the Groningen gas field in the early sixties quickly led to substantial gas exports to France, Belgium, and Germany. Simultaneously, Rotterdam developed into Europe's main trading and refining area for oil and oil products, serving Germany and the Scandinavian countries.

The Crisis of 1973

Had the OAPEC and OPEC action resulted from a carefully timed strategy, 1973 would have been an ideal year in which to strike. Western Europe's dependence on imported oil had reached its height. Even without higher oil prices, nuclear energy, made cheaper by technological advances, and North Sea hydrocarbons would have reduced the share of oil in the total energy economy in later years. Of course, such a Europe-centered perspective overlooks important extra-European developments: the sudden rise in US oil imports in the early seventies; the gradual weakening of the power of the multinational corporations (MNCs) over the conditions for production and marketing in the newly self-assertive exporting countries; and the growing technical sophistication of OPEC, founded in 1960 but not taken seriously for many years.

One of the first organizations to realize the coming danger was the European Commission. In 1972 it resumed its long struggle to persuade the member-states to agree to a common energy policy. Noting that the oil market had now become a sellers' market and that the oil producers were becoming more and more assertive, the

Commission's Memorandum of October 1972 suggested, among other things, a crisis allocation system, a unified oil and energy market, and the need for a structured dialogue with Middle East oil governments.[1] The idea of a common oil market, elaborated in the winter of 1972-73, rested on the following logic: The Community represents the most important single market in the world for oil and a great many other imports. In order to play a role, this market had to be surrounded by a fence, which might take the form of what would amount to a publicly-organized cartel of importing companies. The companies "accredited" to the Community would be required to uphold the rules set by the Community authorities, including an obligation to furnish data on the economics of their operations and to observe "orientation prices" fixed on the basis of this information. At times of scarcity in certain refined products, such as that caused by the "phony" energy crisis in the summer of 1973 because of insufficient refining capacity in the US, price ceilings would be imposed to preclude windfall profits. (It would almost automatically have to be accompanied by export controls to prevent "distortions" of normal supply patterns.) In normal times, price floors would be established to ensure adequate profits to the companies with which to fulfill greatly increased investment needs. The system of Community "accreditation" could be used to bargain with OPEC national companies wishing to establish downstream operations in the Community.

The Commission's October 1972 Memorandum also spelled out the idea of a Community dialogue with the oil producers, which did occur after the oil crisis. The language of the Commission's proposal was ambitious and vague. It argued:

> The economic and social cooperation between the two groups, i.e., EEC and oil-exporting countries in all areas of common interest and based on mutual advantage could facilitate the industrial and economic development of the oil-exporting regions and the establishment of a desirable stability in the relations between equal partners.

And:

> The Commission considers it necessary:
>
> 1. to create a mechanism for a dialogue with the exporting countries; the mixed commissions which are to be established with some of the

countries could be used for this purpose;

2. to send, at the same time, groups of industrialists from the Community to the exporting countries, and vice versa, to examine concrete possibilities for economic cooperation;
3. to negotiate cooperation agreements which should observe the following principles:

— an undertaking by the Community to favor the economic and social development of the exporting countries by making available technical and perhaps financial assistance, as well as to open its markets for the industrial and agricultural products of these countries;

— an undertaking by the exporting countries and the Community to observe certain rules and guarantees for commercial transactions and industrial investments.[2]

The Commission attempts foundered on the resistance of Germany's partners, notably the Netherlands, to share in the cost of supporting a "domestic" coal industry and on Germany's dislike of a *dirigiste* energy policy on the French pattern. At the time of the October 1973 crisis, only two safety measures were in place: a stockpile policy, which obliged member states to build up reserves equivalent to sixty-five days' consumption, and an agreement to introduce domestic measures for energy rationing in a supply crisis. Germany successfully tested the system within weeks after its passage through parliament. In retrospect—and this is important for prognosis of European behavior in a future supply crisis—the panic which followed the 25 percent production cuts imposed by OAPEC and its embargo of shipments to the Netherlands (and the US) was quite unnecessary. European countries had anticipated a planned rise in mandatory stockpile levels to ninety days' oil supply, and a further thirty days were in transit. Actual import shortfalls amounted to about 12 percent of total imports and perhaps 8 percent of total consumption. The use of stockpiles, plus a moderate reduction of consumption and a shift toward coal, would have seen Europe safely through a whole year of the supply cuts exacted by OAPEC.

Why then the panic? One reason was the general feeling of doom which prevailed in political circles at the time. The beginning of the decade saw a marked intensification of the struggle over the distribution of wealth in most European countries. Even in the

Netherlands and Germany wage bargaining had brought settlements well in excess of productivity gains. Inflation was rampant. At the start of the oil crisis there was a general feeling that the population would not easily adjust to a reduction of living standards which would follow if industrial machinery slowed down for lack of fuel. Ironically, the real economic crisis which followed in 1974 and 1975 helped to consolidate the *contrat social,* even in Great Britain.

The great uncertainty among governments about the extent and possible impact of the crisis reinforced the pessimism. Initially, it was conceivable that OAPEC might tighten the oil tap further, or that more countries might be hit by the selective total embargoes. No one could be sure that the oil companies would be able to allocate scarce supplies equitably. Indeed, a tighter control of destinations by Arab exporters would have been technically possible. Uncertainty extended to the precise level and location of stockpiles held by the international companies. The introduction of an extensive information system as part of the International Energy Agency (IEA) a year later owed much to the feeling of helpless ignorance experienced by European (and the Japanese) governments at the time.

Ignorance and lack of confidence in the resilience of the populations thus combined to push European governments into actions which they would rather forget. The attempt of Great Britain and France to play the Arab card and maintain imports at pre-crisis levels, which would have compounded the burden elsewhere, certainly shocked other governments. Apparently, Britain and France also prevented the use of existing, if somewhat rusty, oil allocation machinery—the International Industry Advisory Board of the OECD which had been established after the 1956 oil crisis.[3] Germany's refusal to control the price of oil products, introduced by the partner states, to prevent the oil companies from accumulating windfall profits from existing stocks was a subtle but effective way to gain more than a fair share of crude imports and oil products. The lack of verbal support for the embargoed Dutch was another black mark for the Community, although there was a general feeling among European governments that the Dutch foreign minister should have refrained from pro-Israel comments which helped no one.

European-American Energy Diplomacy

Two and a half years after the October 1973 crisis neither individual countries nor the European Community as a whole had elaborated energy programs which would more than marginally change the status quo. The decline of coal had been halted. Nuclear energy was pursued with a little more vigor. Oil exploration and development in the North Sea was proceeding in spite rather than because of support from public policymakers. Most of the concrete progress in international energy cooperation occurred in the Atlantic/OECD framework under American leadership. Given the dramatic economic and political challenge of the energy crisis for Western Europe, one might have expected equally dramatic policy responses. When these failed to materialize, the observer was easily led to diagnose a lack of political leadership and a failure of government. Given the lack of progress at the Community level, the disappointment extended to the viability of the European Community and its relevance to coping with major challenges.

Yet by a different route, American energy policy had arrived at very similar results. After years of heroic plans, practical politics and practical economics prevented the US government from adopting all but marginal changes in energy policy. If there was a lesson to be learned from both experiences, it was that economic policy can be altered only marginally in response to foreign policy demands, especially when these demands are not literally perceived as vital. "The economy"—the totality of short-term requirements for price stability, full employment, and industrial activity—takes precedence. The difference between the bold American and the pedestrian European approach to energy policy was therefore largely one of style, perhaps arising from the allocation of responsibility for policymaking within the respective bureaucracies and branches of government. In the United States the secretary of state took the initiative in what was largely seen as a foreign policy problem. The Treasury and above all the Congress imposed domestic priorities afterwards. In Europe, from the beginning, the ministries of economics framed energy policy since the issue was defined primarily as one of economics.

The experience of disunity in the fall of 1973 had deeply shaken the mutual confidence of the EEC member states. The plans for the elaboration of a common energy market, fairly advanced by the fall of

1973, were therefore adjourned sine die. For the purposes of energy sharing, the Community almost ceased to be relevant. The oil companies emerged as the unsung heroes of the cutback/embargo period. When they made it clear to the governments that they would be unable to carry the political responsibility for oil sharing a second time, the search for an international political framework passed from the EEC to the OECD level. This, however, raised new and serious policy demands for the Europeans because it implied an alliance with the United States on a major foreign-policy issue, although the underlying divergence of interest, which had become apparent in the fall of 1973, was by no means resolved.[4] Yet Europe needed American leadership and the discipline which only the US could enforce as an alternative to its own lack of leadership and lack of mutual trust. Furthermore, since any future crisis-sharing would require the collaboration of the international oil industry and restraint among all major importers, only a framework which included the US and Japan made sense.

Yet this alliance with the United States had to be handled in such a way that relations with the Arab exporters did not grow unduly strained. This became a major foreign policy task of the Community members in the conduct of their energy diplomacy, in which finance had become an important factor. Two strategies were to serve that end. The first was to modify the alliance, and thus US policy, to minimize its confrontational aspects. The second was to engage in a dialogue with the Arab oil governments to achieve a pattern of relations functionally similar to a "reinsurance treaty." One important element in the conduct of this strategy, which was much less deliberate and planned than the present ex post facto analysis suggests, was to preserve "a European identity" within the reemerging Atlantic context. Thus Henry Kissinger's invitation in December 1973 to key countries for what became the Washington energy conference was countered by the invitees' insistence on participation by all EEC members. A week before the Washington energy conferees assembled (11-14 February 1974), the foreign ministers of the Nine met to work out a common position, which included a commitment to resist any attempt to create a permanent institution for Western energy cooperation. In Washington, under the leadership of Germany which held the presidency of the Council of Ministers, the Eight moved away from what remained essentially a French preoccupation. The logic of the American proposals in a context of rapidly diminishing tensions in the oil crisis proved irresistible to the

Eight. France refused to jeopardize two of its most important foreign policy positions: systematic friendship with the Arabs and resistance to a US-dominated international system. The International Energy Agency (IEA), born nine months after the Washington conference, had direct links with the OECD. This owed much to the European wish to minimize the novelty of the operation and to allow France indirect membership. The readiness of the Eight to go along with the American plans was enlarged by President Richard Nixon's assurances to the OPEC governments of the nonconfrontational character of the Washington Conference and suggestion of a joint producer-consumer conference within ninety days. A commitment to such a conference, which the Community summit undertook in December 1973 in Copenhagen, would thus be implemented in the broader OECD context and preempted by it. At the Washington Conference, however, Kissinger laid down conditions which clearly delayed a producer-consumer conference to the distant future: a solid basis of consumer cooperation had to be established before it made sense to talk to the producers.

On 4 March, the foreign ministers of the Nine, secretly and without consulting the US, sent a memorandum to the Arab League outlining areas of possible future cooperation. Secretary Kissinger reacted with predictable irritation. Unilateral Community attempts to hold a dialogue with the Arabs and/or oil producers were suspended for a year, although individual states continued lobbying, mostly for strictly economic ends. Meanwhile, France tried to wrest the initiative from Kissinger and to commit its European partners to a strategy of cooperation with the producers. It pressed hard for and obtained a "world energy conference." The sixth special session of the UN General Assembly, which met in April 1974, was singularly unproductive. The change of title of the session from energy to raw materials and development, following a suggestion by Algeria's President Houari Boumedienne, yielded major consequences. Instead of a dialogue between a minority of oil producers faced by a majority of consumers, the session turned into a major North-South confrontation on the fundamentals of the international economic order; a new complication had been added to energy diplomacy, dissolving European hopes for a constructive dialogue on energy and reinforcing US skepticism. Nevertheless, a chapter on cooperation with the oil producers became part of the "Agreement on a Common Energy Program," the basic text of the IEA.

By the spring of 1974 the energy problem had ceased to be one of availability and had become one of price and its consequence for the international payments pattern. Again American policy diverged from the European. Throughout the summer of 1974, Secretary Kissinger attempted to "talk the price of oil down." This, in itself, Europeans considered risky. They feared that the conservationist lobby, particularly strong among Palestinian economic advisers to several Arab governments, might be strengthened. If prices fell, oil would be worth more in the ground since oil prices would eventually rise to the level of energy substitutes. More serious from a European point of view was the financial element in the American strategy to push the price of oil down quickly. By a deliberate and not always benign neglect of recycling of petrodollars, the US wanted to demonstrate that the existing price structure was untenable and a mortal danger to the international economic system. Accepting new international recycling machinery would be tantamount to accepting the legitimacy of the new prices. The Europeans doubted the wisdom and efficacy of the strategy and feared a collapse in the very short term of the international trading system. They made strong representations to the US in the annual International Monetary Fund (IMF) meeting in October 1974. At a press conference, US Treasury Secretary William E. Simon admitted the need to study recycling plans, despite the lack of urgency. Yet this concession to European wishes was promptly turned into a tool for strengthening a joint Western stance vis-à-vis the oil producers.

In mid-November, secretaries Kissinger and Simon spelled out the new policy in two speeches in Chicago: the creation of a substantial financial safety-net of $25 billion among the OECD countries with the right to draw on these funds made conditional on a responsible energy policy. In particular, a 10 percent saving of energy was targeted for 1975. As Kissinger explained, "we have to create the objective conditions for a decline of the oil price"; a politically manipulated demand was to be the answer to a politically manipulated price. The day before the IEA agreement came into force, its defensive posture had given way to an offensive policy. This presented the Europeans with new dilemmas. A purely OECD-based recycling arrangement directly snubbed the oil producers. Equally serious, implementation of the plan would take months. By then the international payments structure could be irretrievably damaged. Neither side could know that the recession of 1975 would cure the payments deficits and produce a 10 percent cut in consumption without major effort. In any event, the finance ministers of the Nine, caucusing in London before the January 1975 meeting of the IMF, decided to press for primary recycling through the IMF, which implied cooperation with the oil producers, and to relegate the OECD safety net to a recourse of last resort. They had their way in Washington: the IMF oil facility was doubled to $12 billion and member state quotas were raised by a third. The OECD Fund, designated the Financial Support Fund, was signed on 9 April 1975 to start the long road toward ratification by parliaments.

Meanwhile another diplomatic initiative of the Nine had helped to defuse the confrontation with the producers and restore a measure of harmony within the Nine and the Alliance. After considerable lobbying, especially by German Chancellor Helmut Schmidt, presidents Gerald Ford and Valéry Giscard d'Estaing met in Martinique on 14-16 December 1974. An important compromise was struck. France agreed to participate informally in the IEA, while the US agreed to set a firm date for a conference preparing the consumer-producer dialogue. This agreement incidentally emboldened the Japanese government to endorse Kissinger's Chicago proposals. On the face of it, Kissinger alone had made real concessions at Martinique. France already participated informally in the work of the IEA through the Community caucus, which had quickly established itself and which allowed Commission civil servants to chair two working groups of the IEA, and through French membership in the OECD. A public admission of this fact, however, shored up the appearance of Western unity.

Yet once again Kissinger knew how to use a concession to the Europeans as a stepping stone to closer Western cooperation. In a speech to the National Press Club in Washington on 3 February the secretary of state mentioned three conditions for entering into a dialogue with the producers. Two of these were familiar: an immediate commitment to stringent energy saving by the IEA members and the adoption of the Financial Support Fund. The third was new: the introduction of a floor price for energy. The last demand considerably embarrassed the Europeans, and by the time the preparatory conference with the producers opened in April 1975, only a vague commitment in principle had been obtained within the IEA.

The logic of introducing a common price for domestic energy consumption in all member countries of the IEA was sound. Investments in alternative energy sources were to be assured against the risk, however slight, that international oil prices would fall significantly. Users of energy would be served notice that high energy prices were here to stay and would thus be encouraged to undertake energy-saving investments. In addition, a joint commitment to a floor price would strengthen the coalition of consumers in the coming negotiations with the oil producers. OPEC producers would face the prospect of a stagnating oil market and a declining market share. For Kissinger, however, much more was at stake. If the US was to regain the diplomatic freedom of maneuver required of a superpower, energy autarky was essential. A study by the Federal Energy Agency in November 1974 had shown that the US would achieve autarky by 1985, if the domestic price were $13 per barrel; at $7.00 there would be an import gap of 14 million barrels per day, twice the existing production of Saudi Arabia and half of projected American oil consumption. Significantly it was Thomas Enders, the assistant secretary of state for economic and business affairs, who announced the administration's commitment to a high-price policy. A parallel international strategy would be helpful for two reasons: it would put pressure on the Congress for an early agreement and would prevent a significant gap in industrial competitive strength between the US and its industrial allies.

Most Europeans were highly skeptical of the floor price proposal. For one thing, new domestic sources of energy, notably North Sea hydrocarbons and nuclear energy, were far cheaper than some of the potential US sources, notably shale oil. Secondly, the continental countries were unwilling to give up the option of cheaper oil should it become available. For France, the usual foreign policy objections against an implicit anti-Arab and anti-OPEC policy also played a role. The German policy establishment exhibited its traditional context. Although patent nonsense—oil production can be easily matched to demand—there were references to the "mountains" produced by the Community's agricultural policy. In 1975 these were the makings of a major deal transforming the European Community, a deal comparable to the historic exchange of market access for agricultural and industrial goods between Germany and France when the Common Market was set up. Now the Community could have struck an equally fundamental bargain with Great Britain, exchanging financial support and guaranteed prices on the consumer side for more or less unconditional access to North Sea oil[5] by Great Britain. Neither side was willing to think in these terms.

Great Britain was in a mood of euphoria about North Sea oil which would end decades of industrial decline and international humiliation. Moreover, Scottish nationalism may have contributed to the government's hesitation to "give" something to Europe to which its own claim was disputed. The consumer countries, for their part, saw North Sea development proceed rapidly without government intervention. Two years after the oil crisis, the achievement of energy autarky seemed less urgent.

Instead of becoming a major European issue, the floor price debate deteriorated into the by now familiar pattern of European minimalism versus American insistence on bold approaches. As part of the reluctantly given agreement on the principle of a floor price, the Europeans achieved a significant weakening of the commitment to the IEA. In the provisional agreement reached on 7 March 1975 there was no longer any talk of a single, high, domestic energy price, but of a combination of national subsidies for uncompetitive energy sources, present and future, and great freedom in the way hypothetically cheap oil imports were to be dealt with. This ad hoc approach followed proposals made by the European Commission which, after years of virtual exclusion from energy policymaking, reasserted itself.

There remained, however, the question of the price level below which imported oil would not be allowed to sell. Here the continental Europeans pressed for, and won, the relatively low price of $7.00, which might be said to represent a reasonable safeguard to North Sea profitability. However, the safeguard was seriously compromised by the refusal to index this price level to inflation for fear of creating a precedent for raw-material pricing in the North-South context. Since the Minimum Safeguard Price, as it came to be called, existed for dealing with a hypothetical and far-off contingency, expressing it in nominal terms was quite meaningless. However, most participants hoped or feared that the principle of a guaranteed North Sea price had been admitted and that future adjustments were not excluded.

Significantly, the IEA agreement on the $7.00 floor price was reached only on 19 December 1975, after the twenty-seven-state Conference on International Economic Cooperation (CIEC) ended its first ministerial meeting. Great Britain took the North-South dialogue as the occasion for a forceful, if muddled, attempt to plead for a floor price. Together with a demand for a separate seat at the conference, this led to a minor but bitter crisis with the Eight. Yet the fact that the floor-price issue was raised in such a context demonstrated the ambiguity of the concept. In theory, a high domestic energy price was meant to force down the international oil price. This would allow the consumer countries to reap the balance of payments benefits of lower prices without jeopardizing the goal of energy independence from OPEC. Britain's place, even as a future major oil producer, was therefore within the envisaged protectionist framework of the industrial allies.

On the other hand, some observers had always suspected that the floor price might be a device to keep all oil prices high, in spite of the lonely battle Kissinger had fought for lower prices in 1974. Yet in Kissinger's Chicago speech, which first mentioned the floor price, one sentence spoke of it as "a point of reference" for "an eventual price agreement with the producers." In 1975, several factors made a shift of the US State Department's position toward higher international oil prices plausible. For the State Department, priority had to be given to the goal of energy independence. Yet Congress and the European and Japanese allies had signaled their unwillingness to fix domestic energy levels at anything like the $13 per barrel which, according to official calculations, would lead to energy autarky by 1985. Paradoxically, therefore, the very countries—the members of OAPEC—whose hold over US policies had to be broken in the medium term became important allies in Kissinger's strategy for energy autarky. A more positive attitude toward higher oil prices, which was signaled to the Shah of Iran on his visit to the US in the spring of 1975, did not exclude resistance to them which would have jeopardized the hope for an end to the world recession. However, by 1975, the US had rebuilt its political standing in the Arab world, and the world economy seemed to be coping with the new oil prices. The need for lowering them seemed thus less urgent.

After two years of energy diplomacy, the Community members could at best point to limited successes. The IEA had established an as yet untested mechanism for sharing in a crisis and perhaps facilitated cooperation among its members in the development of new energy technology. The agreement on a minimum energy price was slightly better than the lowest common denominator (i.e., no price) and had prepared the ground for a future deal between Great Britain and the Eight. However, when the Community (Energy)

Council of Ministers, in March 1976, failed to commit France to the $7.00 level, as that government had promised at the Community summit in Rome in December 1975, the attempt to keep France in the fold had proved abortive.

As regards the second string on the Community's diplomacy, the dialogue with the producers, results were even more disappointing. So long as the alliance between the oil producers and the Third World remained intact, the North-South dialogue would remain the forum for an ideological and constitutional debate offering few prospects for creating the sort of political links with the Arab oil states which would be useful in a crisis. Yet such links clearly remained desirable. They would determine whether, in a future crisis, the oil weapon would be used merely symbolically or with intent to harm. The hope remained to create a long-term net of interdependencies which the Arab world would not wish to endanger. While the US could eventually expect to find the oil for its needs within its own hemisphere and even territory, Europeans had to view the dependence on Arab supplies as a long-term prospect. Furthermore, bilateral issues—the way in which petrodollars might be invested in Europe without economic risks and the transfer of technology and related problems of overinvestment in certain petroleum- and gas-related industrial sectors—needed discussion in the short-term. If anything like the planned production of oil products, petrochemicals, steel, and so on was to be realized, serious trade disputes seemed inevitable. Accordingly, the reactivated idea of a formal Euro-Arab dialogue led to three meetings in Cairo, Rome, and Abu Dhabi between June and November 1975. The Arab League and the European Commission acted as secretariats and spokesmen for huge delegations from the respective member states. Working groups were formed to study industrial, technical agricultural, labor, commercial, and cultural relations. Oil was not part of the agenda.

As it turned out, neither the EEC nor the Arab League had the industrial capacity and political authority to exceed a general discussion of the agenda. Moreover, the Europeans were pushed into a manifest defensive posture. The basic flaw in the idea of a dialogue, which Kissinger had recognized, was the great disparity in negotiating power between the sides in the short term. Most embarrassing to the Europeans was the constant Arab intrusion of political demands. The EEC trade pact with Israel dominated the first, and the

European votes on the UN General Assembly anti-Zionist resolutions the third of the supposedly technical meetings. But even the economic demands went far beyond anything the Community could give. Total trade liberalization on the Lomé pattern and export-earning stabilization were clearly out of the question. The dialogue thus helped to undermine the cumulative goodwill of years of patient effort to fashion a working relationship with the poorer littoral states in the context of the Community's Mediterranean policy. By creating a forum where political and economic demands could be made from a position of strength, the Community put itself in the position of having to say no to almost every point of substance. The first ministerial meeting of the General Commission of the Dialogue, planned for the early summer of 1976, promised to bring new Arab demands for political support, embarrass the Europeans, and reveal divergences among the Nine.

Without Grand Designs: Domestic Achievements

European energy policy failed to provide the kind of spectacular initiatives which might have impressed the Arabs and laid the basis for a moderate pricing policy and increased caution with regard to future embargoes. However, strong signals such as a high Minimum Support Price, a crash effort in conservation, or a major acceleration of North Sea development might have angered the Arabs and reduced supply security. More important, the damage to the domestic economy would have outweighed the increasingly hypothetical dangers of dependence on the Arabs. The world recession made government action less urgent. It produced major savings of energy without public intervention—Germany's energy consumption in 1975, for instance, was 8 percent less than in 1973—thus relieving the balance-of-payments problems and forcing the producers into relative moderation on pricing, although this might change in the next economic upswing. Moreover, the recession itself became the major preoccupation of governments. Anything which might prolong it, such as anti-car measures or legally imposed restrictions on energy use by industry, had to be avoided. One could not increase a present danger in order to avoid an uncertain future danger.

This being said, all governments had in fact taken a great many individual measures which would increasingly save energy, produce more domestic energy, and insure energy supplies from non-Arab sources. Most countries already allocate heating oil by quotas, while France, Great Britain, and Germany provide generous tax allowances for insulating industrial buildings. In Germany, plans were in advanced stages to pipe "waste" water from electricity generation through vast regional distribution grids for use in space heating. Most countries, particularly Great Britain, have sharply raised energy prices to users, thus promoting conservation. The British government, in spite of Labour party pressures, has put an end to uncertainty over the extent of government control and financial off-take, which had threatened to slow down oil development in the North Sea. In Germany, the decline of hard coal was halted, and huge new lignite deposits were being developed, although whole villages had to be moved to make this possible.

Next to the North Sea, the largest potential European energy source was nuclear energy. According to Commission projections, almost half of all electricity produced by 1985 would be derived from it. In 1974-75 France especially decided to make a crash effort in the coming years, oddly at variance with its professed belief in Arab reasonableness. However, even in France, where such initiatives were rare, a lively national discussion on the dangers of the nuclear power stations was taking place. In the more densely populated countries of the rest of Europe, utilities were running out of sites for new power plants while citizen groups delayed some projects and managed to prevent others altogether. In 1976 concern over the availability of uranium in the late 1980s, and some doubts about the adequacy of enrichment capacity in the early 1990s, cast another cloud over the future of nuclear energy.

The world economic upswing in 1976-77 might be expected to quicken the pace of energy policy in Western Europe. The rapid deterioration of the payments balances of most countries would lead to renewed efforts to reduce oil imports. A tighter oil market would also reinforce OPEC assertiveness and hence remind governments of the extent of their dependence.

5 *Japan's Long-Term Vulnerabilities*

Masao Sakisaka

Japan weathered the 1973 crisis of interrupted oil supplies. It also managed to absorb the quadrupled price of oil imports, which that year furnished 77.4 percent of the nation's total energy demand. The costs to the Japanese economy were massive, however, in aggravated inflation, prolonged recession, rising unemployment and business failures, reduced private earnings and public revenues, and delayed social and economic reforms. Moreover, Japan's actual and contemplated adjustments to the changed world energy situation could in no significant way lessen its dependence on imported oil or reduce its vulnerabilities in the event of yet another Middle East war and oil embargo. To be sure, Japan's long-term energy outlook was somewhat bolstered by the formation of the International Energy Agency (IEA) with its program for cooperation among the major oil-importing states on price stabilization and energy conservation, on oil sharing in case of a supply crisis, and on joint efforts to expand world oil supplies and develop alternative energy sources.

In the perspective of Japan's dependence on the Arab Middle East for 40 percent of its oil, however, the IEA cooperative effort could be counted as successful only if another war and oil cutback or cutoff could be avoided. Japan therefore faced difficult political as well as economic decisions as it sought to protect established oil supplies while at the same time cooperating responsibly with IEA policies and programs.

The temporary oil cutback in October 1973 created a psychology of scarcity in Japan, accelerating an already virulent inflation. During the one-year period beginning in September 1973, wholesale prices rose 31 percent and consumer prices 24 percent, although the rise in energy costs was only partly to blame. In June 1975 electricity rates were hiked 70 percent, and gas rates in major cities were boosted 40 to 50 percent. By the fall of 1975, the average price of shipments from refineries was three times what it had been before the Middle East war. Even so, petroleum and power companies continued to run deficits in their current operations.

The Tanaka cabinet's oil emergency policy was announced on 16 November, exactly one month after the imposition of the cutback, and was implemented within three days at the vice-ministerial level, through the issuance of administrative guidelines and regulations. The immediate target was to reduce oil and electricity consumption 10 percent under the previous year. The conservation target was raised to 20 percent on 22 December, as the Organization of Arab Petroleum Exporting Countries (OAPEC) announced progressive cutbacks in production, but was dropped to 15 percent on 16 January following OAPEC's lifting of Japan's "unfriendly" designation.

Conservation goals were achieved by requiring eleven major industries to submit monthly reports on energy reductions, subject to audit by the Ministry of International Trade and Industry (MITI). Fuel oil supplies were allocated at the 10 percent reduced level to manufacturers of steel, automobiles, heavy electrical equipment, electronics, petrochemicals, automobile tires, chemical fibers, and other basic industries. The 10 percent reduction in electrical consumption and monthly reporting requirement were applied to all consumers of more than 3,000 kwh maximum flow. These restraints were maintained through the end of 1973, by the invocation of standby provisions under Article 27 of the Utility Company Regulation Act, which also served as the basis for MITI regulation of utility prices.

The Diet responded to the energy crisis by passing two new laws on 21 December. The Oil Supply and Demand Adjustment Act empowered the government to regulate oil consumption, allocate oil to consumers, and require oil importers, refiners, and dealers to submit regular reports on inventories, import shipments received, quantities refined, and import contracts, subject to MITI guidance. The act also laid down guidelines for holding room temperatures to 20° C. (68° F.), limiting highway speeds to 80 kmh (50 mph), closing gas stations on Sundays and holidays, turning off advertising displays at 11:00 P.M., and, after midnight, ending television broadcasts and closing bars, cabarets, restaurants, department stores, supermarkets, and movie houses. An emergency act for stabilizing supply and prices empowered the government to fix prices and regulate the production and import of scarce, essential commodities. Under this act, kerosene and propane gas prices were fixed 11 January 1974, and on 25 January prices were fixed for a number of energy-intensive manufacturers.

In addition, fiscal and monetary policies were employed to achieve "total demand reduction." Government expenditures were cut, the prime rate was raised, and the central bank applied stricter guidance to the city banks. Inevitably, there were inequities in the application of these various restraints. The oil industry, for example, suffered a quadrupling of prices for imported crude, but their retail prices were fixed following ministerial consultations on 4 February with eighty-five business and manufacturing leaders. On 16 March, the oil industry received partial price relief on the basis of the pre-crisis price structure, but most companies suffered operating losses or thin profits through 1975.

Throughout the early crisis period, public scapegoats for scarcities and inflated prices were the foreign and domestic oil companies and leaders of Japanese industrial and trading firms. In the Lower House Diet hearings in February on price controls and unfair business practices, Japanese company presidents who had been summoned to testify were treated as culprits.

* * * *

The Japanese government's rigorous "total demand reduction" policies (both fiscal and monetary) were successful in slowing the inflationary pace. Beginning in the fall of 1975, wholesale prices leveled, even dipping occasionally, and consumer price inflation declined to an annual rate of about 8 percent. However, this success had its costs. The Japanese economy experienced negative growth in the second half of the fiscal year ending 31 March 1976, and in the first half of the fiscal year 1976-77 growth was again expected to be near zero. Furthermore, industrial production dropped 12 percent in the half-year ending in March 1975, resulting in sharp increases in the number of bankruptcies among smaller companies as well as in layoffs and reduced recruiting by large companies. The situation was wholly alien to the high-growth, full-employment patterns of the 1960s and early 1970s. The recession, prolonged by the energy crisis and counterinflationary demand restraints, was the most severe and the longest in Japan's postwar history.

Soaring energy prices and the decline in industrial activity helped achieve one of the government's policy objectives: arresting the growth in energy consumption. The pre-crisis 10 percent-plus annual increase in energy consumption shifted in 1974 to a 2.7 percent decline in shipments from refineries and a 1.4 percent reduction in demand for electricity. Throughout 1975, total energy consumption remained approximately level. Japan also managed its international payments successfully, despite skyrocketing prices for imported coking coal and foodstuffs and crude oil. The 1974 balance-of-payments deficit on an International Monetary Fund (IMF) base of over $4.5 billion ($6.8 billion in the overall account) was recorded primarily in the seasonally adjusted first quarter. Thereafter the deficit contracted, showing a slight surplus in the current and overall accounts in the final quarter; for the whole of 1975 only a slight deficit showed in the current account.

These results were achieved, however, at the cost of stagnating import demand plus a considerable increase in export prices. On the favorable side, export quantity increased, and the capital account benefited from a substantial influx of capital, including petrodollar borrowings. In short, the Japanese economy weathered the oil supply and pricing crisis by ruthlessly damping inflation, prolonging the recession, and achieving economic equilibrium on a smaller scale of industrial and import activities. Beginning in 1975, demand-restraint policies were gradually relaxed, and the underproducing economy began a gentle ascent toward recovery. The next task was to put the economy on a path of stable growth while taking full account of the altered international economic regime, especially in energy, and Japan's own priorities, limitations, and vulnerabilities.

Among the domestic restraints on growth were the scarcity of suitable and acceptable sites for the location of energy-producing plants and energy-intensive manufacturing industries, public fears of pollution and the costs of antipollution measures, and—with the return of normal full employment—actual shortages in important categories of labor, including young trainees. Among the international restraints on growth were the uncertainty of adequate energy imports in relation to growth in energy demand and the realistic limits on increasing domestic energy production. Maintaining a viable balance-of-payments position under these import-dependent conditions was, of course, another important consideration.

In this context the Japanese government drafted a new "Basic Social-Economic Plan" (five-year plan) and a third "National Comprehensive Development Plan" (ten-year plan), both to begin in fiscal 1976. The necessary foundation for these plans was the determination of a feasible long-term growth rate for the Japanese economy. Since assured energy supplies were crucial to this determination, a special cabinet conference headed by the prime minister was created to develop a national energy policy which took account of the realities of the world energy market and was consistent with the policies and prospects of the multilateral International Energy Agency for diversification of world energy sources.

The primary direction of Japan's energy policy was, therefore, to reduce dependency on oil, over 99 percent of which had to be imported, by improving efficiency in domestic energy consumption, and by expanding the reliance on substitute energy sources—all of which objectives were compatible with IEA policy.

* * * *

The long-range outlook for the Japanese economy, published in August 1975 by the Industrial Structure Council of MITI, indicated that the built-in restraints would make it difficult for Japan to exceed 7 percent annual real growth over the next fifteen years (until 1990), although it would be necessary to achieve a stable growth of about 6 percent annually in order to meet social priorities, sustain efficient use of capacity, and provide full employment. The growth projection in real terms was 2 percent for fiscal 1975 (ending 31 March 1976) and 5 percent in fiscal 1976. Beginning in fiscal 1977, a stable average annual real growth of 6.6 percent was projected through 1985. This projection was only half the growth rates of the expansionary 1960s and early 1970s and well below the forecasts made before the 1973 oil crisis.

As indicated earlier, even these modest growth projections depended ultimately on assured and adequate energy supplies. In August 1975 the MITI Advisory Committee for Energy published its report on "Policies for Stabilization of Oil Supplies 1975-85." The report estimated an average annual increase in energy demand of 6.2 percent, down from the pre-1973 level of 10 percent. Yet it also estimated demand growth could be held to 5.3 percent annually, through effective conservation policies.

All these interrelated projections about energy supply and demand were posited on three policy assumptions. First, expansion of domestic energy production would receive high priority, even though the resulting energy would cost more than imported energy. Second, atomic generation of electricity would receive the highest priority because of expected reliability of this energy source. And third, high consideration would be given to maximum diversification of domestic energy production (coal, natural gas, geothermal, solar, and the like) to improve the margin of Japan's energy independence.

Even so, the MITI Advisory Committee projected that the percentage contribution of domestically produced energy (other than nuclear) to total energy consumption would decline from 9.5 percent in 1973 to 8.1 percent in 1980 to 8 percent in 1985. And there were grounds for questioning whether even these goals could be met.

One of the trade-offs to be resolved was between augmentation of domestic energy supply and preservation of the natural environment. This was a political rather than a purely economic or technical decision since the attitudes of local residents could be decisive regarding the siting of new hydroelectric power plants where peak-load use would be economically feasible. Development of geothermal power presented a similar political-environmental problem, since most of the feasible development sites lay in national parks. Hence even the modest MITI projections may be overly optimistic, that the contribution of hydroelectric power would decline from 4.6 percent of total energy consumption in 1973 to 3.7 percent in 1985, and that the contribution of geothermal energy would rise from zero in 1973 to 0.5 percent by 1985.

An equally complex trade-off had to be considered in a revival of domestic coal production. Japan's estimated 1.0 billion tons of exploitable deposits could theoretically be developed at the rate of 20 million tons annually until 1985 at an average cost that would be competitive with the current world price for crude oil. However, actual (rather than average) costs would no doubt increase substantially during this period, reflecting rising wages, safety and environmental costs, with corresponding price increases to consumers. The cost of domestic boiler coal was in fact certain to rise at a much faster rate than the costs of imported coking coal and crude oil.

A more problematical question was whether oil and natural gas explorations on the continental shelf, in the vicinity of the Japanese islands, might prove successful. Small-scale successes were achieved at two points, but the prospect for a major discovery was still uncertain. In any event, MITI projections estimated that domestic coal would make a declining contribution to total energy consumption, from 3.8 percent in 1973 to 1.9 percent in 1985, and that the contribution of domestic oil and natural gas would increase only marginally, from 0.9 percent in 1973 to 1.8 percent in 1985. This left nuclear-generated electricity as the most stable and expansible future domestic source of energy.

* * * *

Nuclear power development presented formidable problems of both a technical and a political nature, and it seemed most unlikely that MITI goals would be met on schedule. Instead of the government's targeted 32 million kw operational capacity by the end of fiscal 1980, 16.6 million kw seems more realistic. The targeted 60 million kw operational capacity for 1985 might be approached only if major decisions were made by 1980 concerning power plant sites. As in the case of hydroelectric and geothermal plant sites, political attitudes (especially of local residents) could be crucial to these decisions. And the longer the delay in starting new nuclear power plants, the more prolonged the dependence on imported energy. For every 10 million kw of nuclear power-generation capacity not realized according to plan, it would be necessary to increase traditional energy imports equivalent to 20 million tons of coal, 100 million barrels of oil, or 10 million tons of liquid natural gas (LNG)—and assurances of supply would be that much less stable.

The optimistic MITI projections forecast an 82 percent dependence on imported energy in fiscal 1985. It would be no easy matter to keep this dependence from going even higher. Japan's unavoidable challenge, therefore, was to secure as stable a supply of imported energy as possible.

* * * *

Stabilization of imported energy supplies entails diversification of the kinds of energy imported and of the countries from which it is imported. The principal options include coal (coking and boiler), natural gas, and oil. Coking coal has been imported principally from Australia, the United States, and Canada. Since Japan's steel production was expected to grow at the rather slack pace of 2-3 percent a year over the next decade, there did not appear to be much difficulty in securing about 85 million tons of coking coal per year from these politically reliable sources, given normal business prudence.

Boiler coal presented a more difficult problem, even though coal is a far more plentiful global resource than oil. It is also becoming a more sought-after resource, in the United States and Europe as well as Japan, raising risky economic consideration for the private utility in the cost differential per calorie between coal and oil. This equation was complicated by environmental considerations, the cost of devices for desulfurization and denitrification of stack gas, and the costs of disposing of powder, dust, and ashes.

One encouraging prospect was that the likely development of practical technologies for coal gasification and liquefaction would serve the interests of the exporting as well as the importing countries. An economically feasible liquefaction technology, for example, would permit the gas and oil derivatives to be processed and consumed locally and the residue (solvent-refined coal) to be exported to Japan as a clean fuel for power generation. Accordingly, the anticipated antipollution costs of developing desulfurization and denitrification devices might prove only temporary, until those technologies were perfected. Meanwhile, Japan would still face the problem of finding acceptable sites and developing antipollution technologies for thermal power plants to consume the projected boiler-coal imports of 4.7 million tons in fiscal 1980 and 14.6 million tons in fiscal 1985. In fact, the site-availability problem suggested it might not be possible to attain the 1985 target.

Natural gas would no doubt take an important place in future energy imports because of its suitability for power generation and city gas, since it contains no sulfur and, when burned, gives off a much smaller quantity of nitrogen oxides than other fuels. Thus it was likely to become a more desirable fuel as environmental standards grew stricter. Although only about 3.0 million tons of LNG were imported in fiscal 1974, future projects that were either firm or in advanced stages of negotiation involved the import of 16 million tons of LNG annually by fiscal 1980. The MITI target for that year was set at 20.6 million tons, apparently a reachable goal. Most of these future LNG-import commitments involved imports from Alaska and Southeast Asia (Indonesia, Brunei, Sarawak), but import opportunities were expected to emerge in Bangladesh and the Arabian Gulf states. Where such long distances were involved, however, it might be preferable to import the gas in the form of methanol.

As in the case of solvent-refined boiler coal, LNG offers economic advantages to the exporter as well as low-pollution advantages to the importer, thus contributing to the probable stability of supply. There were potential problems, however, which could limit Japan's imports of natural gas. One was cost. Under existing contracts, natural gas imports were cheaper than low-sulfur crude. In the future, however, exporters could be expected to demand cost insurance and freight charges in excess of low-sulfur crude prices, reflecting the quality differential between the two products.

* * * *

After all other options are examined, it is clear not only that Japan will continue to depend on imports for more than 80 percent of its energy, but also that Japan's dependence on oil imports will have to expand if current economic growth projections are to be fulfilled. Correspondingly, current projections of energy supply and of economic growth will have to be revised downward if it is found desirable (or necessary) to lower this oil dependence.

MITI projections of 3.0 billion barrels of oil imports in fiscal 1985 (8.25 million barrels a day) were based on the assumptions that price incentives would lead to expanded crude production in non-OPEC countries and in OPEC countries other than Saudi Arabia, Kuwayt, Venezuela, and Libya; that the United States and Europe would make further progress in oil conservation, and that Japan could import at these levels without creating a tight-supply situation.

In fiscal 1975, however, the world oil-market outlook was clouded by broader economic and political developments. As part of the OECD effort to prevent the tying of OPEC crude prices to the prices for industrial goods, Japan was obliged, despite its unique dependence on oil, to reduce its own oil consumption, and thus help insure the recycling of oil dollars in the interest of world economic recovery. The stability of world oil supplies, especially from the Middle East and Africa, remained uncertain because of continuing political instability in the Middle East.

To secure stable supplies of oil over the long run, Japan planned to develop its bilateral commercial relations with the major oil-producing states, including its own comprehensive trade agreements, on the governmental and private levels, for the purchase of crude and the provision to the producer countries of economic and technical assistance. In addition, Japan was exploring the possibilities of diversifying the sources of future oil imports to the maximum possible extent by participating in oil exploration and development in Southeast Asia, Latin America, the Soviet Union, and elsewhere, and by entering into long-term import agreements with China.

As of mid-1976 talks with the Soviet Union on joint Japan-US-Soviet development of Soviet oil and gas fields were stalled on questions of investment costs, dependability of future supplies, and political considerations. In contrast, oil imports from China increased rapidly, beginning in 1973, reaching an estimated 160,000 barrels per day by 1975, or about 3.0 percent of Japan's total imports of 5.3 million b/d. Because of China's growing domestic demand, however, and its export commitments to Third World countries, it has been predicted that shipments to Japan by 1980 probably will not exceed 820,000 b/d, or about 8-12 percent of Japan's imports at that time.

Beyond diversifying the sources of its own oil imports, Japan was being urged also to recognize its obligation to invest capital and technology to enlarge world supply, whether or not Japanese imports were directly involved. For this reason, it would be advisable for Japan's Petroleum Development Corporation and Import-Export Bank to consider abandoning the condition that crude oil developed through their investment and loan assistance be exported to Japan. Japan's best interests would also be served by Japanese contributions to international technology in exploration and development and by additions to world supply capacity in the form of ocean-drilling vessels and oil-terminal equipment in shipyards.

Since, for reasons cited earlier, domestic energy development is unlikely to reach MITI goals for fiscal 1985, I estimate that Japan will probably still depend at that time on imports for about 86 percent of its energy needs. This would mean about 9.0 million barrels per day in crude oil imports, representing approximately 70 percent of total energy needs, in contrast to 75 percent in 1975. In these circumstances, the energy base for continued stable growth of the Japanese economy would rest on such factors as avoidance of another Middle

East war, an effective joint energy policy among the OECD countries, the future production policies of the OPEC countries, international achievements, with Japanese support, in developing new oil fields and expanding total world supply, and progress in Japan and the other OECD countries in framing effective measures for energy conservation and speeding the development of nuclear and other energy sources.

* * * *

Current (1976) energy consumption in Japanese homes, factories, and offices was running 5 to 10 percent lower than in the period immediately preceding the oil crisis. However, sustaining these conservation efforts and generally raising the efficiency of energy use, present a problem in Japan somewhat different from those in North America or Europe. The breakdown in Japanese energy consumption was industry, 60 percent; transportation, 14 percent; and commercial and home use, 26 percent. This was almost the reverse of Western consumption patterns, where industrial use was lower and commercial and home use, proportionately higher. Furthermore, nearly 70 percent of industrial energy use in Japan in 1975 was concentrated in certain energy-intensive industries such as metal, chemical, and ceramic, while the household sector (homes and private automobiles) consumed only 10 percent of total energy, compared to 30 percent in the United States. Since price elasticity was comparatively high in the household sector and comparatively low in industrial, commercial transportation, and commercial sectors, the effect of prices on Japanese energy consumption appeared to be less than in Europe and the United States.

One means of achieving greater economy and efficiency in energy consumption in the industrial sector might come from altering Japan's industrial structure to slow or reverse the growth of energy-intensive industries and stimulate the growth of technology-intensive and other industries which consume relatively less energy. This process would involve, for example, encouraging materials-producing industries, which tend to be energy-intensive, to locate their plants overseas, close to raw-materials supplies, while encouraging imports of the processed materials. Although such changes in industrial structure were under discussion well before the energy crisis, the long-term outlook of the Japan Economic Development Center and the Industrial Structure Council foresaw insufficient progress in this direction to realize significant energy economies in the decade ending in 1985.

Too little study has yet been given to the possibilities for greater efficiency in energy use by means of new technologies in heat control, conversion of production methods, recycling of waste, and the like. The MITI projections suggested possible 15 to 20 percent savings by 1985 over 1973, but another survey was less optimistic, pointing out that such savings might be offset by increased energy consumption for pollution control and safety. Another consideration was that rising Japanese affluence should bring the structure of energy consumption closer to that of Europe and the United States, making even more emphatic the importance of conservation in transportation, commercial, and home uses of energy. This would entail reversing the 1960-72 trend in unit energy consumption, which expanded about 70 percent for passenger transportation and 35 percent for cargo transportation. The reversal could be achieved only by a shift from passenger cars, trucks, and aircraft to railroads, buses, coastal shipping, and other mass-transit modes with a lower unit energy consumption. In the household sector, conservation would require improved housing insulation, district heating systems for group housing, and wider use of solar energy for all residential forms. Inducing such economies would require a variety of tools, including government financing, tax incentives, and regulation or subsidy of utility rates, freight tariffs, and transit fares.

The Japanese government's support of energy research and development extends beyond existing modes of energy supply, such as light-water nuclear reactors and energy-economizing technologies to new types of reactors (fast-breeder and high-temperature gas), centrifugal separation for uranium enrichment, treatment of used fuel, waste disposal, and nuclear fusion. The total government research and development outlay in fiscal 1975 in nuclear power was 85.6 million yen (nearly US $300 million). Under the label of "Sunshine Project," the government also launched a modest research and development effort of 3.7 million yen (approximately US $13 million) in fiscal 1975 in four areas of energy supply: solar, geothermal, coal liquefaction and gasification, and hydrogen.

* * * *

Finally, it is abundantly clear that Japan's energy policies for ten to fifteen years (until 1985-90) would have to be compatible with cooperative efforts among all the OECD states to make more efficient use of available energy, economize on oil consumption, expand world oil supply, and develop substitute fuels. It is only in this international context, rather than a narrow national framework, that Japan can set realistic targets for future economic growth. Because of its dependence on imported oil, the Japanese economy would be vulnerable to large shifts in the relative prices of oil and other primary products on the one hand and industrial products on the other, as these shifts might impose balance-of-payments restrictions on future growth. Indeed, Japan's real energy crisis may emerge after 1985 when actual oil shortages might be expected, with resulting supply and pricing problems. Hence, as Japan's energy vulnerability—and therefore the vulnerability of its economy—increases, the requirement will become absolute for Japanese energy policies to harmonize perfectly with an effective global energy strategy based on producer-consumer cooperation and joint research and development in pursuit of substitute energy supplies.

6 *Access to Oil*

Melvin A. Conant

At the end of World War II, access to Middle East oil was a major objective of a handful of states. Great Britain, France, and the United States were involved, but only Great Britain considered its access to oil to be of the greatest strategic moment. Thirty years later, after the collapse of Western empires, the rise of oil nationalism, and the consequent drastic change in the role of international oil companies, the number of states profoundly concerned with supply includes virtually all. The world's spectacular increase in the consumption of oil in the third quarter of the twentieth century accounts for the heightened concern: 9.7 million barrels were consumed daily in 1950; the total rose to 56 million barrels per day by 1974. The Middle East fueled the far greater part of the increase in use of oil.

The importance of the Middle East in the world's demand for oil was thus dramatic and, in view of the other topics in this volume, even awesome. In the first postwar generation, with the exception of the Alaskan North Slope and North Sea discoveries, all great additions to proven reserves, outside of the Communist world, were discovered in the Middle East. It was highly improbable, at least over the decade ending in 1985, that any new discoveries comparable to the great Middle East fields would be made and developed, thus providing a significant measure of relief from the continuing preoccupation of the nonsocialist world with access to the region's oil.

The world's dependence upon Middle East supply—for as far ahead as we can see—will be a truly primary fact shaping the interests and actions of producers and consumers of oil. How well we conduct our oil relations, how responsive we are to our needs to create a process to insure access on mutually beneficial terms, constitute new challenges for all involved. Peace or war over resources is the issue.

The Role of Governments and Companies

In the furor raised by the sudden emergence of oil-producing states as the masters of their destiny, we have lost sight of the point that importing governments have played the dominant role in effecting access to oil and its terms of supply for much of oil history. In fact, the supportive role of importing governments behind the international oil companies has been a consistent factor in oil although this aspect does not attract the attention it deserves. Before and after World War I, the race for Middle East concessions was run outwardly by the international oil companies. In no case, however, was a concession won by reason of commercial dealings alone. While it was generally the case that supportive governments did not then involve themselves in company decisions on development, production, and price, the concessions could not have been won and retained without home government assistance.

Examples are everywhere; typically, British government support in Persia and Kuwayt and US government in Kuwayt and Saudi Arabia. The companies in some large degree sought this support themselves; in some cases the governments initiated the play. In any and every case, however, government "presence" was important.

The "Seven Sisters"—the giants of international oil—were the predominant creative forces in the system of trade in world oil. Managers of a complex, ever-changing process of great magnitude, their efficiency and technological inventiveness transformed the use of oil. They determined the volumes and prices for oil—and they retained the lion's share of the profits. Unfortunately for them perhaps, in the longer run at least, they were identified by emerging political groups with the interests of the British and US governments. When, after World War II, the Western imperial era ended, the interests of these companies were too firmly linked to those of the discredited imperial system to allow them to become identified with the interests of the producing states. Following the collapse of Western imperialism the associated concessions system drew to its end, and the oil world fell apart.

The producing governments' "early warning" signals came often; access to their oil would have to rest on fundamentally different terms. Beginning with Mexico, then Venezuela, Iran, Indonesia, Iraq, Kuwayt, Saudi Arabia, and Nigeria, the tempo quickened until the negotiations of 1970 led to mounting strain with the dramatic escalation of the pressures upon the companies. With the war and the cutbacks and embargo in the winter of 1973-74 the process of producer-government seizure of control was completed. In the absence of an importing government military response—which would have come fast enough in an earlier age—the old system disintegrated and the building of a new set of arrangements started. When the history of the events of this period is written with the advantage of hindsight, the restraint exercised by several of the key consumers in not seeking early military redress of relief through coups d'état will have to be noted; the military power existed to force a measure of return to the earlier mode, however unwise the effort would have proven.

Fortunately, for all sides, the emphasis has been on the search for accommodation, an acknowledgment that mutually beneficial arrangements are the sine qua non. The interests of the exporters and the importers of oil are so closely intertwined that it may seem almost trite to review them. The interests of the international oil companies reflect the same concerns.

First, the supply of oil—its volume—must be *adequate* to meet the needs of society and to meet the revenue requirements of the developing economies of the producing states.

Second, the supply of oil must be *continuous,* for unlike many other commodities in world trade its flow must not be interrupted—and this is also in the interest of producers who are dependent upon the uninterrupted flow of revenue.

Third, oil must be available at a "reasonable" or "acceptable" price. What that price should be is a matter of unending debate. It may not be so high as to represent robbery—from the consumer viewpoint—nor so low as to waste a producer's diminishing resource. Somewhere in between are considerations of a price which is "equivalent" to or "competitive" with other available energy sources or prospective ones. The "value" of the resource must be preserved in that its price must inevitably be related somehow to sharp fluctuations of price for the goods the producer imports. Several of these concepts are seemingly anathema to some of the consumer governments such as the United States, which is still heard to deny the validity or practicality of applying to energy costs the same escalation practices it implemented widely in its domestic economy. All of these concepts are, however, under active consideration as guides or formulae for the setting of a predictable price.

These three primary interests in the supply of oil are inseparable; the absence of agreement on any one threatens the others. Assurance of an adequate volume in continuous supply at an acceptable price is at the heart of the search for "access." A fundamental part of the change is, therefore, the rising tide of government involvement in the negotiations for access. Inescapably, government's role results from the companies' remarkable success in turning oil from a commercial commodity into a matter of primary national interest. Commercial considerations will no longer be dominant. Industrial governments do not yet possess the competence to conclude arrangements regarding oil supply, but they are acquiring it. Their involvement is now a matter of fact—for only government can represent the broad range of national interests now enmeshed in energy supply.

Transition

Because the old order was passing, one might not assume there were no lingering traces, no remnants of the colonial experience, nothing of the past relationship to shape the future. This could not be the case. Any negotiator for companies or importing governments unfamiliar with the history of oil concessions and insensitive to the convictions of exporting governments could not manage successfully the issues of "access." By the mid-1970s, producers had the power, and progressively the skills, to direct the flow of oil and determine its volume and price.

It could not even be guessed if, over time, the producer governments would see any need to move control beyond their borders and thereby continue to take advantage of the companies for the access to market outlets which they retained. The temptation to producers to move into the international system would be difficult to avoid; yet to discard the companies as soon as possible already seemed an unnecessary, complicating step likely to damage producers and consumers alike.

It seemed more accurate to observe that something of the old and something new were being attempted. The use of oil companies, by producer governments, as service contractors or agents for former concession areas in some cases, and with general access to crude produced anywhere in the country in others, was one approach. Joint ventures between companies and producer governments were most likely to proliferate, for instance, the joint company-producer government tanker ventures in Iran and Saudi Arabia. There would seem to be less interest in 1976 (in a crude surplus market with refineries having high surplus capacity generally) for producer governments (or their chosen instruments) to move directly "downstream" into consuming states or to invest in other promising exploration ventures. Yet the prospect might include the enforced use of producer government tankers or of producer-located refineries even though tankers and refineries were suffering a general surplus capacity. (By such actions the producers would be throwing the burden of surplus entirely on the companies and consumer governments.) Still, joint ventures linking the interests of consuming governments, the companies, and producing countries could eventually be the objective; in time, it would almost certainly be attempted.

North-South/Producer-Consumer Dialogue

While the institutional rearranging was in progress, the other part of the problem in access to oil—the terms on which it would be available—had not been resolved; what was underway was better characterized as the resolve for a *process,* if not yet a formula. The search for a means to resolve questions of volume and price entailed complex considerations. The task would be difficult enough if the principal exporters and importers agreed upon the general approach. They were not so agreed, even within their own camps, and other kinds of initiatives continued to be tested.

Two examples of the differences in approach were the Paris discussions of the Conference on International Economic Cooperation (CIEC) which began in December 1975 and the critical Arabian American Oil Company (ARAMCO) negotiations with Saudi Arabia. Each approach had worldwide significance; each engaged the United States and Saudi Arabia; each reflected a very different approach to "access." The Paris CIEC discussions revolved around its energy, finance, raw materials, and development commissions; the effort was to resolve on a very broad basis major questions of access to raw materials, including oil, in a multilateral forum. From the perspective of the CIEC exercise, the ARAMCO negotiations could be said to resemble the very kind of "special relationship"—perhaps unique in its implications and impact—which the CIEC and the International Energy Agency (IEA) were created in large part to avoid.

From the viewpoint of international oil companies generally, the ARAMCO negotiations represented, at least, a kind of private-industry-producer-government arrangement which was preferable to government-to-government negotiations (even if the outcome set parameters for other company and government discussions elsewhere). The ARAMCO negotiations, however, might be unique in another sense; not only was the magnitude of the volumes and sums unprecedented, but it might be the last such great understanding reached by wholly private companies. In other "access" cases, one or more of the parties on the consuming side was a government-controlled enterprise, and the role of government accordingly acquired some significance. Not all companies in world oil trade had the logistic system and marketing outlets which gave them the clout in negotiations possessed by the ARAMCO shareholders. For such smaller enterprises, government support in negotiations was probably helpful, assuming government interests were limited and close to those of the commercial. Such was rarely the case.

The arguments were many against obtaining access to oil by virtue of a "special" or privileged or preferential relationship reached with a producer. First, such a relationship, to endure, would have to embody a number of interests, on both sides, apart from oil; there might be other commercial or trade advantages sought by either side, but probably mainly by the producer; military or security considerations, which could be of mutual benefit, and larger political interests which might be found on the two sides but were rarely equal and scarcely ever defined similarly. Each of these factors could improve assurance of supply, but collectively they might also be infinitely complicating when the oil relationship was put to the test. When such "extras" are included, the all-around "costs" of the oil are increased. Secondly, it would not be feasible for a single producer state to meet a significant part of a large importer's needs—and neither the importer nor the exporter might wish to be in that position—so the relationship would become diluted from that cause alone.

Thirdly, such special relations as the US has had with Saudi Arabia and Iran tended to be regarded by other states as "exclusive." From the viewpoint of other importing states, such preferential arrangements narrowed down their opportunities, hence increasing the scramble for access. Of course, the durability of the preferential arrangements was important. Political instability was still the ever-present condition in some key producer states. A change in regime which was more than a replacement of the palace guard could destroy a special relationship especially on the inflammatory argument that the arrangement had perpetuated the colonial system in which Western empires continually sought to "sew up" concessions and countries. As a means of obtaining greater assurance of access to oil, "special relationships" are of dubious value; they are politically fragile; they are beset by the pressure of interests other than oil but use oil as their leverage. They tend to be exclusive in fact or by others' interpretation of the relationship. They cannot be based on commercial interests alone. Nevertheless, such relationships were continually being sought by those who found something of value in the prospect which others did not, or could bring some interests to bear which appeared to be exceptional, or sought some admittedly short-term gain. They could not be ruled out for the alternative—multilateral understandings on "access"—might not prove more efficacious and could certainly prove long in the making.

Assuming that the US government was fully apprised of the objectives and tactics followed in the ARAMCO negotiations, it could be argued that there were not only advantages to the private party-Saudi negotiations but that its outcome might bring as much assurance of access as any other approach could achieve. Moreover, it could also be argued that a conclusion to the ARAMCO negotiations might have a salutary effect upon the CIEC talks; it would be an important example of a settlement reached on pragmatic not ideological grounds and with the greatest of the petroleum exporters.

What differentiated the ARAMCO negotiations from those of the earlier, discredited era? On one side was the private company backed, presumably, by its government; on the other side was a sovereign producer state which was not a colony or protectorate but was fully capable of determining the outcome based on its own definition of its national interests.

Nevertheless, since the question of "access" was not one for the United States alone, convincing arguments had to be made that the negotiations over such large volumes, in which US companies alone participated and in which other states' imported supplies were involved, was not, in fact or effect, a "special" or preferential relationship. Of course, the Saudis might find it useful to come forward with their own interpretation. Thus the pursuit of "access" in multilateral forums had to be continued in earnest if only in hopes a scramble for privileged monopolization could be avoided. These multilateral efforts had a usually disappointing record, at least in the light of their original objectives, but perhaps too much was expected too soon.

The list of such efforts is long: General Agreement on Tariffs and Trade (GATT), UN Council on Trade and Development (UNCTAD), sessions of the General Assembly, and the CIEC. Until the developing countries advanced their advocacy of a New Economic Order, and were buttressed by the spectacular gain of OPEC, it did not appear that developing states possessed enough bargaining power or skill to advance their own economic interests.

It was much too early to guess about the CIEC outcome. There might not yet be enough confidence in the commitment of the United States (or agreement within the US government itself) to the process to allow other states to rely on the apparently forthcoming, intelligent, and sensitive definitions of the problems inherent in "access" which had been provided by the US delegation. Having expressed initially serious reservations about the whole exercise, the US turnabout might have seemed to many participants as too good to be true. Doubts persisted also about the cohesiveness and direction of the Common Market states in the exercise. The Japanese were clearly deeply concerned over the potential consequences to them of agreements on raw materials, let alone oil. And no one could pretend to know how the great variety of interests of raw materials' producers, let alone those of the OPEC members, or what combinations of oil and other commodities, would emerge. It might even be the case that the producers were the more sure of themselves and their interests than were their opposite numbers among the consuming states.

There would still be argument over whether oil was so distinctively different from other commodities in world trade that the terms of its supply ought not to be linked with discussions on other raw materials. Whether the relative importance of oil in world trade was the difference or whether the argument was more of a prayer from the consumer side remained unclear. Obviously, the argument would be settled largely by the attitude of oil producers—whether they should want to identify consumer access to oil with consumers' access to other raw materials. (Here the apparent conclusion of an agreement with ARAMCO raised interesting questions about Saudi intentions in CIEC: were the Saudis not going to link access to their oil with progress made on the other producer states' commodities?)

It would be erroneous to think that CIEC represented the last bright hope on earth. It was an important initiative; it might result in general understandings of how an adequate oil supply, at a reasonable price, might be secured. It might find some formula for better preserving the value of the producers' oil revenue or even investments. For the time being, though, CIEC resembled a four-ring circus. To be fair, there was a certain concept behind the undertaking; would the spectator see it? It was not the only show on earth; other multilateral initiatives might be more consequential. Two of these merit mention: the EC-Arab Dialogue and the Lomé Convention.

For as far ahead as one might see, the dependence of Europe upon Middle East oil was to be taken as permanent. There was no prospect of even a significant diminution in their dependence upon that region's oil for the balance of the century. It was essential that no effort go unmade to create a web of relationships with the producers which would bind the two areas in a pattern of interdependent interests solid enough to endure. The "spirit" was undeniably that of cooperation, not confrontation. To that end, the EC embarked on a series of protracted, incomplete, and generally fragmentary talks which had not yet had even a modicum of success. Nevertheless, the ingredients were right and the effort might persist. The natural conjunction of interests—political and economic—between Europe and the Middle East and between Japan and the Middle East, made pursuit of such a relationship wholly sensible and, indeed, necessary.

In the case of Japan, such a relationship with the Middle East is essential. Japan's dependence upon imported oil is one hundred percent with much of it coming from the Middle East. Japan's unrelenting efforts to obtain assured access to this oil, however, have been unsuccessful. There is no "special relationship" of any consequence, although Japan's immense industrial productivity and technological skills are natural assets. Even more serious, and possibly more tenacious, is Japan's feeling of not yet being fully accepted into the institutions and markets of the industrial West. As pointed out in this volume, Japan seems almost to stand apart and to be seeking alone the kinds of relationships sought by the Common Market. Is there to be no possibility of harnessing the unprecedented trade opportunities presented by Japan and Europe to Middle East interest in oil and development?

The Lomé Convention was concluded in 1975 between the Common Market and over forty developing states, largely former colonial territories. Its purpose was to provide financial aid to participating states whose principal export commodities—chiefly agricultural—brought in less revenue than in earlier years. Hence, it was a kind of guarantee of income which would permit receiving states to plan development without fear that an erosion in the market would leave them without financial means. In this fashion, access to their raw materials was better assured, and the developing states obtained certain rights of access to the industrial world's markets for manufactured goods. It was easy to understand why such an arrangement contrasted starkly with the colonial past. It might work. If it did, a precedent might have been set for oil in world trade by this European initiative.

Problems in the Way

Multilateral negotiations spread an initial euphoria over the exercise which concealed, but little more, political and economic realities that persisted and plagued the actors. There was nothing, for example, in the CIEC energy discussions which would alter the Israel issue as a major influence in the use of oil—or the need to be sure of access to it. Nothing in the IEA would probably mitigate the swiftness of some producers' taking up of the oil sword in the event of another Israel war, although the IEA ought to improve its members' ability to cope with the shortfall. Nothing in CIEC, IEA, the EC-Arab dialogue, or comparable undertakings addressed the tensions within the Gulf: Iran vs. Saudi Arabia; Iraq; the survival of Kuwayt; or a Syria contending with others over influence in Lebanon. Not that these particular multilateral efforts were intended in the short run to lessen the dangers of political explosions, but, given time, they might. We were not likely to be given time.

Any one of these issues constituted a real and present danger to the stability of oil relationships. We had become accustomed to think largely in terms of Israel as the focal point of our concerns. There were other issues, however, which plagued us and were rooted deep in Middle East relationships.

Because of the stakes and the US military power, a premium was put on American behavior in the Middle East, the thoughtfulness of our policies and programs, the role of US companies in Saudi Arabia, how the US was seen by others, and the significance and consequences of US special relationships with Iran and Saudi Arabia. There was no other external state which could exercise such power, wisely or ineptly, in the region, with results for all.

The United States possessed important means for helping consumers and producers move through the transition stage from the end of a colonial system to something better. But Europeans and Japanese had the potential to create large opportunities as well. In their several endeavors they were acknowledging that access to oil was a question of enormous significance in itself and with regard to other commodities. At the time of writing, the dimensions of the challenge were just beginning to be appreciated.

II

Changing National Perspectives on the Arab-Israel Dispute

7 American Interest Groups after October 1973

Robert H. Trice

It is difficult to discuss the formulation of American policies concerning the Arab-Israel conflict without considering the behavior and impact of domestic interest groups. Each year thousands of man-hours and millions of dollars are expended by domestic lobbies in an effort to persuade the American people and governmental decision-makers to support one side or another in the conflict. In this study we are interested in characterizing pro-Israel, pro-Arab, and corporate activities during and since the October War of 1973 and evaluating the effects of these partisan efforts on American Middle East policy. We will also engage in a bit of speculation on the role that each of these three lobbies is likely to play in the making of American policy in the near future.

Pro-Israel Groups

The pro-Israel lobby in the United States is composed of at least seventy-five separate groups—Jewish and non-Jewish—which actively support most of the actions and policy positions of Israel's government.[1] The structure and nature of the groups clustered under the pro-Israel heading vary from large social organizations (i.e., B'nai B'rith) and fund-raising groups (i.e., Israel Bond Organization) to labor groups (i.e., National Council for Labor Israel) to explicitly political organizations (i.e., Zionist Organization of America). Two organizations have primary responsibility for holding these diverse groups together and channeling their activities in purposeful, policy-relevant directions. The first is the Conference of Presidents of Major American Jewish Organizations, more commonly known as the Presidents Conference. This "umbrella" group is composed of the leaders of more than thirty different Jewish organizations and is responsible for formulating and articulating the "Jewish position" on virtually all important foreign policy matters. All mass-membership Jewish organizations are members of the Presidents Conference, with the exception of the American Jewish Committee and the Jewish Defense League. Whenever Jewish leaders meet with members of the executive branch or representatives of foreign governments or international organizations, the chairman of the Presidents Conference usually heads the delegation. As it had before October 1973, the Presidents Conference continues to be an important institutional device that allows the pro-Israel lobby to voice its opinions with a forcefulness and unity that generally escapes its domestic opponents.

The second leadership group for the pro-Israel lobby is the American-Israel Public Affairs Committee (AIPAC). AIPAC and the Presidents Conference funnel the bulk of articulate Jewish opinion on policy issues to government decision-makers. Over the years the two organizations have achieved a functional division of political labor. AIPAC serves as the major point of contact between Jewish organizations and members of Congress; the Presidents Conference serves as the primary link between executive branch policymakers and the Jewish community.

The behavior of AIPAC and the Presidents Conference since the 1973 war has been somewhat different than it was after the 1967 war. They have exerted greater energy in the effort to see Israel adequately supplied with American arms than in their attention to developing a peace. One factor likely to have influenced this change in strategy was the differential success in affecting arms sales and diplomatic policies between 1967 and 1973. After the June War, AIPAC and the Presidents Conference waged major campaigns—in the public arena and in private meetings with congressmen and State Department officials—in support of Israel's interests on a number of controversial issues: the sales of Phantom jets to Israel in 1968, 1970, and 1971; the Big Four talks; the Rogers Plan of 1969; and the cease-fire agreement of 1970. During these policy deliberations, Israel's government, finding itself in open conflict with the Johnson and Nixon administrations, encouraged and welcomed the efforts of American Jewish organizations on its behalf. The policy payoffs from domestic pro-Israel activities on specific issues, however, were mixed.

Congress has consistently been more receptive to pro-Israel demands than has the executive branch, with the result that the impact of the pro-Israel lobby has been greatest on those issues on which

Congress plays a significant, independent policymaking role. Between 1967 and 1973, AIPAC found most congressmen willing and eager pro-Israel supporters on arms sales issues. By appropriating the necessary arms sales credits before each of the Phantoms decisions was announced and by publicly defending Israel's requests, Congress prodded the administration toward a pro-Israel course. On diplomatic issues, however, where pro-Israel groups and their congressional allies faced generally unreceptive policymakers at State and the White House and where a policy role for domestic actors was often precluded because of the secret nature of the negotiation processes, they were consistently unsuccessful in getting the policy outputs they sought. It was, therefore, easier and better politically for AIPAC, and to a lesser extent the Presidents Conference, to concentrate on Congress and arms sales and grants.

Another reason why AIPAC and the Presidents Conference have advanced few specific policy positions since the October War is that on several occasions the Israeli embassy has openly discouraged pro-Israeli activities on sensitive issues. The continuing dialogue between American and Israeli officials has developed to the point where the actions of well-intentioned pro-Israel supporters are seen by American and Israeli policymakers as unwanted intrusions into the bargaining process. During the three-year period following the Israeli acceptance of the cease-fire agreement in August 1970, intergovernmental bargaining over American diplomatic and military support for Israel became increasingly routinized. Between 1971 and 1973, American pressure on Israel to negotiate a peace agreement with the Arab states eased somewhat, and the Nixon administration displayed a new-found willingness to maintain a steady flow of arms to meet Israel's defense needs. It appears that within three to five days of the outbreak of the October War there was a clear understanding between Washington and Jerusalem that a major resupply effort would be made by the United States if necessary, and a secret, small-scale arms supply program had been agreed on and was already under way. The famous Kissinger-Schlesinger dispute (or non-dispute) notwithstanding, private discussions with American policymakers had left Israel's leaders with few doubts concerning America's commitment to Israel.

When pro-Israel groups, led by the Presidents Conference and AIPAC, and members of Congress, led by Senator Henry Jackson, began criticizing the administration's cautious public stand at the beginning of the war and demanding a more obvious display of American support, the result was a rare public rebuff by the Israeli embassy. Israel urged its American supporters not to criticize the Nixon-Kissinger policy in the Middle East and to be supportive of American efforts to aid Israel. Embassy officials said they were particularly disturbed by Senator Jackson's attacks on the administration's position and actively attempted to discourage House and Senate resolutions calling for the credit sale of "Phantom aircraft and other equipment in the quantities needed by Israel to repel the aggressors." One reason the Israeli embassy tried to dampen domestic involvement in the arms transfer issue was that negotiations were underway for the administration to *give* Israel the weapons. Obviously, making Israel buy the weapons as Congress and the pro-Israel lobby suggested would only worsen its already acute balance-of-payments problems. Israel's diplomats preferred to let the private discussions take their course, unfettered by domestic interference.

Only once between the 1967 war and the 1973 war did Israeli officials openly split with American pro-Israel groups. That was in 1970, when the embassy argued against massive demonstrations planned during President Pompidou's visit to the United States, to protest the French sale of Mirage jets to Libya. The embassy's warnings went unheeded, and the demonstrations took place. President Nixon was so angered that an imminent decision on Israel's request for more Phantoms was shelved for more than five months. In October 1973, however, the embassy's arguments prevailed, and since then pro-Israel groups have been more cautious in unilaterally advancing specific policy proposals. Although pro-Israel groups have sustained high levels of activity since the October War, the major diplomatic and military decisions that have been made—the Egyptian-Israeli cease-fire and disengagement agreements, the Syrian-Israeli agreement, the "United States proposal" limiting arms and troops in the Egyptian-Israeli cease-fire zone, the American decision to convert $1.5 billion of the $2.2 billion owed by Israel as a result of the October War into outright grants, the US commitment of fifty F-15 fighters, the Lance surface-to-surface missiles, the Sinai accords of September 1975, the American commitment to veto Security Council condemnations of Israel's retaliatory raids, and the American decision to participate in the Security Council debates with the Palestine Liberation Organization (PLO) in January 1976—are almost entirely the products of intra- and intergovernmental bargaining.

In addition to annual fund-raising drives and displays of general support for Israel, pro-Israel activities since 1973 have been concentrated in four major areas: campaigns against the activities of Palestinian commandos; campaigns against alleged anti-Semitism in the United States; efforts to obtain the release of Israeli prisoners of war in Syria and Egypt and to defend the rights of Syrian and Iraqi Jews; and campaigns to counter increasing Israeli isolation in the United Nations. By and large, the primary targets of pro-Israel activities have not been American policymakers but other interest groups in the domestic environment, foreign governments, and international organizations such as the United Nations. As a result, pro-Israel efforts to influence American policy by creating in this country a political climate that is generally sympathetic to Israel have been more successful than attempts to influence the substance of particular policy decisions. A brief review of the activities in some of these areas shows the degree of specialization within the pro-Israel movement and the range of groups that seek to establish and maintain American public support for Israel.

Anti-Terrorism

The dramatic increase in Palestinian commando attacks against Israeli civilians during 1974 produced an outburst of reaction among pro-Israel groups in this country. While the attack at Qiryat Shmonah in April generated only sporadic and short-lived responses among American Jews, it set the stage for the sustained and sometimes violent wave of reactions that followed the Ma'alot attack in mid-May. The day after the Ma'alot attack, 10,000 pro-Israel supporters demonstrated outside the United Nations. Pro-Israel reactions to the Palestinian attacks peaked on 21 May when leaders of the Presidents Conference met with UN Secretary General Waldheim and asked him to help "root out" Arab terrorists operating out of United Nations Relief and Works Agency (UNRWA) camps. After the meeting the chairman of the Presidents Conference said he was pessimistic that the UN would take any action and that the Conference would have to consider asking Congress to cut off American aid for the refugee camps. The following day a group of rabbis and students from Yeshiva University staged a demonstration in the lobby of the UN General Assembly building and youths pelted the Lebanese consulate in New York with eggs.

While these pro-Israel actions reflected Jewish outrage at the terrorist attacks, it is difficult to see how they could have had any significant effect on American policy. The only activities in this area that directly touched on United States policy were after-the-fact criticisms by the Rabbinical Council of America of the American decision in the Security Council to condemn Israel's retaliatory raids on Lebanon following the massacre at Qiryat Shmonah. After Ma'alot there was an eighteen-month lull in Palestinian attacks on Israeli civilians. However, as the Lebanese Civil War spiraled in November 1975, Palestinian commando activities once again increased. During this latter period it appears that pro-Israel groups were concentrating more on activities at the United Nations than on the Israeli-Lebanese border since the new wave of attacks elicited minimal domestic reaction.

Anti-Semitism

Another major dimension of pro-Israel activity after October 1973 has been to uncover and counter alleged anti-Semitism resulting from the war and the Arab oil embargo. The American Jewish Congress and the Anti-Defamation League of B'nai B'rith (ADL) are the two organizations that assume primary responsibility for "monitoring" anti-Semitism in the United States. Both groups conducted extensive studies after the October War on the reactions of virtually all segments of American society to the renewed hostilities. It is not possible here to summarize the findings of these detailed studies.[2] However, while organized labor was praised for its support and Protestants and Catholics were generally found to be more supportive in 1973 than they were in 1967, the list of individuals and institutions charged with anti-Semitism is lengthy, running from Father Daniel Berrigan and Rev. Francis Sayre to the American Friends Service Committee to columnists Rowland Evans and Robert Novak to the *Christian Science Monitor* to Senator William Fulbright to the Socialist's White People Party to the National Black Political Convention to the chairman of the Joint Chiefs of Staff, General George Brown.

Fearing an anti-Semitic backlash from the oil shortage, pro-Israel groups concentrated their efforts on separating the oil embargo issue from the larger Arab-Israel conflict. In November 1973, the ADL launched a nationwide campaign to counter "the Arab politicization of oil, (and) their use of blackmail to dictate" American policy. The core of this program was to counter Arab arguments equating oil shortages with the United States' backing of Israel. Similarly, the American Jewish Committee, the American Jewish Congress, and the Presidents Conference separately issued pamphlets in February 1974 on the "root causes" of the conflict in an attempt to show that the energy crisis was unrelated to the fundamental political problems in the Middle East.

It is very difficult to assess either the effects of the embargo on American public opinion or the effectiveness of the countermeasures adopted by pro-Israel groups. But Gallup polls, taken during and immediately after the October War (1973), and then in December 1973 (after the cease-fire and the imposition of the embargo), showed that the war and its aftermath had little effect on pre-war opinion.[3] Even more interesting were the responses to the following question in a 1975 Harris poll: "If it came down to it and the only way we could get Arab oil in enough quantity and at lower prices was to stop supporting Israel with military aid, would you favor or oppose such a move by this country?" Sixty-four percent of the informed public responded that the United States should not abandon Israel for Arab oil, while only 18 percent favored denying Israel military support in such circumstances.[4]

Prisoners of War and Jewish Refugees

Another area of activity that deserves brief attention is the substantial efforts of pro-Israel groups between October 1973 and the Syrian-Israeli disengagement in May 1974 to secure the release of Israeli POWs. The Presidents Conference sponsored a rally for Israeli POWs in November 1973 that drew 20,000 people to Madison Square Garden and led a mass demonstration outside the Syrian embassy that same month in response to alleged executions of Israeli prisoners. Pro-Israel activity on the POW issue culminated in a January 1974 meeting between a delegation from the Presidents Conference and UN Secretary General Waldheim. The appeals to the United Nations by Jews, demonstrations, newspaper advertisements, and requests for help from the Nixon administration were unsuccessful in getting the prisoners released. Yet, unlike most issues related to the conflict, this one was satisfactorily resolved when the POWs were released shortly after the signing of both the Egyptian-Israeli and Syrian-Israeli disengagement agreements.

Closely tied to the POW issue was the widespread concern among pro-Israel groups over reports that the Syrian and Iraqi governments were displacing and repressing Syrian and Iraqi Jews after the October War. After a brief flurry of pro-Israel activity in 1973 and 1974, the issue appeared to have faded from public view. However, in December 1975 the Iraqi government formally invited all Iraqi Jews who had fled after the 1967 and 1973 wars to return. The invitation sparked a sharp negative reaction from the American Jewish community, with the American Sephardi Federation emerging as the leading opponent. While the reactions reflect the deep concern of pro-Israel groups, it is unlikely they had a significant political impact; the resolution of the POW and refugee problems was largely beyond the control of the American government.

The United Nations

The increasing isolation of Israel in the United Nations since October 1973 has provoked continued reactions from pro-Israel groups and has been one area where the pro-Israel lobby has had a visible effect on American policy. However, pro-Israel efforts and support from Congress and the Nixon and Ford administrations has done little to stem the growing tide of anti-Israel and pro-Palestinian sentiments of the majority of the member states in the United Nations. Pro-Israel groups, led by the Presidents Conference and AIPAC, have used every means at their disposal, from advertisements and letter-writing campaigns to mass demonstrations and warnings of physical violence, to block what they see as the dangerous intrusion of the UN into the Middle East conflict.

Over the strenuous objections of Israel and the United States, PLO leader Yasir 'Arafat addressed the General Assembly in November 1974; that same month the United Nations Educational, Scientific, and Cultural Organization (UNESCO) eliminated Israel from its cultural aid program. Both events sparked mass demonstrations by pro-Israel supporters in New York. In December 1975 the General Assembly passed the "Zionism Is Racism" resolution, and in January 1976 the Security Council debate on the Middle East was convened with the Palestine Liberation Organization seated as a recognized participant. The United States Congress reacted by sending a public letter to President Ford signed by seventy-one senators calling for firm support of Israel and rejection of PLO demands and by supporting AIPAC's demand that the $19.6 million annual American contribution to UNESCO be suspended. Between November 1974 and January 1975, UNESCO received more than 5,000 letters from Americans criticizing the regrouping of cultural areas that led to Israel's exclusion, and the United Nations Association reported more than 100 cancellations of membership. On the opening day of the Security Council debate on the Middle East three lead-pipe bombs were reportedly placed in a subway tunnel beneath the UN library and a propane-gas bomb was placed in front of the Iraqi Mission to the United Nations. In response to Mexico's vote in favor of the anti-Zionism resolution, the American Jewish Congress, the Union of American Hebrew Congregations, and B'nai B'rith canceled more than 128,000 reservations previously made for Jewish tourists in Acapulco and Mexico City for the winter of 1976. What these disparate acts share in common is that they are all less than moderate responses to events over which neither the pro-Israel lobby nor the United States government exerted any significant control. These reactions, in large part born of frustration, beg the question as to whether or not they have isolated Israel and the United States even further from the rest of the world community.

This brief review of pro-Israel activity does justice neither to the amount, the complexity, nor the general success of the efforts exerted in this country on behalf of Israel. After October 1973 pro-Israel groups continue to possess overwhelming organizational and numerical superiority relative to their pro-Arab counterparts. They dominate almost all domestic debates associated with the conflict and continue to be notably successful in garnering support for Israel from less involved groups within American society. We have seen that the pro-Israel lobby has had a significant impact on a number of important issues such as arms sales and others involving the allocation of funds where Congress plays a significant foreign policy role. The question remains, however, whether pro-Israel groups have been able to translate their dominance in the domestic environment into a meaningful role within the American policy-making process on diplomatic issues. This question will remain unanswered until detailed analyses are made of how specific decisions were formulated. To the extent that pro-Israel activities since the October War have centered more on general support functions and issues over which the American government exerted little control (POWs, UN General Assembly) than on specific diplomatic policy options being considered by the administration, pro-Israel interests are less likely to have had a significant direct impact on either American diplomatic policy or the course of events in the Middle East.

The Pro-Arab Lobby

Relative to the pro-Israel lobby, the pro-Arab and anti-Zionist factions in the United States have remained weak and divided. One pro-Arab group, though, the Action Committee on American Arab Relations (ACAAR), has been among the most active domestic groups before and after the 1973 war. Since well before the June War and continuing to the present, ACAAR has almost single-handedly attempted to present the "other side" to the positions advanced by pro-Israel groups. ACAAR's role as a counter-force to pro-Israel initiatives in large part accounts for its high level of public activity. However, its generally antagonistic reactions to pro-Israel activities, its sometimes extreme tactics, and its relative isolation and lack of support from other groups continues to offset the political advantages gained from its extensive public exposure. Some of ACAAR's problems have been eased somewhat since October 1973 by the emergence of a revived Federated Organizations on American-Arab Relations as a consistent and active supporter of its pro-Arab efforts. Also, the Washington-based National Association of Arab Americans, which was established in 1972 and gained significant momentum during and after 1973, has steadily increased its activities. Despite these developments, the pro-Arab lobby has yet to develop into a serious competitor for its pro-Israel counterpart.

Support for Arab States

Pro-Arab efforts since the October War have tended to cluster around three central themes: displays of general support for the Arab states and criticisms of Israel's "intransigence"; attempts to explain the reasoning behind the oil embargo; and campaigns for the recognition of Palestinian rights in the Middle East. In addition to countering pro-Israel demonstrations, the most notable displays of general support for the Arab states occurred during the 1973 war when an ACAAR-sponsored rally in Brooklyn attracted 700 people to hear the Syrian ambassador and when a nationwide letter-writing campaign was successfully organized to urge President Nixon to end American support of Israel. While insignificant in comparison to pro-Israel efforts, the ability of pro-Arab groups to gather more than a handful of people in a public show of support and to mobilize previously inactive Arab-American civic groups for political action appears to have spurred them to adopt a more offense-minded political strategy.

One of the most encouraging postwar developments from the pro-Arab perspective has been the apparent increase in the level of general support displayed by some American politicians. In Congress, traditional advocates of a more "evenhanded" American policy in the Middle East such as former Senator J.W. Fulbright, Senate Majority Leader Mike Mansfield, Senators Mark Hatfield and Henry Bellmon, and Representative Richard T. Hanna have been joined by Senate Minority Whip Robert Griffin, Senator James Abourezk (the only Arab-American in Congress), and Senators Frank Moss and Charles Percy. And although Mayor Abraham Beame of New York refused to meet with Egyptian President Anwar al Sadat on his visit to the United States in November 1975, Chicago's mayor Richard Daley hailed Sadat as a "fighter for freedom and for peace in the Middle East," and the Egyptian was cordially received by Florida's governor Reubin Askew. Again, while the vast majority of congressmen and nationally-known politicians continue to be generally "pro-Israel" in outlook, the "defections" that have occurred since the October War have been welcomed by pro-Arab groups.

Arab Oil Embargo

In late 1973 and early 1974 defense of the Arab oil embargo was carried largely by two sets of actors. The first was the Federated Organizations on American-Arab Relations, which launched a public campaign at the beginning of 1974 arguing that complete Israeli withdrawal from all occupied territories was the "only legitimate basis" for lifting the embargo. The second set of actors was the oil-producing Arab governments themselves. The extent of open participation by foreign governments in the oil-embargo debate added a new wrinkle to domestic activity related to the conflict. The Kuwayti Finance and Petroleum Ministry, the League of Arab States, and the Saudi Arabian Ministry of Foreign Affairs apparently all decided that it was in their best interest to supplement the supportive activities of domestic pro-Arab groups with direct appeals to the American people. In addition to newspaper advertisement campaigns by the oil-producers, the Arab League dispatched a special envoy, Clovis Maksoud, to the United States in January 1974 to carry out a five-month campaign to explain recent Arab political decisions to American audiences. Maksoud, a Lebanese, visited fifty-four cities in thirty-two states and presented the Arab position in a number of meetings with columnists (e.g.,Rowland Evans), congressmen (e.g., Senators Clifford Hansen and Dewey Bartlett), and the mass media (e.g., *Wall Street Journal* and *Newsweek).*

State of Palestine

While the American Palestine Committee has been actively campaigning for some time for recognition of Palestinian rights and the creation of a Palestinian state, one of the most noteworthy developments in this area since the October War was the congressional hearing in April 1974 on alleged maltreatment of Palestinian civilians by Israel's authorities in the occupied territories. Chaired by Rep. Donald Fraser (D-Minn.), the hearings provided a public forum for a number of anti-Zionists such as Dr. Israel Shahak (an Israeli), John Richardson, and W. T. Mallison, to level charges against Israel that included the bombing of civilian targets, the use of anti-personnel weapons, demolition of Palestinian homes, and widescale deportations. More important than the substance of the charges was that pro-Arab supporters and anti-Zionists were using a previously little-used avenue—the congressional hearing—to disseminate their opinions to the American people. The very fact that hearings on the treatment of Arab civilians were even held was but one more small sign that pro-Arab groups may be on their way to assuming a more active political role after the October War.

The January 1976 Security Council debates on the Middle East, in which the Palestine Liberation Organization was accorded a full participatory role, provided pro-Arab groups across the country with a unique opportunity to put their position on Palestinian rights before the American public. In local radio talk shows, newspaper advertisements, and pro-Palestinian demonstrations outside the United Nations, pro-Arab groups exhibited an air of confidence that had been largely lacking in their previous efforts. It is likely that pro-Arab groups will become increasingly active as the Palestinian question becomes more salient to more Americans in the near future.

Corporate Interests

Despite the fact that the political situation in the Middle East during and after the October War has acutely impinged on the operations of some of America's largest oil companies and financial institutions, these corporations have generally declined to use the public stage to make their economic and political preferences known. On those infrequent occasions when corporate actors have formulated policy positions on political issues, they have preferred to convey them to decision-makers through more direct and less public avenues of communication than those used by the pro-Israel and pro-Arab groups. While there has been a relatively sharp increase in corporate political activity since October 1973, in absolute terms their participation in policy debates remains quite low and has been primarily confined to explaining the Arab position on the oil embargo and defending their role in the energy shortage.

One of the persistent goals of American corporations, as organizations, has been to create a political and economic environment in the Middle East that will allow them to maximize profits. Until the June War, the operations of American businesses and American foreign policy were generally viewed by American corporations and host country government officials as two distinct spheres of activity; corporations had little need to engage in foreign policy activities either abroad or at home. After the June War, though, the Arab governments began to tie the continued profitability, and in some cases the independent existence of American firms in the area, to American governmental policy toward the conflict. Since then, American corporations—particularly oil companies—periodically have seen a need to remind policymakers that deviation from an "evenhanded" policy could seriously jeopardize American business operations and investments in the Middle East. The pressures exerted by the Arab governments on the oil companies since

October 1973 to take a more public pro-Arab stand, and the industry's willingness to concede to those demands, represent not so much a new development as a change in the degree of the pressures that have existed since 1967.

While there is substantial evidence to show that the oil shortages from 1972 to 1973 were not directly related to the conflict and that the October War was a convenient deus ex machina that allowed the Organization of Arab Petroleum Countries (OAPEC) governments to cut production, boost prices, and further consolidate their control over their petroleum resources, it is also clear that the outbreak of hostilities produced a bustle of political activity on the part of the major American oil companies. King Faysal's reported threats to Arabian American Oil Company (ARAMCO) officials in May and August 1973, that they might have to bear the costs of America's pro-Israel policies, may have been an important factor in ARAMCO's decision to send a private memorandum to President Nixon on 12 October. The memo, which did not reach the President until after the emergency airlift had been approved, warned that Saudi Arabia and Kuwayt would retaliate against military aid to Israel by cutting oil production and that such an action might have a "snowballing" effect on other producers that could result in a major petroleum supply crisis. In the months that followed, Atlantic Richfield, Standard Oil of Indiana, Exxon, Texaco, Shell, and other oil companies issued public statements that reflected their host governments' positions that a return to normal oil supplies would have to be tied to some kind of "just and equitable" settlement in the Middle East.

In those instances when American corporations tried their hand at partisan political maneuvering they were met with only mixed success, and some efforts quite clearly backfired. For example, in August 1975 it was revealed that Gulf Oil had contributed money to a source in Bayrut for the purpose of underwriting pro-Arab activities in the United States. The pro-Israel Presidents Conference reacted by condemning Gulf's actions and, through the Anti-Defamation League (ADL), demanded a public response from Gulf. As a result, on 21 August 1975, there appeared a half-page advertisement in the *New York Times* which reproduced both the ADL letter and the reply from Gulf chairman, B. R. Dorsey. In the letter of reply Mr. Dorsey publicly apologized for the contribution, which he said had gone for "educational purposes," and assured the chairman of the ADL that "you may be certain that it will not happen again." A vigilant, sensitive, and reactive pro-Israel lobby is one reason why it is unlikely that direct corporate participation in domestic political debates will increase substantially in the foreseeable future.

Corporate groups continue to receive a warmer reception from executive branch officials than pro-Israel or pro-Arab groups primarily because they have succeeded in equating their narrow economic interests with the country's. American exports to all the Middle East countries during the first eleven months of 1974 totaled $4.5 billion, up more than 77 percent from the previous year. However, Israel's share of that export market is steadily declining. During the same period, exports to Israel totaled about $1.1 billion, as compared to $905 million in 1973. While this corporate identification with the country's economic well-being has led to relatively better corporate access to decision-makers, it has also reduced the need for American businesses to assume an active and direct policymaking role as a domestic lobby. Rather—and particularly since the lifting of the oil embargo—American corporations have once again preferred to let their investments serve as a seemingly independent, external consideration in the determination of American policy. Furthermore, when corporate actors have sought a policymaking role they have limited their activities to a very narrow range of issues and have generally couched their political preferences in economic terms. A serious challenge to the continuation of this corporate political strategy has been posed by the recent efforts of pro-Israel groups to get legislation which would impose sanctions on American corporations honoring the Arab League economic boycott against Israel. Whether or not American corporations will seek to debate the merits of such legislation in the domestic political arena remains an important and open question.

The Future Role of Domestic Lobbies

Interest-group activity since October 1973 has shown few dramatic changes in established patterns of behavior and impact. It is my impression that on most Middle East issues, American policymakers will continue neither to seek nor heed the advice of most domestic lobbies. The direct effects of domestic activity on diplomatic issues are likely to be minimized by the general unreceptiveness of executive branch decision-makers and the private nature of the negotiation processes. The result is that in the future, as in the past, interest groups will most likely be forced to react to policy decisions that have already been formulated and announced by the executive branch. The important exception is that pro-Israel policy preferences are likely to be reflected in decisional outputs to the extent that Congress actively participates in decision-making processes—as it does now on most military aid issues.

One of the many things we have not dealt with in this paper is the indirect effects of interest group activities. Although there is no way of gauging indirect impact, I am inclined to believe that the sustained interest of large and easily mobilized segments of the articulate public has made, and will continue to make, some difference in the way American policymakers solve the Middle East problems. To the extent that decision-makers are aware that their actions are likely to elicit some kind of public reaction and to the degree that they anticipate those reactions in their selection of certain policy alternatives, domestic interests will continue to have an impact (albeit incalculable) on policy.

Turning to particular sets of actors, pro-Israel groups are likely to continue to dominate domestic discussions of the conflict in the foreseeable future. Numerically large, organizationally strong, and very active, pro-Israel groups should be able to maintain the visible and widespread support for Israel that has been displayed over the years by large segments of American institutional life. Fears of a significant increase in anti-Semitism are probably exaggerated, but future pro-Israel efforts to equate anti-Zionism with anti-Semitism as a tactic for discouraging public debate are likely to be less successful than in the past. More and more Americans are beginning to develop independent opinions on Middle East issues, and I expect that "blind" support for Israel will gradually be replaced by differential support on various issues. For example, American public support for Israel's annexation of Jerusalem might be less than support for continued military aid to Israel, support for Israel's demand that Arab states formally recognize its right to exist may be greater than for Israel's punitive retaliatory raid policy, and so on.

The October War appeared to breathe some life into the pro-Arab movement in the United States. However, the mild progress that the pro-Arab movement has been making in terms of gaining better access to the media and to Congress, and of increasing coordination within its ranks, is unlikely to make it competitive with the pro-Israel lobby in the near term. Relative to the pro-Israel movement, pro-Arab groups are likely to remain numerically weak and politically divided, and will be forced to continue to operate in an apathetic if not hostile domestic environment.

If and when the next war and the next oil embargo comes, American corporations probably will again scurry into political action in an effort to avoid undesired economic consequences. However, because the nationalization of American oil holdings by Arab host governments has been progressing quickly and smoothly, I expect oil corporations will function less as independent political actors and more as messengers between their host governments and the executive branch. If anything, the period since October 1973 has shown the obvious inability of oil companies to affect the policies of their host governments. The ARAMCO embargo on petroleum supplies to American military forces on demand of the Saudi government, with the consent of the American government, was but the most dramatic of a number of developments that have shown the decreasing international political influence of the major oil companies—a decline that may well be reflected in future domestic political activities as well.

8 Canada: Evenhanded Ambiguity

Janice Gross Stein

Canada, unlike the United States and the major powers of Europe, has had neither major strategic and economic interests in the Middle East nor a long history of involvement in the region. Yet Canada has played an important role in the conflict between Israel and its Arab neighbors. Despite the absence of direct interests, Canadian troops were stationed in the Middle East from 1956 until 1967 and again after 1973 as part of a United Nations peacekeeping force. Canada's policy in the Middle East has been largely a response to external interests.

Immediately after the war in 1948, Canada emphasized support of the United Nations and mediation between the parties. A Canadian policy of "evenhandedness" in the Middle East was necessary and complementary to this policy. A partisan position on the issues of the Arab-Israel conflict was neither consistent with Canada's support for mediation on the international level nor required by the scope of Canadian interests within the region. A one-sided commitment would impair Canada's usefulness as a problem-solver at the United Nations.

In 1956, pursuit of these policies led to Canada's participation as a peacekeeper between the parties to the conflict. The establishment of United Nations Emergency Force (UNEF), largely at the initiative of Canadian Secretary of State for External Affairs Lester B. Pearson, increased local stability by separating the belligerents, and Ottawa's policy of balance in the regional conflict underscored the role of international peacekeeper. Despite the precipitate withdrawal of UNEF in 1967, Canada continued to support UN initiatives; the adoption of Security Council Resolution 242 as the basis of Canadian policy was consistent also with the past practice. After 1967, however, Canada began to accord lower priority to international mediation and peacekeeping and to emphasize the extension of domestic interests abroad. The importance of the Middle East as an arena of foreign policy action receded, and Canada maintained a low profile.

Within three weeks of the outbreak of the October War, however, Canada received a request to participate in a second peacekeeping force in the Middle East and its supplies of oil were curtailed. A serious threat to international peace and security existed and Canada's traditional allies—the United States and Western Europe—were in disarray. The disagreement among allies was compounded in 1973 by competition between the superpowers and a threat to international economic stability. International and domestic concerns increased the salience of the Middle East.

In the first official statement of the government's position, Secretary of State for External Affairs Mitchell Sharp condemned the use of force and reaffirmed Canada's support of Resolution 242:

> Canada has supported Resolution 242 since its adoption in 1967. Our adherence has been total but strictly limited to the terms of the resolution itself and *we have always refused to add anything to it or subtract anything from it* or even interpret it or draw implications from it that were not immediately apparent from the wording. . . .[1] (author's italics)

Sharp's statement reflected traditional Canadian preoccupations: the preservation of international peace and security, support for the resolutions of the United Nations, and emphasis on the necessity for negotiation between the parties. Despite renewed Canadian participation in peacekeeping, however, the policy of evenhandedness was to undergo significant change. Increasingly, Canada shifted its focus from the conflict in the Middle East to its bilateral relations with members of the region. Paradoxically, as Canada moved to encapsulate the conflict, the conflict became an increasingly important issue in domestic politics. Canada redefined evenhandedness as it expanded its bilateral involvement in the Middle East and the Arab-Israel dispute penetrated the political process at home.

Participation in UNEF II: an Obligation

The marked lack of enthusiasm in Canada's response to the demand for participation in a second United Nations peacekeeping force in the Middle East indicates the change in the general direction of Canadian foreign policy. Canadian disappointment in UNEF I was not an isolated experience. In 1972, Canada was a reluctant participant in the International Commission for Supervision and Control (ICSC) in Vietnam and withdrew after six months. In 1973, the government recognized that a clear threat to international peace and security existed, but unlike 1948, 1956, and 1967, made no attempt to mediate between the belligerents; the role of "helpful fixer" was no longer appropriate. Canada did agree to participate in UNEF II but Sharp made it clear that Canada would impose explicit conditions on its participation: progress toward political settlement by the parties, a UN structure for the force, and equitable financing.[2] Above all, he underscored the necessity of the consent of all the parties, and especially the host state, to the deployment of the force. He emphasized that he had personally confirmed the approval of the foreign minister of Egypt to the stationing of UNEF II.

Although Canada's formal demands have been met, decision-makers are reluctant to make an open-ended commitment to participation in the peacekeeping force. This unease is a product of the role the international force performs and of decreasing domestic support. The new secretary of state for external affairs, Allan MacEachen, argued that peacekeeping forces may serve to perpetuate the status quo.[3] However, because of the rate of political progress made in the Middle East from 1973 to 1975—after the second Egypt-Israel agreement—Canada approved participation in UNEF, until 24 October 1976, and United Nations Disengagement Observer Force (UNDOF), until 31 May 1976. Decision-makers were still pessimistic about the prospects of further shuttle diplomacy and MacEachen urged the parties directly concerned to enter into negotiations. Canada would most likely resist an open-ended commitment to participation in the absence of any progress in negotiation between the parties. The presence of peacekeeping forces, it is argued, may sometimes provide an alternative rather than an inducement to negotiation and settlement.

A second difficulty, the financing of international peacekeeping, has been overcome. Canada objected to the inequitable financial arrangements for past peacekeeping forces, particularly in Cyprus. The Security Council decided, however, that UNEF II would be financed by all members of the United Nations through special assessments by the General Assembly. The General Assembly, in an ad hoc arrangement, established a sliding scale of assessment with the heaviest cost borne by the five permanent members of the Security Council who do not participate in the force and the smallest contribution made by those who can least afford the expense. In 1975, Canada was assessed $3.8 million by the United Nations for UNEF and UNDOF. Since Canada contributes the largest contingent to the peacekeeping forces in the Middle East, it also has absorbed over a million dollars annually above the normal cost of maintaining the troops at home. Nevertheless, Canada was satisfied that the costs of peacekeeping were shared by the general membership of the United Nations and not concentrated among those who contribute contingents to the force.

Canada's strongest reservations stemmed from the overextension of its defensive resources. Its commitments in the Middle East and Cyprus strained its personnel to capacity. The secretary of state for external affairs has noted that Canada would be unable to increase the size of its commitment to UNEF, because the army would have to be used for additional security at the Olympic games in 1976. In a period of relative decline in defense spending, the commitment of specialized personnel abroad seriously depleted available manpower. Ottawa emphasized the protection of Canadian sovereignty and the staffing of operations related to these priorities at home as strained. The Department of Defence had not received increases in its budget proportional to the expenses incurred by maintaining troops abroad; this blunted its traditional support for peacekeeping. Nor has the Department of External Affairs been a strong advocate of peacekeeping. The highly unsatisfactory experience in the ICCS, although not comparable to UNEF and UNDOF, was invoked to justify Canada's reduced commitment. The cross-departmental support of peacekeeping has weakened; this reduced bureaucratic support has been matched by a decline in public support for the United Nations and its activities. At the end of 1973 only 36 percent of Canadians thought that the United Nations was doing a good job, down from 42 percent in 1967 and 54 percent in 1961. Since 1973, public support dropped further as specialized agencies engaged in political action. This was a striking decline if only because the previous level was so much greater. Among the public and the relevant bureaucratic elites, the Canadian commitment to the United Nations and its peackeeping activities has been tempered.

Policymakers have concluded that there are no major benefits or costs to participation in peacekeeping in the Middle East. Canada received no credit from its NATO allies for the additional contribution of troops and was not privy to additional information from the United States even though Canadian forces were exposed to danger in the theater of conflict and Canadian policy might have become the target of one of the belligerents. On the other hand, decision-makers felt Canada had a considerable reputation within the Middle East as a result of continued participation in peacekeeping. Peacekeeping was compatible with bilateral economic and cultural relations with states within the region; if anything, participation in peacekeeping facilitated the establishment of cooperative relationships. As Canada devalued the benefits of peacekeeping, it also reduced the constraints on a more active foreign policy in the Middle East, expanded the scope of bilateral relations beyond the conflict, and modified its position on the Arab-Israel conflict.

The Arab-Israel Conflict at the United Nations: Canada Votes

The Arab-Israel conflict increasingly occupied the attention of the General Assembly in the two years following the October War. One of the principal issues was the recognition of the Palestine Liberation Organization as the representative of the Palestinians and its admission as an observer to the United Nations and its specialized agencies. Until 1973, Canada had emphasized the individual rights of the Palestinians and was a major contributor through UNWRA of humanitarian relief. Ottawa has been the fourth largest contributor to the fund. Canada also insisted that the Palestinian question was inseparable from other aspects of the conflict and could be discussed only in the context of a larger settlement; to separate it from the other issues would be to destroy the "delicate balance of obligations" imposed by Resolution 242. Immediately after the October War, Secretary of State for External Affairs Sharp reaffirmed Canadian policy;[4] this policy has undergone some change.

When the PLO was first granted international recognition—when it attended the meeting of non-aligned states as an observer in September 1973—and was recognized as the representative of the Palestinian people, Canada approved. In May 1974, when the Economic and Social Council adopted a resolution inviting the PLO to participate in the world population and food conferences, it again approved. The same month, the World Health Organization (WHO) invited representatives of liberation movements recognized by the Organization of African Unity (OAU) or the League of Arab States to attend the meetings of the WHO as observers. Canada voted favorably. But, in October 1974, when the General Conference of UNESCO invited the PLO to attend as an observer, Canada abstained. On the fourteenth of that month Canada again abstained when the General Assembly proposed to invite the PLO to participate in the debate on Palestine. On 22 November, Canada voted against the General Assembly's invitation to the PLO to attend the General Assembly and all conferences of the United Nations as observers.

Canada derives the parameters of its policy from the simultaneous recognition of the collective rights of the Palestinians and the refusal to judge the issue of their representation.[5] When all national liberation movements which are recognized by the OAU and the Arab League are invited to observe the work of specialized agencies and conferences, Canada supports such participation. When the PLO alone is invited, Canada abstains since it does not accept a priori the claim of the PLO to represent the Palestinians; when such an invitation is issued by consensus, Canada does not dissent. Canada distinguishes, however, the specialized agencies and conferences from the General Assembly of the United Nations. The granting of observer status in the Assembly to the PLO, a nongovernmental body, would accord it a status reserved only for sovereign states or associations of sovereign states and would directly contradict the Charter of the United Nations.[6]

Even on this limited issue of representation, however, Canadian policy is not clear. Secretary of State for External Affairs MacEachen has emphasized the refusal of Canada to decide on the appropriate representative of the Palestinian people. He added that even though, at Rabat, Arab leaders recognized the PLO as the representative of the Palestinians, Israel must have a voice in the selection of the representatives if negotiations are to begin.[7]

Although Canadian policymakers define representation as an issue internal to the Palestinian people, they simultaneously consider Arab and Israel policy on appropriate representation as relevant to the Canadian position. If Ottawa's policy is not internally inconsistent, it is certainly ambiguous. Moreover, it is likely to continue.

On his recent trip to the Middle East, MacEachen found Arab governments divided on the recognition of the PLO. While Saudi Arabia urged Canadian recognition, Egypt did not press the point; Jordan did not initiate any discussion of the issue,[8] and Iraq opposed Canadian recognition of the PLO. Iraq's Foreign Minister, Sadun Hamadi, told Canadian representatives, "I think there is more than one Palestinian organization if we come to the facts.... The PLO is not the central issue in the Middle East dispute."[9] Analysts concluded that recognition of the PLO was not a prerequisite to the improvement of Canadian-Arab relations. Canada is likely, therefore, to continue its present policy with all the attendant contradictions.

The Canadian position on the representation of the Palestinians was only one inconsistency within the larger context of policy on the Arab-Israel conflict. Canada had insisted on the interrelatedness of all the issues in dispute between Israel and its Arab neighbors, and policymakers traditionally emphasized the futility of one-sided resolutions which deal with issues out of context and impede the search for peace. Increasingly, after 1973, Canada acquiesced in the separation of some of the issues in dispute through the practice of abstention.

On 22 November 1974 the UN General Assembly passed Resolution 3236 which reaffirmed the rights of the Palestinians to self-determination, national independence, and repatriation; recognized the Palestinians as a principal party in the establishment of peace; and requested that the PLO be contacted on all matters related to the question of Palestine. Canadian ambassador Saul Rae explained Canada's abstention: "Canada could not support a resolution which makes no reference to Israel as an essential party to the negotiations, nor to UN Security Council Resolutions 242 and 338 as the appropriate framework for negotiation."

However, Rae continued, "Canada fully supports the participation of the Palestinians in a process of negotiations."[10] The first factor dictated opposition to the resolution while the last indicated support; as a result, Canada abstained. This was part of a series of abstentions.

Despite official denials of a change in policy, the pattern of abstentions does indicate a departure from unqualified support of Resolutions 242 and 338. Policymakers seemed to accord as much importance to the participation of Palestinian representatives as to the support of Resolution 242; yet Palestinian participation was only one of several components of 242. If Canada continued to support Resolutions 242 and 338, a consistent policy would be to oppose a resolution which excluded any of the principal components of 242. Canada had occasionally done so. Resolution 3414, introduced in the 30th General Assembly, made no specific reference to 242 or 338 and recommended that aid to Israel be stopped. It condemned Israel's occupation of territory but made no reference to the other issues in dispute. The Canadian delegation considered such an unbalanced resolution would not serve the cause of peace and voted against it. Generally, however, Canada abstained. Abstention replaced substance and evenhandedness became ambiguity.

The examination of Canada's voting record suggests that Canadian policy has changed significantly. First, Canada recognized the individual rights of the Palestinian refugees, as dictated by Resolution 242, and the collective right of the Palestinians to participate in the process of negotiation. Second, Canada no longer insisted on the simultaneous discussion of all issues under dispute. Canadian voting behavior at the United Nations indicated a modification of earlier unqualified support of Security Council resolutions as the framework for settlement. Canada appeared to have reduced the emphasis on legitimacy[11] and increased the emphasis on representation. Not only did Canada modify its policy on the Arab-Israel conflict, but the conflict also penetrated the domestic political arena. The issues of representation and legitimacy are debated in New York and also Ottawa.

The Arab-Israel Conflict in Canada: the PLO

In 1970, Canada invited the Crimes Congress, a United Nations conference, to meet in Toronto in September 1975. A second UN conference, Habitat, was scheduled to open in Vancouver on 31 May 1976. Ottawa extended these invitations before the General Assembly invited the PLO to attend, in observer capacity, the sessions and conferences convened under its auspices. In January 1975, the Secretary-General invited the PLO to participate as an observer in the Crimes Congress. This signaled the beginning of a major domestic debate on Canada's support for the United Nations, its opposition to international terrorism, and the evenhandedness of

Canadian policy on the Arab-Israel conflict. Foreign policy was politicized and decision-makers could not abstain.

In March, the first mobilization of domestic pressure to bar the entry of the PLO observers began. The Canadians Against PLO Terrorism (CAPLOT) organized to demand the Canadian immigration law be applied. Under Canadian law, the PLO is considered a terrorist organization and its members are barred from entry; members of the PLO can be admitted only through the exercise of ministerial discretion. By the time a decision was finally made in July, a broad range of interest groups, political parties, and government and civil leaders expressed their opposition to the admission of the PLO. The Law Society of Upper Canada, the governing body of Ontario's legal profession, voted to withdraw its facilities if the PLO were admitted, and Canadian Jewish groups promised massive peaceful demonstrations if the PLO were granted visas. All the federal and Ontario opposition parties, the provincial and federal Liberal caucuses, the premier of Ontario, and the chairman of Metro Toronto demanded that the government prohibit the entry of members of the PLO. They argued that Canada's laws and strong opposition to international terrorism precluded the admission of members of a terrorist organization.

Those who favored the admission of the PLO argued that Canada's evenhanded policy in the Middle East and support of the United Nations were at issue. George Hajjar, a leader of the Canadian-Arab Federation, warned that Canada would jeopardize its economic and cultural relations with Arab governments and sacrifice its reputation as a supporter of the United Nations if the PLO were not admitted. Spokesmen for the Canadian-Arab Federation also noted that Arab ambassadors in Ottawa had been in constant touch with the government urging the admission of the PLO. A third group, mainly editorialists in the big metropolitan dailies, argued that Canada must implement the decisions of the United Nations, even if these were distasteful.

The Department of External Affairs recommended to the cabinet that the government proceed with the congress and bar only those members of the PLO known to be terrorists. MacEachen met on 9 July with the Canada-Israel Committee and on 14 July with the Canadian-Arab Federation; he did not make a commitment to either group. On 18 July the Minister consulted with the Secretary-

General in New York and on 21 July he announced that Canada would seek a postponement of the conference for one year. Although he cited the protests against the admission of the PLO, MacEachen offered as the principal reasons for postponement the likely politicization of the congress and a possible reescalation of violence in the Middle East.[12] These reasons were not convincing: the public outcry would undoubtedly exist one year later, as would extraneous political considerations and a possible escalation of violence in the Middle East. On 26 July, the government added to the confusion by announcing that members of the PLO other than those who were known terrorists would be admitted to Canada by minister's permit for attendance at UN conferences or on invitation by reputable Canadian organizations; this position was reiterated over the next several months.

Government policy satisfied no one and clarified nothing; postponement substituted for abstention. Those who opposed and those who favored the admission of the PLO were dissatisfied with the absence of a clear government position. The contradiction between opposition to international terrorism and the contravention of Canadian immigration laws, on the one hand, and the implementation of UN decisions, on the other, was ignored rather than confronted. Although policymakers had anticipated that the principal costs of government action would be international, the major costs were domestic. The PLO had threatened reprisals, but MacEachen found during his trip to the Middle East that Canadian policy on the PLO was no barrier to the improvement of economic and commercial relationships. Though the Crimes Congress was transferred to Geneva, the United Nations agreed formally to the holding of Habitat in Vancouver and Israel agreed to attend the conference. At home, however, the foreign policy bureaucracy disapproved strongly of the penetration by domestic interest groups of their sphere of competence. Some academic commentators noted that the domestic policy of multi-culturalism was not intended to apply to foreign policy, while others contended that the higher level of participation attested to the increasing involvement and sophistication of the Canadian public and should be encouraged.

Paradoxically, as the Arab-Israel conflict became a domestic political issue, the government attempted to reduce the importance of the conflict in its relations with the states of the Middle East. The government hoped to encapsulate the conflict abroad and expand its bilateral ties. The encapsulation of the conflict was consistent with abstention at the United Nations and postponement at home.

Beyond the Arab-Israel Conflict: Canada in the Middle East

Until October 1973 and the increase in the price of oil, Canada had only modest economic relations with most of the states in the Middle East. Canada imported some oil; exported principally pulp, paper products, and wheat flour; and maintained embassies only in the "confrontation" states—Israel, Egypt, and Lebanon. The government had decided to expand the scope of diplomatic representation in the Middle East before the October War, but the international economic crisis sharply accelerated the pace of implementation. In December 1973, Ottawa announced the establishment of an embassy in Saudi Arabia, and in February 1974, Canada established diplomatic relations with Bahrayn, Qatar, 'Uman, and the United Arab Amirates. An embassy was also opened in Iraq, Jordanian representatives now reside in Ottawa, and an ambassador from Saudi Arabia is expected in the near future.

Canada is a trading nation. Like other industrial states, however, Canada runs a deficit in balance of payments; this has spurred the effort to increase bilateral trade and expand exports. In April 1974, the minister of industry, trade, and commerce led a trade mission to Iran, Iraq, and Saudi Arabia. Iran agreed to the establishment of a Canada-Iran Joint Commission which met in July 1975 and initiated projects valued at $1.3 billion. In 1974, Canadian trade with the Middle East as a proportion of total trade doubled; it increased from 1.1 percent in 1973 to 2.6 percent in 1974. That year, Canada exported goods and services of $62 million to Iran, $52 million to Israel, $19 million to Iraq, $18 million to Saudi Arabia, and $14 million to Egypt. In the first half of 1975, Canadian exports to the Middle East—principally to Egypt, Iraq, and Iran—continued to grow, and a new task force was organized within the Department of Industry, Trade, and Commerce to survey the prospects for joint ventures.

Secretary of State for External Affairs MacEachen began a tour of five Middle East states in January 1976. In Cairo, he made explicit the new emphasis on conflict encapsulation and increased economic and commercial links; for too long, Canada had perceived

Egypt principally as a party to the conflict.[13] In addition, MacEachen announced that Canada would contribute $1 million to the reconstruction of the Suez Canal zone and that "active consideration" would be given to the invitation of bilateral technical and financial assistance for Egyptian development projects.[14] The minister also announced that Ottawa would explore the possibility of long-term arrangements for the sale of wheat to Egypt. In Riyadh, Saudi Arabia and Canada agreed to establish a Joint Committee for Economic and Technical Cooperation which met in Ottawa in the summer of 1976. All four Arab countries—Jordan and Iraq as well as Egypt and Saudi Arabia—expressed an interest in Canadian expertise, particularly communications technology, and an expansion of commercial ties.

If significant joint ventures are to be financed, banks, commercial insurance companies, and the Export Development Corporation (EDC) will have to expand their activities. Two Canadian banks recently opened offices in Cairo and in 1974 the Export Development Corporation insured $47 million—one-eighth of total Canadian exports—to the area. Although Canadian exports to the Middle East were only 2.6 percent of total exports in 1974, the $47 million insured exports accounted for 5 percent of the total EDC insurance commitment on Canada's global exports. The EDC admitted, in 1975, that it inadvertently had insured some contracts with boycott clauses; such action is clearly inconsistent with the expansion of bilateral ties with all states in the region, the declared policy of the government, and with traditional Canadian emphasis on trade liberalization. In April, Mitchell Sharp, as acting prime minister, expressed the government's grave concern about the matter and reported that the EDC had been asked to present a review of its practices. Despite repeated questions in the House, however, no report was issued. Although Canada had emphasized that commercial relations with Israel should not and do not impede the improvement of economic relations with Arab states, Ottawa did not formulate a clear policy on the Arab boycott.[15]

Although Canada promoted trade, investment capital from the Middle East was not actively pursued. Troubled by the extent of foreign ownership of its economy, Canada set up procedures to review all foreign investments which might acquire control of Canadian corporations. Canada prefers foreign funds to enter the economy as debt instruments rather than as equity, and unlike most of the industrial economies, Canada did not solicit petrodollars.

During his tour of the Middle East, the secretary of state for external affairs emphasized the new direction of Canadian foreign policy. MacEachen noted that the principal purpose of the trip was the strengthening of bilateral relations. Participation in peacekeeping facilitated the improvement of relations, and Canadian policy on the Arab-Israel conflict did not constrain economic and commercial initiatives. The conflict, moreover, could be contained within the broader structure of expanded relations; the Arab-Israel conflict could be put in perspective.

* * * *

Canadian foreign policy in the Middle East changed significantly after the October War. Ottawa no longer responded principally to the traditional stimuli of disagreement between its allies and a UN presence in the field, although these factors were present. Canada did not emphasize the overriding importance of the United Nations in conflict-management, and support of the United Nations was no longer an automatic reflex in Canadian foreign policy. Nor did Canada seek to mediate between the parties to the conflict. On the contrary, Ottawa reduced the importance of the conflict and upgraded the importance of bilateral relations. Secretary of State for External Affairs MacEachen made explicit Canada's limited interests in the Arab-Israel conflict: "Canada is not a party to this dispute; and not being a great power, it has no immediate political interests in the Middle East conflict."[16] This reduced emphasis on the conflict and the expansion of bilateral relationships was the most important change in Canadian policy.

Even within these more narrowly-defined boundaries, Canada's perspective on the Arab-Israel conflict had shifted. Although Ottawa continued to affirm support of Resolution 242 as the basis for settlement between the parties, in practice Canada acquiesced in the separation of issues which were interlinked by the resolution. This was a marked departure from past Canadian policy. Voting at the United Nations had focused on legitimacy and representation as issues of the conflict. Canada had changed its position on representation: Ottawa now recognized the collective right of the

Palestinian people to be represented in any process of negotiation. Policymakers continued to reaffirm their commitment to the legitimacy of all states in the area. When UN resolutions referred to representation and ignored legitimacy, however, Canada abstained. Ottawa replaced the traditional emphasis on creative conflict management with a strategy of deliberate ambiguity and conflict avoidance. But a continuing strategy of evenhanded ambiguity cannot be in the best tradition of Canadian foreign policy.

9 *The Strategy of Avoidance: Europe's Middle East Policies after the October War*

Hans Maull

At the time of the outbreak of the fourth Arab-Israel war in 1973, Europe's interaction with the Middle East had been thoroughly reshaped by two opposing trends. The first was the decline of Western European capabilities to project power and exert influence over events in the area; the second was the growing imbalance in the international oil market.

After World War II, French and British colonial remnants in the Middle East were rapidly swept away by the tide of Arab (and Jewish) nationalism and a series of failures to influence events since the last imperialist effort in the 1956 campaign demonstrated Europe's dwindling power in the Middle East. Great Britain still maintained its quasi-colonial political and military presence in the Persian/Arab Gulf until 1971 and France still cultivated illusions about, and allusions to, its former Great Power status in the region, but this provided no more than a nostalgic comment on Europe's fundamental political weakness in the area.

While Europe's influence in the Middle East declined, another, not unrelated development began to shape the structure of interaction between the two areas: the ascent of oil power. Growing demand for oil (culminating in the simultaneous boom in the industrial countries in 1972-73) and the relative or absolute decline in importance of traditional oil-producing areas (US production peaked out in 1970, and the country began to enter the international market as an importer of large quantities) shifted bargaining power in the international oil market to the Middle East and the Arab world. Supply interruptions began to become a severe political threat.

Europe, devoid of any means of actively controlling events in the Middle East, became highly vulnerable and dependent on this area. Moreover, the disequilibrium in the international oil market had become so pronounced that Europe, at least in the short term, could not offer sufficient economic incentives to secure the oil imports it needed from the Middle East; it therefore had to rely on political incentives. This had profound consequences for European attitudes toward the Arab-Israel conflict.

Historically, this dispute has from the very beginning affected the international oil market: The establishment of the Jewish state in 1948 led to the interruption of the pipeline to the export refinery of Haifa, and in 1956 and 1967 a combination of deliberate measures of the oil producers and transit countries (Syria and Egypt), as well as the repercussions of the fighting, affected oil supplies to Europe. In 1956, the Suez Canal was closed and the pipeline from the Iraqi oil fields to Lebanon was interrupted by Syrian action. Saudi Arabia declared an embargo on France and Great Britain, and strikes and sabotage affected oil exports from other Gulf oil-producing countries. In 1967, key Arab oil producers halted exports altogether and then decreed selective embargoes against Great Britain, the United States, and Germany, and the Suez Canal was closed again—this time for several years.

In 1956 and 1967 the crisis turned out to be manageable: Its core was not a physical shortage of oil, but the reallocation of available supplies. The Western Hemisphere possessed substantial standby capacities, and other oil producers were willing and able to increase production. Additional supplies from Venezuela, the United States, and Iran helped overcome the shortfall of European imports from the Arab world.

Both crises nevertheless demonstrated the linkage between instability in the Arab-Israel zone and European oil supplies and Europe's vulnerability. In 1956, oil rationing had to be reintroduced in Great Britain and the cost of European oil imports increased. Between 1967 and 1973, Europe's vulnerability increased considerably while growing cooperation of the Organization of Petroleum Exporting Countries (OPEC) oil producers and the erosion of standby capacity outside the Arab world lowered the capacity of the international oil market to deal with supply interruptions. Politically, the realignment of the Arab world around the Cairo-Riyadh axis substantially strengthened the linkage between the Arab-Israel conflict and the oil market. It is therefore hardly surprising that Europe began to react to this situation by shifting its attitudes toward the Arab-Israel dispute.

Yet one should avoid simplistic conclusions about European appeasement policies of "selling out to the Arabs." A closer look at Europe's economic security interest in Middle East oil would reveal the following aspects:

Stable and sufficient oil supplies from this area could be threatened by accidental interruption, deliberate producer action outside the framework of a regional crisis, instability in the area involving intended or unintended supply interruptions, or Soviet interference with oil trade or direct influence in producer countries. While the first possibility may be discarded, the second is conceivable but relatively unlikely: The need to cooperate in an action group, the partly uncontrollable consequences of interference with oil supplies, and the producers' lack of control over the international distribution system which confronts producers with all consumers rather than with a specific target all imply a very strong and commonly held policy objective. Such a possibility would only appear likely in connection with a regional crisis. The third possibility, Middle East stability (regionally and domestically), is therefore a key element in European economic security—and one, though not the only, source of instability in the area is the Arab-Israel dispute which repeatedly has demonstrated its capacity to spill over into the international oil market. The European security interest, then, makes a solution of the Arab-Israel dispute necessary—which is not the same as saying it requires appeasement of the Arabs.

The threat of a disruptive Soviet role in the Middle East—possibility four—(interference with oil trade may be considered unlikely since it would either be of minimal impact or a direct confrontation with NATO) points to a second ingredient of European security interests in the Middle East: freedom of access including access to the Middle East market since that would be the only possibility to pay for the oil. (For European-Middle East trade patterns, see Table 1, p. 113.)

Soviet penetration in the Middle East may appear as a potential danger to European access there, but given the limited attractiveness of the socialist countries as economic partner, this seems unlikely. Eastern European—and Soviet—oil markets (though growing) are not alternative to Western European markets, and the USSR and other socialist countries are less well equipped to assist the Arab world in the solution of its economic problems. Still, the

Table 1

EUROPEAN TRADE WITH THE ARAB WORLD AND ISRAEL, 1973 and 1974
(millions of dollars)

	United Kingdom		France		Holland		Italy		West Germany	
	Exports	Imports	Exports	Imports	Exports	Imports	Exports	Imports	Exports	Imports
Arab world, total										
1973	1,176.8	2,455.6	2,307.1	3,484.4	436.7	1,415.8	1,182.0	3,095.1	1,416.6	2,928.2
1974	1,973.2	6,695.2	3,758.8	9,135.2	615.1	786.4	2,287.8	8,384.0	2,813.8	6,712.6
% world total										
1973	3.9	6.4	6.4	9.3	1.7	7.7	5.3	11.1	2.0	5.1
1974	5.1	12.3	8.2	17.3	2.2	2.8	7.6	20.5	3.1	9.1
Israel										
1973	451.3	168.8	164.6	72.9	115.1	30.2	148.1	50.0	364.3	159.5
1974	515.1	184.9	201.9	104.2	100.5	48.1	217.0	62.4	481.7	167.6
% world total										
1973	1.5	0.4	0.46	0.19	0.45	0.10	0.67	0.18	0.52	0.28
1974	1.3	0.13	0.44	0.20	0.4	0.2	1.10	0.26	0.54	0.24

Source:

Middle East Economic Digest,
27 December 1974 and 26 December 1975

Arab-Israel dispute played an important role in the increase of Soviet influence in the Middle East. The solution of the dispute could help to dissuade the Soviet Union from attempts to dominate parts of the area while continuing instability in the Middle East might provide the USSR with opportunities and temptations to follow a quasi-colonial policy.

As already noted, Europe's capabilities to protect its economic security interest in the Middle East are very limited. Europe can no longer exercise military power in the area, nor does it possess any significant leverage on Israel or the Arab states. Politically, the protection of stability and access rests ultimately with the United States since any solution of the Arab-Israel dispute needs Washington (and possibly also Moscow) to guarantee the agreement.

Economically, however, Europe's resources were considerable, and it was its economic power which made it an important partner for the Middle East. Concealed under the disequilibrium in the international oil market, there existed a second, reverse, imbalance: the imbalance between industrial countries and the developing oil producers. In the longer run Middle East oil producers depend on European markets as much as the Europeans on their oil supplies, and they also need the Europeans to diversify their economies, develop their societies, and ultimately to sell their industrial products once their development and industrialization strategies have succeeded. It is this economic interdependence which restricts—and will further restrict—the potential leverage of the oil weapon: the costs of applying it become higher for producers the more intensive and diverse their links and interactions with consumers. This economic power even translates into some political influence: it provides the Arab world with a focus for its desire to reduce dependence on the superpowers (which are widely seen as aspiring to some kind of neo-colonial domination of the Middle East). The very weakness of Europe, in terms of military power, has thoroughly eroded its past imperialist image in the area and thereby provided a new, much more diffuse, but nevertheless tangible, form of European influence: traditional links, cultural affinities, and economic strength made the Arab world turn naturally to Europe as a political ally, and Arab desire to intensify relations certainly constituted one of the bargaining assets of Europe.

Europe's economic power and its concomitant political influence was not without direct and indirect implications for the Arab-Israel conflict itself. First, Europe's offer to assist the Middle East effectively in economic and social development could increase the incentives to come to an agreement; second, its "persuasive" (as opposed to its previous "coercive") political influence could contribute to produce a milieu more amenable to compromises between Israel and the Arab world; and, lastly, Europe could play an important role in cementing any final agreement in the Arab-Israel dispute economically, say, by helping to build a viable Palestinian state.

* * * *

When the Arab-Israel conflict erupted once more in open warfare and the oil weapon was applied, Europe saw its economic security directly threatened. The consequences were serious tensions and ruptures within the European Economic Community (EEC) and the Western alliance. While procedural shortcomings and the absence of strongly institutionalized forms of crisis-management played a role in both respects, the core of disagreement within the Western alliance lay in different degrees of vulnerability and dependence (see Table 2, p. 116), which led to different perceptions of the crisis. Europe tried to secure access to oil on a national basis and to promote the reestablishment of stability in the area; the United States was mainly concerned with the East-West aspects of the crisis and Soviet attempts to exploit the Middle East situation in order to gain unilateral advantages. Both sides combined justified preoccupations with partial misapprehension of the position of the Atlantic ally and a failure fully to understand its situation. The United States did not see that British and French policies actually benefited all consumers; as the oil companies provided some minimum economic security by sharing out available supplies relatively equally, actual rates of production became the core of the supply crisis, and any further embargo (which no doubt would have followed had Great Britain and France taken the US position and assisted in rearming Israel) would have further reduced total available supplies. Washington also failed to appreciate the vulnerability of Western Europe.

European behavior during the crisis exposed some of the limitations and restrictions of EEC foreign policy: the absence of military and political power; the difference involved in reconciling different national decision-making processes, objectives, and interests in a unanimously pronounced position necessarily confining European foreign policy to long-term strategic and non-crisis aspects of foreign policy, while capabilities for crisis-management are virtually nil.[1] Initially, the EEC countries fell back on national

Table 2

IMPORT DEPENDENCE ON ARAB OIL, 1973

	BeLux	Britain	Denmark	France	Germany	Holland	Ireland	Italy	EEC Total	Japan	U.S.
(1) energy consumption (mill. t)	48.370	213.093	19.284	159.391	252.620	57.223	7.154	115.854	872.991	289.811	1,702.877
(2) oil consumption (mill. t)	25.938	94.637	16.904	109.496	135.171	20.518	4.775	88.088	495.562	222.202	754.522
(3) net crude oil imports (mill.t)	35.647	113.541	9.719	134.920	110.493	70.381	2.460	125.798	606.164[a]	249.246	161.175
(4) oil products: imports (+) or exports (-), net (mill.t)	-4.817	+1.127	+8.693	-6.109	+32.166	-31.962	+3.052	-23.854	-22.296	+21.323	+127.606
(5) Arab crude oil imports (mill.t)	25.940	80.290	5.760	103.610	79.200	47.910	.940	100.280	443.930	111.670	35.190
(6) (5) as % of (1)	53.6	37.7	29.9	65.0	31.4	83.7	13.1	86.6	50.9	38.5	2.1
(7) (5) as % of (3)	72.8	70.7	59.3	76.8	71.7	68.1	38.2	79.7	73.2	44.8	21.8

[a]gross imports

Sources:

lines 1, 2, 3, 5: UN Statistical Papers, Series J
line 4: Comité Professionel du Pétrole, Pétrole 1974

policies to cope with the crisis, and these national reactions, in turn, produced severe tensions within the Community and the Western Alliance. It might well be the peculiar character of European Community foreign policy which could explain the eventual approach to the Arab-Israel conflict: EEC policy focused on the elimination of the Arab-Israel conflict by suggesting and supporting a scheme of mutual concessions designed to meet the requirements of an overall solution of the conflict, but it paid little attention to the practical needs of the intermediate efforts necessary to arrive at such a solution. One of those needs was certainly to start the negotiation process on a roughly equal basis; a substantial military defeat (or victory) of Israel would have increased the dangers to stability in the Middle East. Equally, the EEC failed to recognize the importance of the East-West element in the crisis and the ultimate connection with Europe's own security interests.

The initial reaction of the European countries to the outbreak of the Middle East war in 1973 was confused, incoherent, and very much characterized by *sauve qui peut* attitudes. Its evaluation ranged from Dutch accusations of Egypt and Syria as unilaterally breaking the de facto truce, to French Foreign Minister Michel Jobert's famous phrase: *"Est-ce que tenter de remettre les pieds chez soi constitue forcément une agression imprévue?"*[2] Britain refused to cooperate in attempts to arrange an early cease-fire along the pre-October lines and declared an arms embargo against all Middle East states involved in the conflict. Several countries imposed export controls on oil products, and there was no effective solidarity with the embargoed Netherlands. The disarray within the Community was reflected in the refusal of Denmark and the Netherlands to authorize Great Britain and France to speak on behalf of the EEC in the UN Security Council. Similarly, all European countries except Portugal (which relied heavily on its Angolan oil) refused to cooperate in the US airlift to Israel, although Bonn turned a blind eye to the use of US supplies and bases in Germany in American efforts to rearm the Jewish state, until the war itself was over. The German government protested strongly only after the war, when US arms were directly loaded on an Israeli ship in a German port.

The Community institutions, and in particular the EEC commission, were hardly in a position to cope with the crisis. There was no common energy policy framework, and consequently only a marginal role for the commission. Joint attempts to react to the

Arab-Israel conflict, therefore, had to come through foreign policy coordination. Although the initial call of the Nine for an end to hostilities was made on 13 October (before the application of the oil weapon), the EEC reaction did not come until 6 November in a resolution by the foreign ministers of the EEC—a resolution at the time widely interpreted as a "surrender to Arab blackmail."[3] The resolution urged Israel to return to the cease-fire line of 22 October (a demand then made by Egypt and the Soviet Union) and upheld the following principles for a settlement:

(a) the inadmissibility of the acquisition of territory by force;
(b) the need for Israel to end its territorial occupation;
(c) the respect for sovereignty, territorial integrity, and independence of every state in the Middle East and their right to live in peace within secure and recognized boundaries; and
(d) a recognition of the legitimate rights of the Palestinians.

To arrive at a settlement, the resolution suggested international guarantees and demilitarized zones; finally, the resolution was explicitly linked to the Mediterranean policy of the EEC, already hinting at the strategy the EEC was to pursue after the crisis had subsided.[4]

While this resolution did represent a significant further step in the EEC attitude toward the Arab-Israel conflict, it was not exactly the volte-face it was widely thought to be. The crisis rather accelerated and crystallized changes which had been going on for some time within the EEC, on a national and an EEC level. It could be argued that the real turning point was in 1971, when foreign ministers of the then Six member states agreed on a joint position paper on the Arab-Israel conflict. This paper was not published, but its contents were leaked to the press. The paper suggested demilitarized zones between Israel and the Arab states, the stationing of UN troops to separate the opponents, an Israeli withdrawal from all occupied territories (with the possibility of minor adjustments), the internationalization of Jerusalem, and a solution of the refugee problem through repatriation in stages or compensation under the supervision of an international commission. While some differences of interpretation appeared to persist about this paper, German Foreign Minister Walter Scheel, pressed hard by Israel on his visit to Jerusalem, refused to renounce the principle of withdrawal from all territories.

* * * *

Two aspects appear remarkable about the substantial change of

European attitudes toward the Middle East conflict: first, the sensitivity with which European foreign policies reacted to the ascent of oil power and, second, the fact that, as early as 1971, the Community members found it advisable to formulate joint policies within the framework of Community institutions—the foreign policy coordinating process in the case of the position paper on the Middle East conflict and the Commission in the case of the Mediterranean policy (an attempt to come to a series of bilateral agreements between the EEC and all Mediterranean countries, launched in 1972).

There can be little doubt that awareness of the realities of oil power, and of Europe's vulnerability, constituted a major factor in shifting European policies toward the Arab-Israel dispute jointly as well as individually (though not in all cases). The coincidence between the Libyan action in 1970 (demonstrating the oil producer's strength) and the Tehran negotiations in 1971 (the first time a group of oil producers threatened supply interruptions as a means to increasing bargaining power) and formulations and reformulations of European Middle East policies is hardly coincidental. The swiftness of European reaction was impressive if one compared it with US inaction during the period leading up to the October War of 1973.

This sensitivity and swiftness of reaction, and even the fact that part of the European reaction to the ascent of oil power was formulated within the EEC framework, do not imply unanimity. Differences between member states, and inconsistencies within Middle East policies of the single members, continued and were indeed exacerbated in some respects. While before the 1973-74 crisis those differences and inconsistencies could be deemphasized, they became painfully clear during the crisis itself.

To understand the sensitivity and early insistence on the Community framework as a means to formulate an EEC Middle East policy, and also the differences between and the inconsistencies within national and EEC Middle East policies, we have to turn to the domestic dimension of foreign policymaking, briefly surveying some of the Nine countries.

The only internally consistent Middle East policy within the EEC has been the French policy: since 1962 (the end of the Algerian War) and more pronouncedly since 1967, Paris pursued a pro-Arab line. This policy was formulated by Charles de Gaulle, and its fundamental objectives and tactics have changed little under his successors Georges Pompidou and Valéry Giscard d'Estaing. The pillars of this policy were in line with de Gaulle's global vision of the international system and his view of France's role within it. The main objectives of French Middle East policy since 1967 can be summed up as:

(a) defend and pursue French national interests;
(b) prevent superpower "collision or collusion,"[5] and try to weaken polarization in the Middle East, thereby creating a sphere of action and influence for France;
(c) enlist maximum support from the great possible number of Middle East, in particular Mediterranean, countries by projecting a Great Power image, an alternative to their alignment with the Soviet Union or the US and thereby actually improve their status in the international system toward such a Great Power role; and
(d) try to gain a role in the political settlement of the Arab-Israel dispute.

Those basic objectives were pursued essentially by deemphasizing the (continuing) links with Israel and abandoning the previous alliance; increasing independence from the major international oil companies by developing Algeria's oil resources and fostering a special relationship with this country and by direct competition of French oil companies with the majors, and by oil diplomacy in the Middle East at large; and suggesting four-power initiatives to solve the Arab-Israel dispute.

The remarkable consistency and flexibility of French Middle East policy under de Gaulle (who managed to turn France into a country widely acclaimed by the Arab world for its benevolent attitude only five years after the end of the Algerian War) stemmed from the fact that it was largely formulated by de Gaulle himself—in line with his fundamental convictions but with hardly any interference of domestic politics. Though French Middle East policy was occasionally adjusted so as to attract maximum popular support at home, in essence this support was immaterial to its formulation—and rather weak in any case. Public opinion in France was largely pro-Israel; support for French Middle East policy came from very diverse corners of French society: the Communist party, the new left and the intelligentsia, left-wing Gaullists, and the foreign policy bureaucracy of the Quai d'Orsay. The political center, the Socialist party, the right wing (the former Algerian settlers), and the armed forces have traditionally supported Israel. Although there have been some changes in domestic alignments behind, or against, French Middle East policy (the most interesting being a split within the Socialist party, with a new left group clashing with the traditionally pro-Israel party leadership), the 1973 war proved that Israel still enjoys strong public support in France. This has led to some ambiguity of French declarations if compared with the straightforward pro-Arab stand taken by de Gaulle in 1967—a symptom which demonstrated the growing influence of domestic politics on French Middle East policy. While de Gaulle had been able to effectively insulate the formulation of his Middle East policy from domestic pressures and influences, the weakening of the Gaullist system under Pompidou (who sought to increase the power base of his regime by gaining support from traditionally pro-Israel sectors of French society) began to have its effect on the consistency of French Middle East policies. Still, the strong bureaucratic element, and the centralization of power in the hands of the president, made those linkages relatively weak.

Therefore, while French Middle East policy since de Gaulle by-and-large maintained its internal consistency, it suffered from another weakness: the gap between French objectives and capabilities. France did not possess any political leverage on Israel (and could not hope to play an important role in the settlement of the Arab-Israel dispute), and though it could serve as alternative supplier of arms, its ultimate credibility as ally was limited by its military and economic weakness in comparison with the superpowers. It was this dilemma which largely accounted for the failure of French Middle East policy and made France look for allies to project a more credible Great Power image. At this point it was only natural that Paris should turn to the EEC as a vehicle of its ambitions. France, therefore, became the most ardent advocate of a common EEC Middle East policy.

For somewhat different reasons, French aspirations about a common EEC policy met with German approval. Germany was one of the advocates of far-reaching European integration, and it probably saw, in a Community Middle East policy, a useful way of avoiding the burden of unilaterally moving away from its previous pro-Israel policy. As a consequence of the extinction campaign under Hitler, guilt and a moral commitment of public opinion and government policies to the Jewish state had become important political factors shaping an entirely pro-Israel Middle East policy. The Christian Democrats, in power since 1949, caused an almost complete rupture with the Arabs by their inept handling of relations with Israel and the Arab world and their insistence on the Hallstein doctrine (the claim exclusively to represent the German state, demanding automatic severance of relations with countries which established contacts with East Germany).

When the Sozialdemokratische Partei Deutschlands/Freie Demokratische Partei (SPD/FDP) coalition government under Willy Brandt came to power in 1969, it declared its support for UN Security Council Resolution 242 and its desire to establish good relations with both sides in the Arab-Israel dispute. A spokesman for the foreign office later appeared to interpret Resolution 242 as a call for Israeli withdrawal from virtually all occupied territories. This new attitude, which signaled the beginning adjustment of German Middle East policy, reflected a certain change in public opinion: the strong moral commitment to Israel shifted from unconditional support for Israel's policies to unconditional support of Israel's existence in secure and peaceful boundaries, which did not necessarily imply total agreement on the means of achieving this objective. Only a politician of Brandt's moral stature, and a party so little incriminated by the Nazi era as the Social Democrats, could give expression to this shift in public opinion in government policy. Even so, Germany in no way questioned the "special relationship" with Israel and maintained that this relationship was in no way affected by Germany's overtures to the Arab world. This internal inconsistency in German Middle East policy was one element separating Germany from France; a second element was the different emphasis of security links with the United States. As it turned out, during the crisis of 1973, Germany's overtures to the Arab world could not always be reconciled with a policy of close cooperation with the United States. Up to 1973 those inconsistencies could be concealed by ambiguity and by maintaining a low profile. The US provision of European security formed only a background factor in the formulation of German Middle East policy: détente and multipolarity in the international system, as well as a new German self-confidence in view of its economic strength and its political reintegration in the international political system, changed Germany's previous strict adherence to US policy lines into a somewhat more independent, though still closely coordinated, stance.

The expansion of the Community in 1973 induced a further pro-Arab element in the Common Market—the United Kingdom—thereby strengthening the French position in this respect. The Conservative government under Edward Heath had, shortly after its election in 1970, set out the principles of its Middle East policy in a speech by Sir Alec Douglas-Home. Those principles have dominated Conservative Middle East policy ever since, and the party in opposition—under the new leader, Margaret Thatcher—has continued to follow the pro-Arab policy. During the 1973 crisis, this led to British refusals to let the US use Cyprus bases to rearm Israel and to an arms embargo on all Middle East states involved in the Arab-Israel dispute—a measure which clearly favored the Arabs. As in the French case, this policy has met with widespread criticism among the public, but the strong foreign policy bureaucracy and the powerful position of the government (which, as in Germany, through its majority in parliament and strict party discipline virtually controls parliament, and not vice versa) largely decoupled foreign policy from domestic politics. While the Labour party traditionally has had close links with Israel, since 1967 a split within the party has developed on the Arab-Israel dispute, with a small group of pro-Arab Labour MPs now being organized in the Labour Middle East Council. When Labour came back into power in 1974, its Middle East policy differed from the Conservatives' only in emphasis and nuance and not in substance—despite the continuing, though lessened, dominance of pro-Israel attitudes within the party. The Foreign Office bureaucracy again would appear to have played a role in this constancy.

In 1973, then, three key countries within the Common Market favored a policy of neutrality or neutrality with a pro-Arab tilt. Two countries, Germany and Great Britain, had shifted their position considerably as a consequence of changes in government; they had no doubt been helped by an important tradition of étatism in foreign policy. The strong foreign policy bureaucracies and the position of the executive within the political systems in those countries have virtually removed foreign policy from direct domestic influences and intra-government rivalries. In comparison to the United States, whose decision-making process in foreign policy could be described as "open" and "social," the three described European cases contain a strong element of étatism in the traditional sense. This could well account for the remarkable sensitivity of the European reaction to the largely undramatic but fundamental shift in power to the oil producers in the Middle East around 1970. All three countries agreed on the usefulness of a common EEC Middle East policy, though for different reasons; again, the relative remoteness of foreign policy from domestic politics and the tradition of foreign policy bureaucracies made such a move easier.

Of the "big three" within the Community, Germany remained one step behind in the consistency of its policy and in the degree of adjustment toward Arab positions. This was partly a consequence of Germany's special relationship with the Jewish state and partly it reflected greater sensitivity toward its vital security link with the United States. But undoubtedly even Germany's Middle East policy has been changing since 1970.

At the other end of the spectrum, within the Nine's Middle East policies, one would find the Netherlands—a case of high inconsistency and very strong interrelations between domestic politics and Middle East policy. Only a few months before the outbreak of the October War, a new coalition government had come to power—the first with a socialist prime minister since 1958. The new government was distinctly less Atlanticist and European than its predecessors; it favored global redistribution of wealth and anti-colonialism. Traditionally, the Netherlands had been strongly pro-Israel for much the same reasons as the Germans, the Danish, and the French: sympathy with the Jewish lot in Nazi-dominated Europe combined with a feeling of guilt for not having prevented some of the crimes committed by the Germans. After 1967, however, the traditionally pro-Israel Middle East policy had been somewhat moderated into a more evenhanded approach. Still, the issue was largely peripheral to Dutch interests.

During the 1973-74 crisis, the government followed an erratic line between condemnation of Arab violation of the de facto truce, a refusal to call for Israeli withdrawal from all occupied territories even after the joint declaration of 6 November, and attempts to convince the Arab world that the embargo against the Netherlands had been founded on a misunderstanding. In fact, it appears as if Foreign Minister Max Van der Stoel tried to appease Arab oil producers and to assure his own party that he had not capitulated to the Arabs. The left wing of the Labor party, though sympathetic to the Arab cause, accused the foreign minister, a fellow party member, of having abandoned Israel under Arab pressure—a tactical move designed to force the resignation of Van der Stoel (who was disliked by the left because of his Atlanticist views and was maintained in office only because the government needed the support of two Christian Democrat parties who sustained the foreign minister precisely for his Atlanticist views). These vicissitudes of domestic politics and coalition jockeying for power largely account for the meandering of Dutch Middle East policy, which, somewhat ironically, was perceived as being staunchly and consistently pro-Israel and pro-American. The adherence to the November 6 resolution of the Nine certainly constituted a modification of Dutch policy—in spite of later attempts to interpret the resolution in line with previous Dutch attitudes on required Israeli territorial concessions. The motivation for this adherence to the common declaration was the hope to gain European solidarity with the embargoed Netherlands and probably also to remove some of the domestic pressure resulting from such a shift in policy. European solidarity, however, was at best clandestine even after the November resolution.

Thus the growing dependence on Arab oil and the imbalance in the trade relationship between consumers and producers put the European states under pressure to react to the Arab-Israel dispute in a way which would appease the Arabs and assist in the establishment of a permanent settlement in order to eliminate a constant threat to European oil supplies. EEC countries did indeed react to this pressure jointly and on a national level, but differences still existed. While France and Great Britain went furthest toward Arab positions, most of the other countries tried to keep a low profile as the easiest way to reconcile diverging influences such as strongly pro-Israel public opinion and close ties with the United States.

Both trends continued after the 1973 crisis had ended. There was further adjustment of Middle East policies, but this time mainly in response to changes in the conflict itself, and while differences within the Community continued, there were certainly some further compromises to come. Once the crisis had subsided, the EEC could move out of the area of crisis management and pursue a different, longer-term strategy toward safeguarding its oil supplies: the development of closer economic ties with the oil producers on a national and on an EEC level which would eventually lead to such a high degree of interdependence as to make further supply interruptions counterproductive for the producers. Inevitably, this strategy would encounter political obstacles, thereby demonstrating the continuing divisions within the Community. It did, however, provide a new area open to intensified common efforts.

* * * *

The aftermath of the 1973-74 Middle East crisis brought substantial changes which made it easier for the Community to pursue a new strategy.

First, the shift of the United States toward a mediating position in the Arab-Israel conflict provided a realistic prospect of eventual solution of the dispute. Washington had finally come around to what Europeans saw as one essential aspect of their future economic security: a vigorous attempt to establish peace between Israel and the Arab countries by trying to persuade Israel to make substantial concessions. Since the oil weapon was directed against Europe as a hostage to put pressure on Washington, rather than with any real Arab hopes that Europe itself might be able to play a decisive role in any settlement, the EEC found itself under little direct political pressure once the US-sponsored negotiating process started. The crisis-management aspects of the problem had been taken care of by Henry Kissinger in a way which increased the compatibility of Western policies toward the Middle East conflict. Washington now recognized the need for putting pressure on Israel.

Second, the Arab objectives vis-à-vis Europe shifted from political to economic questions partly as a consequence of US mediation efforts and successes and the realization that Europe could do little to assist the Arabs in achieving their aims in the Arab-Israel conflict and partly because economic aspects constituted an important factor in the strategy and motivations behind the oil weapon. This underlines the argument that the link between the international oil market and the Arab-Israel conflict is essentially a negative one; the elimination of the latter was necessary for the oil producers, in particular the conservative Gulf states, to concentrate their efforts on economic and social development based on stable and high oil revenues, assured markets, and cooperation with the West within a modified framework.

Third, the character of the Arab-Israel conflict has changed considerably as a consequence of the 1973 war. Paradoxically, the efforts of the moderate Arab governments to eliminate the Arab-Israel conflict by triggering a political process ultimately designed to reach a compromise with Israel focused the conflict sharply on the Palestine issue. What dissolves the paradox is of course the fact that once the Arab-Israel conflict moved into the area of realistically defined, limited political objectives and tactics based on political rather than military means, dissention within both camps would be mobilized. A stable solution required acceptance by a vast majority on both sides, and in order to achieve a majority sufficient to eliminate the effective veto power of dissenters, the Arab efforts necessarily had to turn to the Palestinians. The focus of the conflict therefore shifted away from territories and toward the very core of the Arab-Israel dispute, the competing territorial claims of two peoples, the Israelis and the Palestinians.

Those changes after the end of the 1973-74 crisis facilitated for Europe the task of reacting and developing its Middle East policy. Politically, Kissinger's diplomacy was very much in Europe's interest and therefore generally supported by the Nine, though not without some sour remarks by the French. The US efforts helped to bridge the gap between Europe's primary interest in a settlement and its lack of power and influence to assist in its negotiation. The EEC member states continued, though with different emphasis, to uphold the principles for a final settlement mapped out in the 6 November declaration of the foreign ministers. But while these principles were seen by Kissinger, at the time, as an interference in US attempts to arrange negotiations, they did prove to be fairly realistic in terms of requirements for a stable peace settlement. In that sense, one could see US-European differences as a useful division of labor, with the Europeans advancing positions which the United States could not take, but eventually would have to take, if a settlement was to be achieved. This division of labor may also be seen in French and British arms sales to Arab countries. While Washington finds it difficult to supply arms to Egypt, French and British arms sales could provide Egypt with a limited alternative to Soviet weapons and, therefore, help to contain Soviet influence in the area. France agreed with Egypt on a package deal worth about $1.0 billion, including Mirage F-1 aircraft, AMX 30 tanks, Crotale surface-to-air missiles, and anti-aircraft guns. The French were also to assist Egypt in building up and developing its arms industry. Great Britain also supplied arms and contributed toward an expansion of Egypt's arms industry.

With the exception of France, the EEC member states tried, after the 1973 crisis, to return to a low political profile in the Middle East, emphasizing the difference between economic and political problems and between the Arab-Israel and the North-South aspects of the oil equation. Changed circumstances helped them to pursue such a low profile, and, on the whole, the Arab states contented themselves with affirmations of the EEC position taken during the crisis. The EEC, however, did not fully succeed in eliminating politics from its attempts to pursue closer economic cooperation, and this led to internal friction within the Community and posed obstacles to European-Arab negotiations. The first intrusion of politics into the European-Arab dialogue came with the Arabs' insistence on the participation of the PLO. A second stumbling block for the dialogue was the trade agreement between Israel and the EEC, which Israel's foreign minister Yigal Allon interpreted as proof that the EEC "cannot be pushed around by the Arabs." While this trade agreement was initially threatening to delay the second round of the dialogue scheduled for June, the talks did take place, demonstrating Arab interest in its continuation.

In other instances of economic interaction, the same basic picture emerged: the European countries managed to deemphasize political aspects and concentrate on economic and commercial cooperation, thereby pursuing immediate economic needs and interests to reestablish some balance in trade as well as the longer-term objective of reducing dependence on the Arab world by increasing interdependence. The second part of the EEC policy toward the Middle East was the increased attention paid to the Mediterranean policy of the Community, which, until 1973, had not achieved very much. Negotiations for association agreements were speeded up and resulted, in early 1976, in a series of agreements with North African states. Again, politics marginally interfered in the form of the Arab boycott of companies dealing with Israel. Again, the EEC had to accommodate this intrusion of politics in accepting unilateral declarations by the North African states which allowed them not to break their commitment to this boycott. The North African countries did, however, accept a nondiscrimination clause in the agreement; their reservations took the form of unilateral declarations subordinating nondiscrimination to national security priorities.

A large part of European economic interaction with the Arab world was based on bilateralism, and bilateralism flourished particularly strongly during and immediately after the crisis. It continues to be an important element in Europe's approach, but the emphasis has shifted from oil-for-goods deals to broader bilateral agreements of economic cooperation designed to attract a maximum of Arab oil revenues. Possibly even more than on the multilateral level, some countries succeeded in separating economics from politics. Great Britain, for instance, did not have to take a cooler attitude toward Israel as a price for economic cooperation when Foreign Minister James Callaghan visited Saudi Arabia in November 1975. The Netherlands, also, did not appear to suffer unduly from its pro-Israel image in the Arab world. Dutch industry gained a significant share in the growing Middle East markets, partly as subcontractor of German firms. Italy and France, however, the two traditionally most pro-Arab states within the EEC, did declare their support for Israeli withdrawal from all territories and a national home for the Palestinians in joint communiques sealing bilateral economic agreements.

The internal crisis of the European Community during the October War has, all in all, given way to greater coordination and harmonization of its policy toward the Middle East. The joint position formulated under the direct pressure of the oil weapon was not eroded in spite of the change in government in Great Britain, where the traditionally pro-Israel Labour party succeeded the Conservative government. Britain did not change its attitude substantially, even though the Labour government tried to be vague about its position toward the Arab-Israel dispute. Germany at the beginning of 1976 came round to supporting Israel's complete withdrawal from all occupied territories, including, so it was specified, Jerusalem and the Golan Heights, and the creation of a Palestinian state. While the government refused to talk about the change in its Middle East policy, the adjustment certainly constituted a major evolution toward neutrality. Bonn refused, however, to recognize the PLO until it, in turn, accepted the existence of Israel and refrained from terrorist acts. The government spokesman also specified that a Palestinian state would not necessarily mean a PLO state.

Still, the change in German policy reflected a general evolution of European attitudes in line with the shifting focus of the conflict between the Israelis and Arabs themselves; the Palestine question began to play a growing role in the formulation of European Middle East policy. France, of course, went furthest in this direction, with the meeting between Yasir 'Arafat and Foreign Minister Jean

Sauvagnargues, interpreted by the "Voice of the Arabs" as a de facto recognition of the PLO. But Italy, and later Germany, explicitly supported a Palestine state, while Great Britain, though acknowledging the need to go beyond the solution of a refugee problem as suggested in the UN Security Council Resolution 242, preferred to call for a settlement providing a "personality" for the Palestinians. Informal contacts between European governments and parties of the PLO intensified; there are now PLO representatives in Bonn and London and information offices in Paris and Brussels.

Increased coordination and cooperation within a Community framework was most pronounced in the area of economic relations. While bilateralism continued to play a role, the Community succeeded in concluding a series of association agreements with North African states within the framework of its Mediterranean policy; similar negotiations with the Mashriq (Arab East) states were under way. Those agreements are essentially bilateral economic trade and aid pacts between the Commission and the Arab states involved; a potentially more significant development has been the Euro-Arab dialogue. This was launched at the Copenhagen summit of the EEC in December 1973, when four Arab oil ministers arrived, unexpectedly, with the suggestion of broad and far-reaching European-Arab cooperation. The dialogue is supposed to incorporate three stages; preliminary talks, establishment of joint working groups, and a full-scale conference of all member states of the Arab League and the European Community on the ministerial level. After two preparatory meetings in 1974, the dialogue began to move into substantive discussions—and almost immediately ran into political difficulties over the issue of PLO participation. While France and Italy were prepared to accept the PLO, the other EEC states maintained that only states should participate in the dialogue. This split within the Community led to the postponement of the first meeting of the permanent general commission of the two sides in the dialogue. Eventually, however, a compromise formula was found which proved acceptable to all concerned: each side was given a free hand to choose its own delegation for the working groups, which were brought forward, pending the political decision about PLO participation in the general commission.

A first round of talks among experts from both sides took place in Cairo in June 1975; a second meeting convened in Rome in July. The third meeting in Abu Dhabi (November 1975) brought the preparatory stage of the dialogue to an end. The next major step would be the convening of the general commission, for which the compromise formula concerning PLO participation in working groups had been accepted. In the meantime, seven specialist groups set up by the Abu Dhabi meeting would continue expert discussions.

The talks in Abu Dhabi were largely economic, and the suggestions made by the Arab side were of a fairly specific and far-reaching nature: trade conventions abolishing duties and other export restrictions for Arab goods (without offering reciprocity), financial guarantees for Arab investments in Europe, technical assistance to develop and diversify exports, and a stabilization scheme along the lines of the Lomé Convention between the EEC and forty-six African, Caribbean, and Pacific developing countries. This appeared to be far removed from what the EEC was willing to grant, but it did indicate some progress of the dialogue along the lines desired by Europe: the separation of politics from economics and, thereby, of oil from the Arab-Israel dispute.

The Euro-Arab dialogue offered a microcosm of Europe's problems, strategies, and objectives after the 1973-74 crisis. It posed the dilemma of reconciling the Atlantic with the Arab dimension of European foreign policy. The United States had initially objected to the dialogue, but the Community agreed to exclude oil (particularly the price of oil) from the discussion and to consult the United States during the development of the negotiations. The dialogue forced the Europeans to further develop and harmonize their positions on the Arab-Israel issue by acceptance of the PLO as a participant. It also marked the success the Community had had in separating politics from economics. Although political questions could not be fully excluded (but would, by agreement, continue to play a role in the dialogue), a preoccupation with economics was already apparent, while politics played a remarkably small role in spite of the presence of Palestinian delegates. The dialogue finally provided a key example of Europe's strategy vis-à-vis the oil producers and the Middle East at large: to create a tight network of links and interactions which would preclude certain forms of conflict between the European states and those countries (the oil weapon) and ultimately among those countries and within them (regional and domestic violence).

The extent to which the Arab states have been willing to follow Europe's strategy has been remarkable. While the Arab summit meeting in Algiers in November 1973 decided secretly to demand far-reaching further adjustments of European Middle East policies (no restrictions on arms sales to the Arab world; severance of trade, economic, and communication links with Israel),[5] the Arabs in fact accepted the adjustments made in the 6 November declaration, and subsequent modification of policies regarding the Palestinians, as sufficient. They did not insist on separate Palestinian participation in the Euro-Arab dialogue, they accepted the virtually complete exclusion of the Middle East conflict from these negotiations, and they did not use the trade agreement between Israel and the EEC as a pretext to discontinue or even postpone the dialogue. This was in line with Arab readiness to accept political compromises in bilateral agreements either between single nations or between Arab states and the EEC within the framework of the Mediterranean policy.

This preparedness to accommodate European positions reflected, no doubt, the economic weight and the diffuse political influence which Europe had in its relations with the Arab world; it also pointed to the already mentioned imbalance underlying the present disequilibrium in the international oil market—the imbalance between developed and developing countries, which rendered the oil power of those countries fragile and vulnerable.

There was, then, a strong mutuality of interest in continuing the dialogue and in developing a dense network of interactions and interdependencies. It appeared, however, as if the interests within such a framework differed considerably and that the main obstacles in the Euro-Arab dialogue were yet to come. These difficulties might sometimes be political in the sense of an intrusion of the Arab-Israel issue (particularly if no further progress was achieved in the American-sponsored negotiating process), but they could equally, and more likely, be economic. While there can be little doubt that the Mediterranean, and the Middle East including Iran, will be a region of growing European influence and activity, this development might lead to painful adjustment processes within the Community. It appeared as if developments drew the EEC onto a course of rapidly increasing links with the Middle East without a clear notion about how far the Community was willing to go. If such a dense network of interactions between the two areas should indeed come about, it would seriously affect the economic and social structure of Community members and require a fundamental change of EEC institutions. As Middle East countries begin to compete in industrial and agricultural production, as industries like refining and petrochemicals are shifted to the Middle East, Europe will be affected by structural unemployment (presumably regionally concentrated) and massive problems of industrial policy to successfully move into new industries (presumably posing questions of relative competitiveness between Community member states). This will have far-reaching implications for the Community's agricultural and regional policies. Alternatively, there was the danger that the Community was fostering illusions among Middle East countries as to the acceptable degree of cooperation and the possibilities of development with European assistance. To break off the dialogue or attempt to halt it at a low level of increased interaction, might create strong resistance and therefore be politically impossible for the Community.

The Community strategy appeared precariously based on the assumption of stability and was probably seen as a means to increase such stability. But while one can reasonably assume that intensified interaction and expanded links would make the interruption of oil supplies more costly for the producers and therefore less likely, this assumption fails in situations of serious instability where more irrational modes of behavior could easily prevail or where long-term economic objectives could be deemphasized for short-term political goals. This was true about the Arab-Israel conflict and about other regional and domestic sources of conflict. A crucial question would appear to be whether the development momentum could be maintained successfully over a longer period or whether economic and social distortions created by this process of development, and a series of failures within it, would not lead to severe political tensions in some countries—tensions which could easily spill over into regional conflicts.

While the pace of European policy seemed, to some extent, to be determined by external events, with the Community drawn into a course of action as much as being in control of it, it was generally quite successful in terms of its objectives; the temporary separation of the oil issue from the Arab-Israel dispute and of economic aspects from political questions was sufficiently achieved to reconcile the Middle East dimension of European policy with its Atlantic dimension. There was also a considerable harmonization of positions within the EEC with regard to economic cooperation and the Arab-Israel conflict. On the strategic level, the crisis strengthened

European cooperation rather than weakened it. On the tactical level, however, the Community was less successful in coordinating policies.

The differences and disagreements continued. It was significant that the Community failed to coordinate its members' voting behavior in the UN with regard to the Arab-Israel dispute, while such coordination had been quite successful in other areas. France and Italy were the only EEC members to vote for PLO participation in the Palestine debate in the UN General Assembly, and both countries abstained when the General Assembly decided on a committee to work out a program for the implementation of Palestinian rights. The rest of the EEC voted against this proposal. The Community did abstain jointly in the General Assembly vote on recognition of the PLO and jointly opposed the resolution equating Zionism with racism.

Such tactical differences reflect traditional foreign policy orientations, influences of domestic politics and public opinion, and different emphases on other dimensions of foreign policy, particularly relations with the United States. "Atlanticism," as well as Germany's moral commitment to Israel and Labour's traditionally pro-Israel attitude, have effectively prevented these two countries from developing a coherent and comprehensive Middle East policy able to reconcile the various pressures and objectives involved. In Denmark and the Netherlands, it is public opinion and the complexities of coalition politics which have produced ambiguity and a desire for low profile. Geopolitical factors and cultural affinities or distances certainly explained some of the differences within the Community regarding the Middle East. From this point of view, it was hardly surprising to find that Mediterranean France was the only EEC member with a reasonably consistent Middle East policy and that the second traditionally pro-Arab state within the Community was Italy. Italy pursued an international oil policy along lines similar to the French example, and the political influence of Ente Nazionale Idrocarburi (ENI), the state oil company, within the ruling Democrazia Cristiana party (DC) produced a conservative, pro-Arab element within the government much as in the case of France. Italy's policy, however, was much less outspoken than the French equivalent. Domestically, the absence of a strong bureaucratic element and the obscurities of coalition politics (within the ruling coalitions and the DC, which itself was divided in a number of factions) have worked toward a general attempt to maintain a low profile; internationally the alliance with the United States and the weight of Germany constrained Italy's Middle East policy (apparently, Italy secretly cooperated to Washington's satisfaction in the US rearming of Israel in 1973).

The most conspicuous case of low profile, given its previous Great Power role in the Middle East, was Great Britain. While the Labour government declared its readiness to play a constructive role in the Arab-Israel negotiating process, it always hastened to add that the United Kingdom would not force itself on the parties and only step in if asked by both sides.

* * * *

The shift in European Middle East policies began about 1970 in a remarkably sensitive reaction to fundamental changes in the international oil market. The evolving Middle East policy of the Community and the individual policies of some key countries demonstrated this flexibility because of strong bureaucratic and étatist elements in the foreign policy formulating process. To assess the effectiveness of those changes—as opposed to their swiftness—posed a difficult problem: on the one hand, they did not shelter Europe from the impact of the oil weapon or the Netherlands from an embargo. But given the structure of the international oil market and the European alliance with the United States, Europe could hardly avoid being affected—partly by the general shortfall as a consequence of production cutbacks, partly as hostage to exert pressure on the US. On the other hand, the most-favored-nation status given to France and Great Britain (and later to other Community members) helped all consumers by increasing available amounts of oil. Appeasement might not have been a very effective means of countering oil power, but it was preferable to confrontation.

Another conclusion to be drawn is that European Middle East policies evolved more gradually than was normally perceived. The crisis in 1973-74 only highlighted changes which had been under way for some time—though there was no doubt the crisis had a crystalizing and catalyzing function. Equally misleading was the impression that the crisis divided Europe permanently; this impression was created by the initial disarray and the inability of the Community to agree on joint measures of crisis management, a role the Community was badly equipped to play. The crisis brought to the foreground areas of dissension and conflict within the Community by exacerbating the disparate elements influencing European foreign policies: the Atlantic and the Middle East dimension of European military, political, and economic security. Concealed was the extent the Nine had been able to agree on a Middle East policy before the crisis; it also obscured the further harmonization, particularly with regard to the Palestinian issue, after the crisis. Nevertheless, disagreements within the Community continued, predominantly on the tactical level, and member countries also continued to pursue bilateral policies outside the Community framework. The degree to which the Nine decided to use the Community framework appeared more remarkable than the degree to which they used national channels for Middle East policies.

Once the need for crisis management was removed by American mediation in the Arab-Israel conflict, the European strategy was quite successful. The Nine managed to separate economic from political questions, to reconcile the dialogue with the oil producers with coordination and cooperation with the United States, to prevent any erosion of their political commitment to the right of Israel to live in secure and recognized boundaries and their economic, political, and cultural links with the Jewish state. While it was true that this was achieved only because the international environment had changed as a consequence of new American policies in regard to the Arab-Israel conflict and (somewhat later) the energy issue, Europe continued to be exposed and affected by the international climate—with limited influence on it.

Ultimately, the crisis opened a new dimension for the expansion of Europe's role: the Middle East from Morocco to Iran. While Europe's economic dependence on this area was the obvious motivation, and it had been complemented by a need to use European resources and know-how for development, there were also traditional cultural links and a desire to escape dependence by cooperating with Europe, the "civilian superpower." While the balance in coercive power clearly favored the oil producers, this was to some extent offset by the more diffuse political influence of the Community in these countries and their long-term need for European resources, technology, and markets. The conflicting interests of both sides posed extremely complex bargaining situations and required considerable structural changes for Europe for the expansion of interaction to succeed. The strong mutual interest in maintaining and developing this interaction could be seen as the most important factor of stability, but sources of instability were numerous and largely outside the influence of Europe. Growing interaction with the Middle East will continue to pose problems for Euro-American relations, and the reconciliation of those fundamental dimensions of European foreign policy can be expected to demand considerable effort and skill.

10 Japan's Tilting Neutrality

Kazushige Hirasawa

The dependence of Japan on the oil-producing states of the Middle East far exceeds that of any other advanced industrial state. Japan's economy relies more heavily than any other industrial state's on oil for primary energy (79.1 percent).[1] Moreover, 99.7 percent of Japan's oil must be imported, and of these imports, 80 percent originates in the Middle East—half from Iran and half from Saudi Arabia, Kuwayt, and other Arab states. Despite its economic vulnerability, public opinion in Japan and Japanese diplomacy have been slow to manifest direct concern over Middle East tensions and conflicts. The reasons were several: the seeming remoteness of the area from Japan; Japan's very modest trade, other than oil, with the region; the fact that the oil trade has been conducted almost exclusively through foreign intermediaries (especially the US and British oil majors); and the presumption that it was a task for the United Nations to prevent Arab-Israel disputes from erupting into a major world conflict.

Israel was the first Middle East state with which Japan established diplomatic relations (May 1952) after Japan regained its sovereignty with the coming into force of the San Francisco Peace Treaty. This early initiative reflected in part the popular enthusiasm in Japan for the United Nations, which had been instrumental in the birth of the state of Israel. It also reflected romantic interest in Israel's nation-building on the part of Japanese youth, a number of whom went to Israel in the 1950s to live and work in kibbutzim. It also reflected the general passivity of its diplomacy in an era when Japan was content to follow the US lead on most international political issues.

Diplomatic relations were established with Egypt in December 1952, with Saudi Arabia in 1954, and with Iraq in 1955 (the year Japan was admitted to UN membership). Relations with Iran were opened in 1956, Libya in 1957, Kuwayt in 1961, and Algeria in 1962. But not until 1971 were emissaries exchanged with 'Uman, Bahrayn,

Qatar, and the United Arab Amirates. Surprisingly, there was no Japanese embassy in 'Amman (Jordan) until July 1974.

Japan's first significant involvement in Middle East crisis diplomacy was, in a sense, an accident of UN parliamentarianism. As a nonpermanent member of the Security Council in the fall of 1967 and with its representative, Ambassador Senjin Tsuruoka, in the presidency of the Council during October, Japan had a responsibility to participate in the protracted and often heated debate which followed the third Middle East war of June 1967 in the search for a peace formula.

Moreover, law-trained Tsuruoka was deeply interested in the problem and enjoyed the active support of then foreign minister, now prime minister, Takeo Miki. Both perceived the danger that, in the absence of a Middle East settlement, another war might lead to a more serious superpower confrontation and a threat to world peace. The Japanese government also saw in the "occupied territories" issue a parallel with Japan's long-standing complaint about the Soviet Union's occupation by force, since the close of World War II, of two northern islands which are part of Hokkaido and two southern Kurile islands, all of which are historically Japanese territory. The Security Council debate continued into November 1967, when Tsuruoka passed his gavel to Lord Caradon of the United Kingdom. The Japanese representative worked closely with his UK colleague as the Council sessions stretched into the early morning hours in search of a formula which would gain unanimous Security Council support and would, therefore, have a chance of working.

The final result, adopted at 3:00 A.M. on the morning of 22 November 1967, was Security Council Resolution 242, with its deliberately ambiguous text, calling for "withdrawal of Israeli armed forces from territories occupied in the recent conflict" and for "respect and acknowledgement of the sovereignty, territorial integrity and political independence of every State in the area and their right to live in peace within secure and recognized boundaries. . . ." The Resolution contained two ambiguities. It was unclear whether *all* occupied territories were to be evacuated; nor were Israel's rights as a state explicitly declared. Nonetheless, in his remarks congratulating the Security Council for achieving a unanimous agreement, Tsuruoka emphasized "the inadmissibility of the acquisition of territory by war and the need to work for a just and lasting peace in which every state in the area can live in security."

* * * *

With the coming of the fourth Middle East war in October 1973, the Arab oil strategy forced the Japanese people and government to face the issues more directly. The Arab states, determining that Japan's self-styled neutrality in the Arab-Israel conflict was "unfriendly," precipitously reduced oil supplies to Japan as it had to the other industrial states other than the US and the Netherlands—to which oil shipments were totally interrupted. The reaction in Japan, as in Western Europe, was panic. Oil-dependent industrialists faced the nightmare of forced cutbacks in production and lost foreign markets. Consumers began scare-buying and hoarding products (including toilet tissue) which they feared would be affected by oil shortages. Some unscrupulous oil dealers and commercial firms, taking "once in a lifetime" advantage of mass ignorance and fear psychology, resorted to unfair business practices to reap windfall profits.

On the diplomatic front, the Tanaka cabinet's response was to tilt Japan's neutrality closer to Arab views in the hope that this would induce a lifting of the oil-supply restrictions on Japan. This new posture was announced publicly on 22 November 1973 by Chief Cabinet Secretary Susumu Nikaido in a statement to the press. The statement set forth Japan's insistence that Israel's forces be totally withdrawn from "all the territories" occupied in the 1967 war; that the "just rights" of the Palestinians, based on the UN Charter, should be recognized and respected (Resolution 242 had mentioned only a "fair solution of the refugee question"); and, in a concluding passage, that "the government of Japan will continue to observe the situation in the Middle East with grave concern and, depending on future developments, may have to reconsider its policy toward Israel.

Nikaido also called for respecting "the integrity and the security of the territories of all countries in the area" and "guarantees" to that end. His statement nonetheless had wide repercussions at home and abroad. In particular, there was speculation about the meaning of the word "reconsider" in terms of future Japanese-Israel relations. Did this imply the possibility of severing economic relations, recalling the Japanese ambassador, or severing diplomatic relations?

The Nikaido statement, however, failed to persuade the Arab oil states to remove their restrictions on supplies for Japan. Prime

Minister Tanaka then asked Deputy Prime Minister Miki to visit the Middle East as a special envoy of the government in a second-stage effort to have the restrictions lifted. Special Envoy Miki left Japan on the tenth of December, returning home on the twenty-seventh. In those seventeen days he visited eight states: Abu Dhabi, Saudi Arabia, Egypt, Kuwayt, Qatar, Syria, Iran, and Iraq. The crucial encounter was with King Faysal of Saudi Arabia, Japan's primary oil supplier and dominant political force among the Arab oil states. There was a happy meeting of minds between the two austere but gentle leaders, especially on the problem of those developing Asian states which had become dependent upon Japan for petrochemical fertilizers to expand their food production. King Faysal's favorable decision was critical in lifting the restriction. However, the goodwill of the other Arab states, especially Egypt, was also essential for Japan in its search for release from the Arab oil-supply restrictions. Obtaining this goodwill was the further objective of the Miki diplomacy.

At the time, one American newsweekly reported that Special Envoy Miki had $1.0 billion in his pocket to "buy" Arab favor. In fact, his pockets were empty. But he did go out on a political limb to pledge to Egypt a credit of 38 billion yen (about US $127 million) toward the first phase of the project to widen and deepen the Suez Canal, plus a 30 billion yen (about US $100 million) commodity and project aid credit. On the former, an implementation note was exchanged between the two governments in April 1975, and on the latter a note was exchanged in July 1974 to implement one quarter, 7.5 billion yen (US $25 million), of the pledge. The offer rested on a personal political judgment and an earnest hope that future diplomatic developments would permit the reopening of the Canal and that this achievement would also contribute to peace and regional development.

Japan was transferred to the list of "friendly" states, and the supply restriction was lifted before the special envoy had left the Middle East. On his return to Japan, however, Miki still had to "sell" his Suez pledge to his colleagues in the Tanaka cabinet.

* * * *

The next test of Japan's oil diplomacy was to accommodate Japan's new posture to that of the United States, whose energy situation was the strongest among the major industrial states. Immediately after returning home, Miki flew to Washington for lengthy talks with

Secretary of State Henry Kissinger on problems of Middle East peace and of harmonizing energy policies among the industrial democracies. At the outset this was a difficult assignment because of US insistence that effective negotiations with the oil-producing states would be possible only after the oil-importing industrial states had reached a united front. The oil-producing states, in turn, viewed this approach as an invitation to confrontation. Japan was caught in the middle.

Japan's early dilemma was eased as the United States and the oil-producing states moved toward reconciliation on pricing and supply issues and also politics. Indeed, measurable progress, however painstaking and limited, was accomplished after the October War, mainly through Secretary Kissinger's initiative in negotiating transfers of territory and reducing the dangers of a fifth round of war in the Middle East. Even so, gaps remained between US and Japanese vulnerabilities, attitudes, and policies in relation to the Arab-Israel dispute. Japan continued to be uniquely vulnerable among all the industrial democracies in terms of the dependence of its economy on oil as a primary energy source and terms of its overwhelming dependence on Middle East oil. Because of oil imports, Japan's trade with the Middle East oil states was much greater than with Israel and Egypt and the gap grew massively wider following the steep rise in prices, as the table on page 143 demonstrates.

Where national survival was the issue, Japan's national interest clearly lay in accommodations which would sustain its essential energy sources without doing violence to its equally important political commitments. Japan's political commitments in the Middle East situation were substantial. The rights of all states, including Israel's, had to be respected. So had the rights of self-determination of the Palestinian people to be respected. Nor could Japan condone the terrorist activities of the Palestinian guerrillas against innocent civilians and children.

In May 1972, three young Japanese ultraradical guerrillas affiliated with the so-called "Red Army," a splinter group then collaborating with the Palestine liberation movement, attacked the Tel Aviv airport, causing death to twenty-six persons and injury to seventy, many of them foreign tourists. Within twenty-four hours the Japanese government issued a statement deploring the "sheer insanity" of the act and extended "deep and sincere apology and condolences for

JAPAN'S TRADE WITH SELECTED MIDDLE EAST COUNTRIES

	US $ million		
	1972	1973	1974
Saudi Arabia			
from Japan (steel manufactures, synthetic textile fabrics, misc.)	238	389	677
to Japan (crude oil, misc.)	901	1,386	5,238
Egypt			
from Japan (machinery and steel manufactures)	17	14	74
to Japan (raw cotton and crude oil)	33	48	168
Israel			
from Japan (steel manufactures, machinery and tools)	44	58	89
to Japan (diamonds, fruits, chemical fertilizer)	59	80	65
Iran			
from Japan (steel manufactures, synthetic fiber, machinery)	322	484	1,014
to Japan (crude oil)	1,490	1,922	4,766

Source:
MITI, Trade White Paper, 1975

those who were killed or injured." Soon thereafter Dietman Kenji Fukunaga was dispatched to Israel as a special emissary, with a solatium of $700,000. Japan's concerns for national and human rights continued as strong as ever, even with the tilt in its diplomacy.

* * * *

The government of Prime Minister Miki gave high priority to Japan's Middle East diplomacy. This was underlined when Mr. Miki began his first policy speech as prime minister, at the ordinary session of the Diet in January 1975, with a discussion of the Middle East question. In the tradition of such policy speeches, this represented an unprecedented emphasis on a foreign policy matter. Miki suggested there were two deficiencies in UN Security Council Resolution 242:

1. Although the Resolution acknowledged the right of all states in the region to coexist peacefully, it mentioned no country by name. Miki expressed the view that this principle should apply to "all parties concerned, including Israel."

2. The Resolution was inadequate in that it dealt only with the refugee question, avoiding any mention of Palestinian rights. On this matter Miki urged: "What must be achieved is the recognition, in accordance with the United Nations Charter, of the legitimate rights of the Palestinians, together with a solution to the Jerusalem problem, through peaceful negotiations." Miki reiterated these views as basic to Japan's approach to the Middle East question in September of that same year, in his policy speech before the extraordinary Diet session.

Nonetheless, Japan's position came under attack from all sides. Pro-Israel Americans criticized Japan for yielding to Arab pressures and leaning excessively toward the Arabs. The Arabs criticized Japan (under the Tanaka cabinet) for abstaining in November 1974 in the UN votes on the resolution concerning Palestinian rights of self-determination and the resolution concerning the granting of observer status to the Palestinian Liberation Organization (PLO). On the first resolution the major democracies abstained, with the exception of the United States which voted against. On the second, Japan, France, and Sweden abstained, but the other major democracies voted against. In November 1975, Israel criticized Japan for abstaining on the UN resolution defining Zionism as a form of "racism." All the other major democracies voted against.

The future direction of Japan's Middle East policy was implicit in three initiatives undertaken in early 1976. Minister of International Trade and Industry Toshio Komoto, a close associate of the prime minister, spent a fortnight in four Middle East states, beginning on 4 January. His consultations in Iran, Iraq, Egypt, and Saudi Arabia explored proposals for economic cooperations with Japan. Further proposals for economic cooperation were likely to be one of the pillars of Japan's Middle East policy.

On 14 January, Japan's permanent representative to the United Nations, Ambassador Shizuo Saito, made an indicative statement before the Security Council, which was then considering the Middle East question. Although the Security Council adopted no resolution at that meeting because of a US veto, Saito's statement confirmed that another pillar of Japan's Middle East policy was a strong stance on the Palestinian question. Ambassador Saito emphasized that the Palestinian question was central to a resolution of Middle East problems and that there could be no settlement until the Palestinian issue was resolved according to principles of self-determination under the UN Charter. He added that the states concerned should use the forum of the Geneva Conference for consultation, and that, in order to expedite a peaceful settlement in the Middle East, Israel and the PLO should open a dialogue in some form or another.

The third initiative was also in a UN context. On 24 March, Japan's deputy representative, Ambassador Masao Kanazawa, amplified Japan's policy in light of disturbances in Arab areas under Israel's control:

> The basic position of the government of Japan with regard to the occupied Arab territories and Jerusalem is that Israel should withdraw from all the territories occupied since 1967. The government of Japan therefore firmly opposes any attempt to annex those territories and any change, physical or demographic, or other actions and policies intending to alter their legal status.

Regarding Jerusalem, Kanazawa declared that "the great historical heritage which it has brought to the world should be protected for the benefit of all mankind, without distinction as to race or religion." He praised the decision by the Supreme Court of Israel which banned Jewish prayer at the Haram al-Sharif, sacred to Islam, and urged "all the parties to refrain from any action that would further heighten the tension."

* * * *

Japan had become deeply enmeshed in Middle East affairs, incapable of retreating to its earlier distance. Continuing energy dependence on Middle East oil for at least another decade was one determining factor. Another was Japan's recognition of the critical importance to world peace and stability, as well as international economic prosperity, and of steady progress toward a durable peace settlement in the region. Japan's direct contributions to this objective were necessarily limited, but they were meant to be constructive. There was probably no direct role Japan could play in negotiations among the principals to the disputes, but it could promote those political considerations which it believed most likely to yield fruitful negotiations. This Japan was attempting to do, especially in the discussions at the United Nations.

Japan also had the capacity to contribute directly, under favorable political conditions, to international cooperation on the economic development of the region. The opportunities were vast and challenging: revival of the Jordan River international development plan, agricultural rejuvenation of large areas of the Middle East, creation of an international solar-energy research institute which would pool the brains, technologies, and funds of many countries in an effort of common benefit, and a broadening of the industrial base for the Middle East economies.

Yet there were abiding fears to be abated before these opportunities could be realized to any significant degree. These included Israel's fear of extinction, Arab fears of Israel's expansionism, Palestinian fears that their national aspirations might be forgotten by the rest of the world, and the fears of all the peoples of the region of adverse intervention by outside forces. These fears will not be overcome nor will negotiations be advanced by a mere choosing of sides by Japan or the other interested states. Japan, I am confident, will continue a Middle East policy of active, rather than passive, neutrality, tilting to the extent it believes it can constructively advance the causes of reason and justice, and encourage the forces for negotiation, accommodation, and the realization of a stable peace in the Middle East.

III

Oil and Politics in the Middle East

11 *Petrodollars, Arms Trade, and the Pattern of Major Conflicts*

Paul Jabber

This chapter focuses on the likely courses the flow of arms to the Middle East will follow during the balance of the seventies, the scope of feasible arms-limitation measures in light of existing political quarrels in the region, and the factor of greatly increased revenues for Middle East oil-producing countries. I have chosen to look at the problem from the perspective of its linkages to regional political realities and of operative influences at both the supply and demand ends of the arms transfer process, largely neglecting its quantitative aspects which are abundantly treated elsewhere.[1]

Since the 1940s, the Middle East has been synonymous with conflict, in many cases active military conflict. During much of the post-World War II era, the stage on which these confrontations unfolded was largely restricted to the Palestine area and its immediate environs. But for the past dozen years, violent disputes, accompanied by the development of major arms contests, have occurred in several other parts of the region as well. This process has been aided by altered political factors and the burgeoning of local economic resources. As a result, any review of the armaments situation and speculation about future trends that would do justice to the complexity and variety of the subject cannot be limited to the Arab-Israel conflict area; it must encompass the other important locus of arms rivalry, the Persian Gulf. This is particularly appropriate if we are to look at the problem from the perspectives of its impact on North American-West European-Japanese relations, which is exercised mainly through the venue of the energy issue, and its interaction with the vastly expanded Middle East oil revenues.

The arms buildups in the Gulf and in the Arab-Israel conflict zone are closely linked by several factors other than geographic proximity. Three are of particular importance: first, a number of countries in the Gulf area that have been acquiring substantial amounts of advanced weaponry may become directly engaged in a fifth

Arab-Israel war—Iraq and Saudi Arabia played a minor role in the October 1973 hostilities which is suggestive of future possibilities. Second, it is becoming clear, from statements by Middle East leaders and actual events—such as the loaning of Mirage fighters by Libya to Egypt in 1973—that oil-rich countries are or may serve as conduits of military hardware and financial aid to Arab states that are frontline participants in the Arab-Israel confrontation. Third, any prospective arms-transfer control measures aimed at curbing the Arab-Israel arms race will have to include countries beyond the immediate conflict zone if they are to be effective or at least acceptable to both sides. US Secretary of State Henry Kissinger has expressed this publicly.[2] For arms control purposes, the larger Middle East area may have to be considered as a unit, a necessity that will complicate further the already difficult task of achieving arms regulation in that part of the world.

Arms and Conflict in the Persian Gulf Area

The situation in the Gulf epitomizes the complexity of the pattern of local conflicts characteristic of the Middle East as a whole. Most existing disputes—revolving mainly around boundaries, jurisdictional claims, dynastic issues, and ideological differences—are not new. What gives them increasing relevance, from a military point of view, are two developments: the withdrawal in December 1971 of the British military presence, which for over 150 years had determined the course of events in the region and underwritten its stability; and the tremendous increase in local arms after the October War which was made possible by the influx of sharply increased oil revenues. This has resulted in the launching of several tangled and multi-tiered arms races, as the local states have endeavored to acquire the means of defense against internal threats and external attack and, for some, the military muscle necessary to fill the vacuum of power in the manner most favorable to their interests.

Briefly, one may single out three main axes of interstate conflict—largely nonviolent though not without occasional flare-ups—which may easily take on large-scale military form in the future. Perhaps the most important is the Iraqi-Iranian situation. The various issues of contention—from border disputes in the Shatt al-'Arab and other areas to the Kurdish problem, rivalry over Gulf hegemony, and ideological hostility—are well known. They foreshadow a continuing antagonistic relationship for the foreseeable future despite the settlement of various differences. On paper, Iranian superiority would appear overwhelming and still on the increase. Iran holds a three-to-one advantage in population, a six-to-one advantage in GNP (1974), and a ten-to-one margin in military expenditure (1974-75). Furthermore, the Shah has acquired or placed orders for large shipments of the most advanced equipment in Western arsenals, including 2,000 Chieftain battle tanks, over 300 Phantom fighters, 80 air superiority F-14 fighters, and an array of modern warships. On the other hand, the Iraqis, together with the Syrians, have moved to the forefront among Arab recipients of Soviet military equipment; a Soviet-Iraqi Treaty of Friendship and Cooperation was signed in April 1972, and all Arab states have expressed solidarity with Iraq at times of crisis in Iranian-Iraqi relations.

A second axis of conflict in the Gulf region is that of Iraq vs. Kuwayt and, indirectly, Saudi Arabia. This dispute developed around Baghdad's claims to Kuwayti territory. Iraqi access to the Gulf was cramped, and Kuwayt's oil fields were an obvious attraction. The problem began in 1961 when the Qasim regime activated the Iraqi claim; the incident in March 1973, when Iraqi troops temporarily occupied a small portion of Kuwayti territory, was its latest but probably not its last manifestation. In 1973, Saudi Arabia was reported to have sent troops to Kuwayt, and Iran and Jordan offered military aid. Though there was a great discrepancy in terms of military power between these two countries, with the balance tipped strongly in favor of Iraq, Kuwayt embarked on a very substantial effort to build up its armed defenses. This was primarily for deterrent purposes or, if deterrence failed, to force an invader to mount a major military campaign, which undoubtedly would bring in neighbor states and the Arab League in general. In July 1973 the Kuwayti parliament authorized an arms purchase program of $1.4 billion over the balance of the seventies. Since then, Kuwayt has placed orders for twenty Mirage F-1 fighters (destined for Egypt according to some reports), thirty-six US A-4M Skyhawk attack planes, and a Hawk missile defense system.

The Kuwayti-Iraqi relationship also exemplifies a problem facing other small shaykhdoms in the Gulf area: that of territorial claims being a potential area of conflict. (Historically, perhaps the most notable of these has been the recently-settled dispute between Abu

Dhabi and Saudi Arabia over the Buraymi oasis and other oil-rich portions of Abu Dhabi territory.) Similar quarrels over offshore waters, islands, and border territories exist between Iran and several United Arab Amirates shaykhdoms, within the UAA itself, and between Sharjah and 'Uman. Some of these disputes flared up in the sixties and seventies and led to sporadic armed clashes and, with petrodollars becoming plentiful, the building up of military establishments. (Abu Dhabi, for example, boasting a population of 90,000, has, since 1973, purchased a squadron of Mirage fighters from France and a Rapier missile defense system from Great Britain.) As local arsenals burgeon, the large number of inter-dynastic rivalries and territorial quarrels may provide grounds for increasingly frequent military conflicts in this strategic area.

A domestic factor is also present. All the small oil principalities on the Gulf are ruled by families or clans in whom tribal leadership has been invested for generations. Their rule is of the absolutist-traditional type, and mediating political institutions are virtually nonexistent (Kuwayt and Bahrayn being notable exceptions). The populations of these Gulf states have a large proportion of immigrants from outside the area who form most of the working force, owe no allegiance to the traditional rulers, and are socially and ideologically a factor that militates toward radical political change. In this situation, the loyalty of the armed forces is the mainstay of the traditional regimes, and the drive toward the modernization of military equipment and enlargement of the defense establishment aims at keeping the soldiers happy yet also enhancing the regime's ability to remain in power against internal enemies. Of course, this approach does entail the danger of catapulting the military into a position where they may become active promoters of political change, and this is why most of these shaykhdoms have in the past relied on foreign mercenaries or military personnel, detailed by friendly governments, to man many of their command positions and operate sophisticated military equipment. But as this situation changes, the existence of strong military forces in the oil-rich states of the Arabian peninsula will loom progressively larger as a source of domestic instability.

The third main axis of potential conflict along which arms races may be evolving is the Arab Gulf states against the non-Arab regional power, Iran. Such a military confrontation would arise if the Shah were to flex his enormous military muscle—which he began acquiring in the early seventies and continues to build at a rate of some $2-3 billion per year—to establish control over the strategic exit from the area via the Strait of Hurmuz or to interfere actively in the internal affairs or interstate relations of the Arab countries on the western shores of the Gulf. Historically, there has been no love lost between the two camps, and their relationship has been one of antagonism on religious and ethnic as well as political grounds. The Shah's forcible seizure of several Gulf islands claimed by Sharjah and Ras al-Khaymah rankles with the Arabs, who eye Iranian designs of regional predominance with great suspicion. Moreover, the existing situation can be destabilized overnight by a change in the political regime in the Arab camp by forces leaning toward radical nationalism or socialism—a development which, the Shah has threatened, would prompt Iranian intervention. Were this to happen, an Arab-Iranian confrontation would be likely to develop; the magnitude of the Arab response would be dictated largely by the status of Iraqi relations with the conservative regimes in the area—particularly Saudi Arabia—and of the Arab-Israel conflict in the west.

What arms-related developments can be forecast for the medium-term future in the Persian Gulf areas?

It seems clear that the outstanding elements of the situation in the Gulf are such that we may not see any change in the current trends of increasing arms transfers and high military expenditure for the remainder of the seventies. The oil factor, as a source of wealth outstripping local capacities for useful absorption and as a bargaining or pressure tool; the relative instability of the strategic-power situation in the area, where the status quo is challenged in terms of the relationship of predominance between the major local powers, against a background of more pronounced Soviet-American competition—particularly in the adjacent Indian Ocean area; the previous absence of large military establishments, which are in the process of being built up; the inner dynamics of arms races, which makes it almost unavoidable that a large influx of arms to one regional country will trigger acquisitions in the neighboring states; the political-diplomatic and domestic economic imperatives in the arms supplying countries—all these presage no let-up in the present arms flow.

Whether these bulging arsenals will be put to actual use in combat will depend primarily on political changes of regime in one or more

Gulf states, which might give rise to interstate confrontations along ideological lines; on an aggressive campaign by Iran to establish itself as the uncontested regional policeman; or on a recrudescence of frictions between Iran and Iraq. The success of OPEC over the past few years has produced, among its Middle East members, a strong momentum toward compromise and improvement in bilateral relationships. While this trend may continue, it does not rule out political quarrels. OPEC basically has one simple and limited objective: stabilization of oil prices at levels desirable to its membership. There is no compelling reason why even a state of war between two or more OPEC members should lead to a breakdown of an arrangement which is in the best economic self-interest of each individual member and which requires for its continued operation a minimal amount of coordination that can be carried out indirectly and inconspicuously. Indeed, OPEC scored its most impressive gains in a period when several of its most prominent members were engaged in limited military hostilities against one another (Iran vs. Iraq and Iraq vs. Kuwayt in 1973-74).

The Arab-Israel Race

The Arab-Israel conflict remains the primary potential flash-point and the locus of greatest political and military instability in the Middle East area.

The arms competition between Israel and its neighbors is the fiercest and most expensive of any generated by international conflicts outside the industrial European-North American quadrangle. The resources devoted to it by local participants, both in absolute values and in relative terms, have no parallel elsewhere. Since 1950, published military outlays in Israel and Egypt alone have absorbed some $45,400 million—of which about $24,000 million was spent from 1973 to 1976. It is also the most unstable of arms races: it is extremely competitive, with adversary states procuring offsetting armaments in a continuous action-reaction process; new arms accretions have repeatedly involved generational jumps in the quality of armaments, at periodically faster rates and with sharp increases in military expenditures; and each side aims not at equilibrium, but at achieving a preponderance of power.

The political issues that lie at the core of the Arab-Israel conflict and have prompted this violent arms race are too well known to require description here. In terms of the arms race per se, one could even say that the logic of periodic all-out wars and military deterrence has taken over; the process has become impervious to any but the most radical changes in the existing political situation. In 1967 and 1973, the warring parties were able to replenish their arsenals very shortly after the end of the hostilities and bring their overall strength to a level not only equal to but superior to that obtained at the outbreak of the war. Qualitatively and quantitatively—and cost-wise as well—the arms race has been spiraling upward at an increasingly rapid pace.

Furthermore, though more movement toward an eventual Arab-Israel peace has been recorded in the two years following the October War than at any other time since 1949—a movement reflected mainly in changed attitudes and positions, but nonetheless real and significant—the situation is very unstable. As a result of the October War, the deterrent effect of Israel's superiority lost much of its credibility. The Egyptian and Syrian armies fought well and regained their prestige and self-confidence, thereby restoring to the political leadership a feasible military option that appeared lacking between 1967 and 1973. The Arabs' resort to arms yielded handsome political and diplomatic dividends and even resulted in the recovery of some of the occupied territories, which may tempt them to follow the same path again. Their ability to attack Israel first proved extremely successful, and will almost certainly result in Israel's returning to a preventive or preemptive war posture.[3]

Thus, like Janus, the new Arab-Israel strategic balance is double-faced. It offers better chances of a negotiated peace; but, if diplomacy proves sterile, it presages an increase in the tempo and scale of armed violence. In either case, the situation has had a serious accelerative impact on the arms race. On the Israel side, the substantial margin of military superiority perceived to have existed prior to 6 October 1973 was shown to be inadequate for deterrence. On the Arab side, despite the success of their surprise attack and their much improved battlefield performance, the Egyptian and Syrian forces could not register a military victory. A virtually irresistible incentive exists for all parties to seek a substantial increase in their military power. The advent of a new generation of conventional weapons which combine high accuracy with low cost and afford considerable versatility in deployment has introduced novel elements of uncertainty that may be highly detrimental to stable deterrence.[4]

In short, current trends in arms acquisition may be expected to continue into the 1980s, barring major changes in the status of the political dispute. The arms flow clearly is a dependent variable in the Arab-Israel situation. The independent variable is the outcome of the diplomatic maneuverings for a political settlement that have taken place since the October War. In very general terms, three alternative futures, ranked here in ascending order of conflict-potential, are possible:

1. One future would be characterized by gradual but perceptible progress toward a state of normal, peaceful interaction between Israel and the Arab countries. This process would be slow and drawn out over a number of years because of the enormous psychological readjustment it will require. It is predicated on the achievement of a comprehensive peace settlement acceptable to all major parties to the conflict. It would lead to an increasing integration of Israel within the system of Middle East states, both economically and politically. As mutual confidence develops and diverse networks of transnational relationships multiply, the military confrontation and weapons contest would wind down. A number of complementary arms control measures might be instituted such as a political settlement of standing issues which would permit the lifting of military pressure and, because of a presumable desire by each party to ensure that the other side keeps its share of the bargain, the imposition of limits on war-waging potential. The economic advantages of constraining the arms race are obvious. One may reasonably expect that demilitarization of border regions, international policing or inspection of sensitive points, and communications links (hot lines) between the parties will be instituted as part of any political settlement package; the presence of UN forces on the Syrian and Egyptian fronts and of American cease-fire surveillance personnel as well as unmanned sensor stations in Sinai are examples of feasible arrangements. It is likely that steps would be taken to regulate the qualitative and quantitative inflow of new weaponry into the area to discourage the buildup by either side of an imbalancing superiority and to increase military stability by injecting only arms that enhance the defensive capabilities of the recipients and their ability to deter surprise attacks. Furthermore, partial disarmament measures such as reductions in the stockpiles of costly weapons and the dismantling or civilianization of military industries could become feasible in time. Regionally self-imposed curbs on arms production acquisition and on military budgets under some form of mutual inspection might also be negotiated.

2. An alternative future would be one of peaceful, but heavily armed and suspicion-riddled coexistence. The psychological breakthrough envisaged in scenario one would be absent here. Even if the issue of diplomatic recognition might have been transcended, Arab-Israel economic, political, and human relations would remain severely limited. Continuing Arab suspicions of hegemonic Zionist designs would be counterbalanced by Israel's fear of Arab nationalist irredentism. Although some formula expected to solve the Palestinian plight might have been worked out, the arms race would continue at a high level, with large percentages of the parties' national wealth spent on armaments and with an unceasing escalation in the lethal quality and sophistication of the weapons sought. Eventually, a nuclear balance of terror might come into existence, thus bringing to a climax the logic of military deterrence that would undergird this particular state of relations. Despite its grimness, this could be a considerably "stable" situation in the sense that it could last many years. The less comprehensive the settlement that might be reached under the momentum created by the October War and the larger the number of important issues separating the contending parties that are left unresolved (status of Jerusalem, final border, Arab economic boycott), the stronger the probability that this situation of hostile coexistence, of a long-term "cold-war," would develop.

3. Finally, a third possible kind of situation might develop that would be more prone to break down over the short term and would also permit no scaling down in the ongoing arms race. It would come about under either of two sets of circumstances. One, the interim Egypt-Israel agreement of 1975 is followed by a diplomatic stalemate rather than by further significant steps toward a negotiated settlement. Two, a settlement is reached with a high built-in quotient of potential instability. The pivotal issue would be the formula governing the return of Palestinian territories. Assuming that any likely political solution will give the Palestinian people some form of autonomy, what would be the status of the new Palestinian entity, its relationship to Israel and Jordan, the degree of its politico-economic viability, and the collateral arrangements governing the future of the refugees and other Palestinians now living outside the confines of this new entity? Given the historical roots of the Arab-Israel conflict, the demographic composition of Israel and Jordan, and the foreseeable requirements of economic survival in that area, it would be an enormous achievement if any stable arrangement

could be negotiated. Ironically, there is substantial agreement on this matter between the current official Israeli position, which contends that there is no place for more than two states in the Palestine-Jordan area, and the more radical component of the Palestinian Resistance, the so-called "rejection front," which argues that a small state on the West Bank and Gaza portions of Palestine could be only a paralytic, Bantustan-type satellite and therefore one that the Palestinians cannot tolerate for long as the expression of their natural aspirations.

Supplier Incentives: Old and New

Why are the weapons-producing countries so willing—indeed, so eager—to supply such enormous quantities of arms to an area where political quarrels are at such a pitch that there is a high likelihood that all available weapons will indeed be used in anger? What are the incentives that prompt the major arms sellers—they are a small group; the US, the Soviet Union, France, and Great Britain thus far have cornered the heavy-weapons market for all intents and purposes—to pour arms into a region whose stability is deemed *by them* to be vital to world stability from strategic and economic points of view? In the Arab-Israel context, at least, the record does not support the familiar argument that adequate defenses will prevent the outbreak of wars—that elusive "stability through military balance" that Washington has unsuccessfully sought for decades as a cornerstone of its Middle East policy. The map of the area has been repeatedly altered by the use of force. From an economic perspective, every Middle East war has been accompanied by disruptions to the vital flow of oil and to the channels of trade and communication that cross the region. Clearly, other considerations prevail and provide some rational justification for these paradoxical circumstances; for example, the United States sells or grants several billion dollars worth of arms to a number of Middle East countries at the same time as the American Secretary of State—in an unprecedented fashion—devotes months of frenzied activity to obtaining a cease-fire over a few hundred square miles of territory.

Autonomous, international arms merchants largely went out of business by the end of the Second World War. Since then, there has been a crucial change in the nature of arms transfers: they have become an explicit instrument of state policy, wielded directly by national governments as a legitimate means to the attainment of foreign policy objectives. As the character of the phenomenon has changed so have its underlying motivations. The mercantile impulse that motivated the arms trafficker of yore has been replaced by a complex of interconnected incentives and interests that have prompted the governments of most arms-producing countries to maintain, and at times vigorously promote, large-scale programs of military exports. Only partially invested by a profit orientation, these interests and incentives range from the need to maintain a viable domestic arms industry to the belief that arms grants and sales secure valuable ideological or political influence in the inner councils of foreign governments. They also include the desire to strengthen the military potential of allies and friendly regimes, to secure important quid pro quo's such as base rights, to preempt arms acquisitions by recipients from rival suppliers, to extend the umbrella of symbolic deterrence in regions witnessing power competition by adversary blocs, to buttress friendly governments in domestic trouble, to gain the allegiance of uncommitted governments, to dispose of surplus matériel or obsolete equipment, to compensate partially for heavy defense expenditures, to develop and maintain domestic technological expertise in the area of weapons production, and to redress balance-of-payments problems.

In the Middle East of the seventies, all these stimuli are in evidence. Though one could easily give examples of each, only two of the most important—one political, the other economic—are sufficient by way of illustration.

Starting with the major arms deal concluded between Egypt and the Soviet bloc in 1955—the famous "Czech" arms deal—the pattern of arms supplies to the area witnessed a remarkable polarization. Egypt, Syria, Iraq, and the Yemeni Republics became armed exclusively with Soviet weapons. The remaining countries of the region had arsenals almost totally made in the West. As a result, both suppliers and recipients became locked into an exclusive relationship that served as a major cause for large-scale supplies of arms. For one, the prestige of the suppliers from a military-technological standpoint was at stake. Neither the Soviet Union nor the United States was willing to let its respective clients be defeated in a test that unambiguously pitted American technology against Russian technology. Moreover, because arms sales had been the venue for Soviet political entrance into the region, and continued to be the mainstay of their Middle East presence, a change of suppliers by a regional government came to be perceived as tantamount to crossing the threshold between one camp and the other. Furthermore, the tight arms relationship helped thrust the suppliers into the role of principal diplomatic patron of their arms clients and entangled them even deeper in regional crises. This political polarization reached its apex with the Six-Day War and was maintained and reinforced during the six long years that preceded the October War. All these factors have tended to strengthen the bargaining counter of Middle East clients in their arms acquisition efforts and to make it extremely difficult for the suppliers to initiate any unilateral policy of restraint without jeopardizing their entire political relationship with their respective clients.

From an economic standpoint, the incentives to sell arms have been even more compelling; by their very nature, they are more tangible and usually bear fruit much more immediately. In Western Europe (Great Britain and France in particular) they have included the need to maintain viable independent domestic industries in the defense sector, which, given the high cost of research and development of advanced weapons systems, they could not assure without lowering costs by selling part of their production abroad. In the United States, balance-of-payment problems, particularly since the peaking of the Vietnam War, have provided a standing stimulus to bolstering exports by means of arms sales.

However, neither these long-standing incentives nor the enormous losses in equipment sustained by both sides in the October War are sufficient to account for the five-fold increase in arms transfers to the Middle East area which has taken place since 1973. Two novel stimuli, of apparently overwhelming strength, have come into play and account for much of the current surge in weapons supplies. They are both petroleum-related and have become well publicized. One is the industrial countries' need to assure an adequate supply of oil from the producers. This they are attempting to do, in part, by concluding very sizeable agreements which entail either directly or indirectly the exchange of oil for Western arms as well as industrial goods and technology. The other is the desire to recover some of the vast capital that had begun to flow from the developed countries to the oil producers as a result of the drastic increases in oil prices, and which has magnified balance-of-payments problems and is viewed as posing a major potential threat to the stability of the world financial structure. An easy and available means of doing this is to sell to the oil producers large quantities of the latest military equipment while sharply increasing the price tags on these weapons (the Shah appears to be paying 50 percent more for each of his F-14 planes than the US Navy is).

Faced with this new crisis, the major Western arms producers have assigned most of their policies of restraint in the arms supply field to the back burners. France has lifted its seven-year-old embargo on sales to front-line countries in the Arab-Israel zone—which had been the only exception to its vigorous arms export program—and in February 1974, the then-Finance Minister and later President of the Republic, Valéry Giscard d'Estaing, exhorted the armaments industry to try to "put in a thirteenth month for the export market." In the US, the aerospace industry was added to the list of fifteen top-priority government-aided export industries; the participation of American arms-makers in international exhibitions and trade fairs was officially encouraged; and in December 1973 a Presidential directive ordered the establishment of an interdepartmental committee on export expansion in the military sphere. The Department of Defense promoted an extensive arms-selling effort for more than a decade, with American advisory and training missions stationed overseas doing a very effective job as sales agents in the field.[5] The results of these concerted efforts are reflected in the table.

U.S. MILITARY SALES AND AID TO THE ARAB STATES, ISRAEL AND IRAN, 1950-1974
(US $ thousands)

	1950/63	1964/70	1971	1972	1973	1974(est)
Iran	818,593	1,049,329	467,035	564,960	2,075,997	3,794,000
Israel	9,821	759,724	340,006	548,593	255,054	2,117,000
Jordan	95,338	309,776	43,029	98,525	93,620	163,502
Saudi Arabia	117,364	188,075	105,665	340,364	66,580	587,000
Other Arab States	207,692	229,265	27,882	31,174	31,100	130,000
Total	1,248,808	2,536,169	983,617	1,583,616	2,522,351	6,791,502
Yearly Average	89,200	362,310				

Source:
DOD figures, which include foreign military sales, military assistance program, MAP excess defense articles, commercial sales, and security supporting assistance.

What effects can the unprecedented revenues going to Middle East oil producers be expected to have on the arms flow to the area for the remainder of the seventies? Quantitative prognostications regarding the magnitude and cost of the flow would be foolhardy. However, the following general predictions are probably safe:

1. It is unlikely that the current policy of almost unrestricted supply will be reversed by arms-producing governments as long as there is a large imbalance in trade figures in favor of the oil suppliers and a strong demand for arms. In the Persian Gulf area, the actual impact of recent arms procurement on the course of existing or potential quarrels will not be felt fully for another three to four years—until these arms have been delivered and assimilated into the local military machines. By that time, the arms buildup in the area will be well under way, with further purchase orders already made for the next loop in the cycle. Though US sales of arms are justified in terms of the need to ensure the security of this vital region from outside interference and to reinforce domestic stability in the oil-rich states, the current policy may in fact conjure up the very evil it wishes to exorcise by fueling interstate fears and suspicions and providing the means to back up an activist foreign policy on the part of local powers with hegemonic designs. The primary threat to stoppages or drastic reductions in the flow of oil may be armed hostilities in the Gulf area itself and not the Arab-Israel conflict.

2. The availability of greatly expanded oil revenues to Arab producers has practically eliminated what was previously expected to become a major brake on the Arab-Israel arms race: economic constraints. By the early seventies, the cost to Israel and Egypt of the military competition had reached the range of 20 to 25 percent of their respective GNPs. It could not rise much higher without major domestic dislocations and hardships. The arms race was approaching a qualitative threshold beyond which any desired improvements in major weaponry would require the acquisition of the latest types of arms in production—which would be much more expensive than previous generations. Compare, for instance, the cost of an F-4 Phantom aircraft ($4 million) with that of an F-14 ($20-25 million), which Israel purchased as a replacement. The 1973 war (which Egypt would not have launched without assurances of Saudi financial backing) and subsequent developments indicate that, for the time being, these economic problems have been circumvented by the injection of Arab oil money into the Egyptian and Syrian

rearmament efforts on the one hand and the initiation of large-scale US military assistance to Israel on the other. The availability of money already has, and undoubtedly will continue to have, influence over Soviet willingness to transfer arms to the area by adding the incentive of hard-currency profits to the already existing motives of political influence, ideological access, and strategic advantage.

3. The vast increase in oil profits, coupled with the willingness to invest heavily in the Arab military effort evinced by the Arab oil producers, will alter drastically the patterns of arms acquisition developed since 1955. The front-line Arab countries are now able to diversify their sources of procurement, thus escaping to a degree from past limitations on their freedom of action—in military and politico-diplomatic spheres—imposed by their exclusive reliance on the Soviet Union. Egypt, for example, has purchased with Saudi aid several squadrons of Mirage fighters from France and has obtained a commitment of French technical aid in building a number of military industries; has acquired Sea King ASW helicopters and is negotiating the purchase of Jaguar strike jets and Chieftain tanks from Great Britain; and is expected shortly to obtain Hawk SAM missiles, TOW anti-tank missiles, and military transports from the United States. Furthermore, the main combatants can have access to more Western armaments by drawing on the expanding arsenals of other Arab states in case of need.

4. From an arms control perspective, the new situation will have its obvious complicating effects on any effort to restrict the transfer of weaponry to the region. A control system would have to involve a much larger number of supplier and recipient countries. A mere Soviet-American agreement, fully or partially, to withhold arms from Egypt, Syria, and Israel, which might have been sufficient to put a cap on the arms race between 1967 and 1973—and which appears to have been an officially stated but never aggressively sought objective of US policy in the interwar period—would probably be woefully inadequate. Furthermore, the demonstrated readiness of the Arab oil producers to use their petroleum as a "political weapon" in the Middle East conflict has given the arms recipients a powerful means of deterring the suppliers from "ganging up" and imposing any concerted embargo or slow-down on arms sales to the area. In short, too many interests are too well served by the continuation of arms sales to expect advocacy in favor of limitations to carry the day in governmental circles.

Still, while sweeping controls are not feasible, the possibility of reaching limited agreements, and of removing from the area certain highly destabilizing weapons-systems, such as surface-to-surface missiles, high-performance aircraft, and nuclear arms, is not to be excluded. Some of these weapons are already being manufactured in the region, which means that not only transfers from without but also local arms industries and capabilities have to come within the purview of limitation agreements. No such control initiatives are likely to succeed, however, unless certain preconditions are met. Principally, a propitious climate for negotiations must be established by substantial progress on the political-settlement front; moreover, the negotiating process should include suppliers *and recipients,* so that the resulting accords will not be coercively imposed but consensually arrived at and willingly implemented.[6]

12 *The Abiding Threat of War: Perspectives in Israel*

Yair Evron

There are several variables affecting Israel's approach to war and the interactions between war and politics. The possible developments can be viewed in two time ranges: a "short" one and a "long" one. An Arab-initiated war will very probably occur within the next five years—1976-80, the "long" time range. This war might be averted by intensive continuation of the defusion of the conflict which began with the three partial agreements between Israel and Egypt and Syria. The probability of a war initiated by Israel, on the other hand, has probably diminished because of the constraints—perceived by Israel's decision-makers—placed on their freedom to maneuver.

Throughout Israel's history, war has been seen as an instrument for the defense of the existence of Israel and its political integrity. (Since the 1967 war, the territories conquered were also seen as being an area to be defended by force against an attack.) Apart from this general political objective, the majority of the political elite have perceived the use of force as having strategic and military objectives. Israel's cabinet has never discussed beforehand the possible political gains to be made from or following an Israeli military victory. Only on occasion, and in a rather haphazard way, have decision-makers contemplated the political payoffs of the use of force. (The three obvious examples are: the rationale for some of the retaliatory attacks during the first half of the fifties; the political objectives of the 1956 war, though the strategic and military objectives were probably more important; and the rationale for the deep penetration bombing of Egypt during 1970.)

This non-Clausewitzian approach, the realization of the lack of direct correlation between military success and the achievement of political aims, was based on a solid understanding of the constraints on Israel's freedom of behavior. These constraints were seen as restricting the time "allowed" by the superpowers to the exercise of war as well as the political gains to be accrued from the action.

After the 1967 war, different schools of thought emerged. Some members of the political elite tended to believe that the superpowers' constraints were partly removed, and hence Israel could hope to hold on to some of the territories conquered in 1967 and also impose Israel's political demands on the Arabs. Others, however, realized that the superpowers' constraints were still operative, and the ability to impose on the Arabs a political settlement based on battlefield successes, without the superpowers' intervention, was slim. Some of the latter also doubted the possibility of imposing—by compellance strategies—a political settlement on the Arab side even if no superpowers' constraints had been applied.

At the same time, throughout Israel's existence, an Israel-initiated war was perceived as a legitimate and even advantageous instrument of strategy in four cases: the preventive mode, when there was a danger that the military balance might shift in favor of the Arab side in the short or medium range; the anticipatory mode, as in 1967 when there was a large threatening concentration of Arab forces along Israel's borders; the preemptive mode, in case there was a very high probability of imminent attack by the other side; and, lastly, as an instrument to enhance Israel's deterrence posture. All these however are strategic objectives and not political ones.

The situation after the 1973 war was different in two senses: first, two of the strategic objectives (to enhance deterrence posture and the preventive mode) increasingly seemed not to be worth the risks of war—although differences of opinion did exist. Secondly, and more widespread, the realization of the political nonprofitability of the war had deepened. All this was not to say that Israel shrank from war, but it did mean that the likelihood of a war initiated either directly or indirectly by Israel had diminished.

This attitude was dictated partly by the growing dependence of Israel on the United States and by the realization that in most possible future wars, the firepower and attrition rates would be considerably higher than in the past. These higher rates would mean both a high level of casualties and a considerable loss of matériel, probably even higher than in the 1973 war. Needless to say, such a loss of matériel would lead to increased dependence on the United States.

While these attitudes characterize the position of the central decision-makers in Israel, there are probably other members of the political and defense establishments who perceive war as an important and beneficial instrument of policy. Furthermore, their considerations are shared by many in the rank and file. First, there was the desire to have another round of war to once again demonstrate the superior military capability of Israel—superiority which existed and was proven during the 1973 war, but which was blurred by the unfortunate conditions of the initial stage and by the intervention of the superpowers and the imposition of the cease-fire. Underlining this attitude is the feeling that the unclear results of the war are the real sources of the troublesome international situation in which Israel finds itself. Coupled with this attitude is the misunderstanding of the relations between politics and force in the Arab-Israel context. Although the government of Israel, with some exceptions, views war in non-Clausewitzian terms, their attitude is not shared by the "man in the street." The latter believes—as did some of Israel's decision-makers—that, provided Israel's army were to hit the Arab armies hard enough, Israel could compel the Arabs to accept Israel's peace conditions. He overlooks the constraining role of the superpowers and the fact that, although it can defeat the Arab armies militarily, Israel cannot occupy Arab countries and control large Arab populations. Yet, without such control, there is little hope of forcing the Arabs to accept Israel's conditions (and even then it is highly debatable).

Two additional arguments were voiced which favor war: first, that the Arabs may have come to the conclusion, following the 1973 war, that Israel had lost its military superiority; hence, Israel's deterrence had eroded. According to this argument, to reestablish a credible deterrence, Israel would "welcome" another round of hostilities and, following a more devastating Israeli victory, the deterrence posture would be reconstructed. The second argument states that within the bargaining process with the Arab states about a political settlement, it is important to show that Israel is not afraid of war, and such a position also implies that under some condition of crisis, Israel would react forcefully to limited Arab probes. The argument continues that a limited and swift military operation might be conducive to strengthening the hands of Israel in future negotiations.

Indeed, maintaining a forceful posture with signals of readiness to go to war if necessary, would probably be viewed by the central decision-makers as important within the political bargaining process. The existent division of opinion relates to the question of what level of brinkmanship Israel is ready to accept in a situation of crisis in the bargaining process.

A word of caution is needed here: many members of the political elite have not fully developed their positions on these problems. Some would probably change their attitudes with a change in circumstances. Furthermore, although there is some overlapping between attitudes about war and attitudes about the preferable future for the territories conquered in 1967, one should not overemphasize such overlapping. Those who are in favor of the return of the territories in exchange for a peace settlement will in most cases view war as not beneficial to Israel. Their attitude is caused not by fear about the military outcome of the war, but rather about the lack of possible political gains from a victory. Even the position of some moderates might change if war was seen as an instrument to enhance Israel's deterrence posture or to strengthen its hand in the bargaining process.

It is even more difficult to try to link positions about the role of war with the differences between formal political parties. All of Israel's parties are divided about the future of the territories, the best procedure to achieve a settlement, and the level of concessions that Israel should make. It is also difficult to establish the attitudes of political parties about war and its uses. As a general assumption, one could perhaps contend that the right-wing party, Herut, would probably be ready to lower the threshold for war in a crisis and that various moderate parties and groups such as MAPAM and Yad would probably recommend pushing this threshold up. But beyond these general observations the dividing lines seem to be more fuzzy and difficult to ascertain. Moreover, some members of the Herut Party would claim, and some of them genuinely, that their political platform is the real hedge *against* war; any concession by Israel would lead to the whetting of the Arab appetite and eventually to an Arab attack. Precisely those who are against war—so would their argument go—must endorse the tough and unrelenting Herut position. They would add that they are against war and that is the reason for their political position.

In the Labor Party—the main political body in the country—attitudes are again sharply divided as to the political solution to the ongoing conflict. One can find the whole spectrum of opinions there. As regards to the role of war, a question which is again difficult to measure and assess, the positions apparently differ. My previous discussion of attitudes to war in the political elite reflects divisions inside the Labor Party. One of the difficulties in tracking such a diversity of views is that, in the last analysis, no Israeli would welcome war. The question is more complex and relates as aforementioned, to thresholds and crisis behavior.

The Problem of Surprise Attacks

In three Arab-Israel wars, those of 1956, 1967, and 1973, surprise played an important role. Although, in the final analysis it did not decide the military outcome of the wars, the surprise element showed the overall military capability of the opponents. For example, in 1956 and in 1967, Israel launched the surprise first-strike and won the war; in 1973 it was the Arab side which launched the surprise attack but lost militarily. While the element of surprise is important in affecting the nature of the initial first stage, what is perhaps more important are the perceptions of the defense and foreign policy establishments about the central role of surprise in the development of the war. It appears that many among both sides' leaderships consider surprise the single most important variable in the conduct of the war. Thus, in Israel after the 1973 war the element of surprise was seen as a decisive factor affecting the whole course of the war. Then again, and in the same vein, Israel's decision not to launch a preemptive air attack on the Egyptians and, primarily, the Syrians on 6 October was seen as a major mistake which cost Israel a significant number of casualties. In retrospect, it seems that although the surprise in timing was important in the initial stage of the hostilities, there were two other important "surprises" that the Arab side had prepared for Israel: first, the effective use of anti-tank and air-to-surface weapon systems, limiting the effectiveness of Israel's tanks and attack aircraft, and second, the launching of a full-scale war with only limited military objectives but with far-reaching political consequences.

Indeed, the surprisingly effective use of the weapons systems would have made a preemptive air strike by Israel inconsequential. Apparently Israel's Chief of Staff was aware of this but still considered—and possibly rightly—that on the Syrian front the air strike would have had some impact.

Because of the importance attached to surprise by the defense establishments of both sides, the mutual fears about surprise attacks in a situation of crisis are multiplied and by themselves could increase the likelihood of either side launching a surprise attack.

Analytically, there appear to be two basic reasons for a surprise attack: a preemptive strike (mainly in a situation of intensive crisis) or a premeditated strike for any one of many strategic and political objectives. Bearing in mind Israel's interests and objectives, it would seem that an attack by Israel, "out of the blue," would be highly unlikely for several reasons. The political utility of wars has diminished in the perceptions of Israel's leadership. Thus a premeditated war for the attainment of political objectives is less and less likely. The other broad possibility is a preventive war, likely in case of a perceived gradual change in the balance of military power. From 1976 to the early 1980s, such a strike seems highly unlikely. Israel's military superiority in conventional arms seems secure for this period of time; beyond that, no one can make any valid projections. Moreover, much depends on political variables which are difficult to assess, such as the level of unity in the Arab world and the readiness of the oil-producing countries, primarily Saudi Arabia, to give substantial sums of money to the confrontation states.

A third reason for the unlikelihood of a premeditated surprise attack by Israel is Israel's growing dependence on the United States. The US would most likely view another war in the Middle East as a very dangerous development, one which might threaten American objectives. The war might bring about confrontation with the Soviet Union, something which both superpowers dread; it might trigger another oil embargo; adversely affect the delicate and precarious emerging American-oriented Tehran-Riyadh-Cairo axis; and it might cost the United States billions of dollars to resupply Israel's forces.

Under such circumstances, the United States would probably oppose very strongly a premeditated attack by Israel. If this opposition failed to deter the attack, the US would probably try to keep Israel's forces from a complete destruction of the Arab armies, and would also be reluctant to support Israel's position in the postwar negotiations. It seems unlikely that this American opposition to war, of which Israel is fully cognizant, will change in the foreseeable future.

One can only add that a surprise strike by Israel is also not very likely because of the military and technical problems involved. In order to launch a full-scale war, Israel's forces must be mobilized or, at the very least, be in a stage of advanced preparation for mobilization. Although in 1973, Israel was able to mobilize its forces at an amazing speed, and since then has made successful efforts in hastening the process, mobilization, nevertheless, *does* take time. Furthermore, it cannot be done in secret. Mobilizing the units, moving them to the front lines, and moving large amounts of war matériel cannot go undetected for more than an extremely short time. Once they are detected, the surprise element is lost.

The possibility of launching a surprise air strike remains an option and it can be followed by quick mobilization, but it is dangerous because it means starting a war while one's forces are not yet mobilized. The Arab side, with its standing forces, is in a much better position to launch such surprise attacks, although after the experience of October 1973, Israel will probably always err on the side of overcautiousness and mobilize at any sign of a threatening Arab deployment.

Preemptive or anticipatory strikes remain a possibility, although the likelihood of such an attack would diminish if large demilitarized buffer zones were to be established between Israel and the Arab states. Such a measure would apply most successfully to the Sinai; its relevance to the Golan Heights would be more limited because of the narrowness of the Heights.

Short-Range Scenarios (1976-77)

Any prediction of the likelihood of war is hazardous—the level of uncertainty is high; circumstances can change very quickly; and surprising interferences can affect any system. Bearing in mind these substantial limitations on any forecasting of international events, one can only speculate on the future. The previous discussion provides some indication of the factors and circumstances which could affect a decision by Israel to initiate war. These factors should be considered against the background of some possible future developments.

The most important potential political developments during this period, within the context of the Arab-Israel conflict, relate to the continuation or discontinuation of the conflict-defusion process initiated by the Israel-Egyptian disengagement agreement of January 1974. In 1976, more than two years after the agreement was passed, further moves toward defusion of the conflict had been developed, but major problems still remained unsolved. Moreover, the form and structure of the negotiating mechanism was thrown into doubt, thus increasing the dangers of war. The most likely scenario of war would therefore be linked to a stalemate in the process of political settlement.

A Syrian decision to begin military operations against Israel because of a stalemate in the political process is a permanent possibility. The Syrians probably calculate that once hostilities with Israel start, Egypt would find it impossible to stay out of the campaign, even though this is not the declared Egyptian policy. One of the ways to draw Egypt in is to initiate a static war with the assumption that a counterattack by Israel would be seen by the Egyptians as an Israeli attack. A static, limited war would also be convenient for the Syrians because of the more limited risks involved and because, if Israel did decide to counterattack and escalate the war, the Syrians would be able to fight a defensive battle. Given the density and depth of the Syrian fortifications on the Golan Heights, an Israeli offensive would not be an easy operation.

How would Israel react to a Syrian-initiated static war? In military terms, Israel could sustain a limited static war for a long time. But Israel's General Staff would have to consider the possibility that the longer the war the more difficult it would be for Egypt to stay out of it. Under such circumstances, Israel would have to mobilize on the southern front as well. Thus, a limited static war in the north, even if not immediately bringing about Egyptian participation, might nevertheless force Israel to mobilize, especially considering the psychological impact of the 1973 war, in which the initial delay in the mobilization of the reserves adversely affected Israel's performance. Precisely this line of reasoning leads to the conclusion that instead of a long period of mobilization and static war, Israel should try to apply its tactical offensive doctrine: offensive on the northern front, hitting hard at the Syrian army before possible escalation on the southern front.

A fast attack by Israel on the northern front would enable Israel to stay on the defense on the southern front with the hope that Egypt would not join the war; should Egypt enter the conflict, this plan enables Israel to defend real estate in the south (which covers most of the Sinai) and, upon conclusion of the war in the north, to counterattack in the south or to deescalate the conflict there.

The ongoing civil war in Lebanon also might escalate into a military confrontation between Syria and Israel. Israel warned that, if Syrian military intervention passed tacitly defined limits, Israel would also intervene, and as of the time of writing the deterrence seemed to be working. And though a new political framework appeared in Lebanon which might bring an end to the civil war, there is still a great potentiality for resumption of internal strife. If the situation escalates again, there is the possibility of an Israel-Syrian confrontation.

The Long Range (1976-80)

If the danger of a major war in the short range is somewhat limited because of Egyptian interests and their contractual undertakings in the September 1975 agreement, the dangers of war in the long-range period, from 1976 to 1980, resulting from insufficient progress in the political settlements, are very high indeed. Five years is probably the limit of time within which most of the outstanding political issues must be settled or at least contained. Within this time period several significant political steps must be accomplished in order to avert an Arab-initiated war. These should combine Israel's withdrawal with Arab political concessions and adequate security measures such as demilitarization of buffer zones and external guarantees. If war breaks out it would probably engulf all the Arab confrontation countries. Whether the rest of the Arab world would join in a military campaign is very hard to determine. If one extrapolates from the 1973 war in a simplistic linear way, then the probability of non-confrontation Arab states sending part of their forces to participate in the war is quite high.

The Egyptian army is still the most important single Arab military machine. Although Syria, Jordan, and Iraq can put together formidable forces to be used on the northeastern front of Israel, they still cannot compare with the Egyptian army. Moreover, they suffer from the obvious difficulties of conducting joint operations with three (or more) different armies with divergent political objectives and lacking coordinated training and a unified command system. What they could accomplish is to tie down a large part of Israel's forces and make it difficult for Israel to concentrate the majority of its units in an attack on the Egyptian forces. But the ultimate outcome of any war depends on the performance of the Egyptians.

The concentration of firepower in such a future military confrontation will be enormous. One possibility is that the Arab side will probably favor a static campaign again with the objective of considerable attrition of Israel's manpower and matériel. Such a battle would probably strain Israel's capabilities. On the other hand, such a campaign would also allow Israel to be more flexible with its more limited manpower resources. It could absorb the war on one front and divert a larger portion of its military capability to the other front, and vice versa.

Another possibility is that if parts of the territories conquered in 1967 are already demilitarized (primarily in the Sinai), then the Egyptian forces will have to rely more on mobility and hence on forward offensive tactics. The Egyptian forces will try to "jump" over the demilitarized areas in order to get to Israel's line of defense and begin a mobile battle. On the basis of this analysis one can envisage a static war along one front and a mobile war on the other.

The Balance of Military Power

As noted, the politico-strategic context determines to a large extent the patterns of possible future crises and the outcomes of wars which might result from them. It is important, however, to consider very briefly the military aspects of the balance of power. This balance is of course burdened with several uncertainties: to begin with, it is very difficult to assess those unquantifiable and intangible qualities such as morale, motivation, the efficacy of command and control systems, and organizational capabilities. Moreover, the scope of a future confrontation is also difficult to predict: will it encompass large parts of the Arab world, just the confrontation states, or perhaps only one or two of the latter? Will social and economic developments in the Arab world affect to a considerable degree the military capacity of the Arab armies? And what are the time ranges involved? Still another factor is the question of tactics in the battlefield: who will take the offense and who will be on the defense? Last but not least, what are the possible effects of the revolution in the technology of conventional weapon systems on the battlefield and, hence, on the ratio of military power between Israelis and Arabs?

There are no definite answers to these questions, and one can only speculate about them. It appears that the lessons of the 1973 war do not indicate a critical change in the relative capabilities of either side in terms of the mentioned intangibles. Bearing in mind the very slow and complex impact of modernization on the structure of these societies, it seems highly unlikely that, in the time dimension considered in this article, the intangibles—which have usually been favorable to Israel—will be changed in a way that will affect the ratio of military power.

Both sides have received huge quantities of military matériel and hardware since the last war. The details of these transactions are not clear and many are classified, but from the open, available sources, it certainly does not seem that the ratio of military power in terms of hardware has changed against Israel. If anything, it is the other way around, especially when one considers the ratio of military power between the two main opponents, Israel and Egypt. Even a major decision by the Arab states to unite in a meaningful way for preparation for war against Israel, by diverting huge amounts of financial resources and by creating a meaningful unified command system—eventualities which seem very improbable—would hardly change the ratio between Israel and the Arab world in the five years until 1980. Such developments might, on the other hand, make such a change more likely in longer-range periods.

The effect of the technological revolution in conventional weapons systems is also not clear. Would the appearance of precision guided munitions (PGMs) and "area weapons" benefit the offense or the defense? Would tanks and attack aircraft be less effective? Would the motivation for surprise first strikes increase? The answers are not clear, but the majority of observers, including the author, would agree to favor the defense, although this change would become clearer after a few years. The effect of these advances on the ratio of military power between Israel and the Arab states is even less clear. The resolution of this uncertainty is related to what tactics the two sides would adopt and the nature of their respective command and control systems. If, for instance, large buffer zones were to be demilitarized and Israel reverted to mobile defense tactics, a technological change favoring the defense probably would only enhance Israel's superiority. Then again, because of the intangibles mentioned before (such as flexibility and organizational capability), Israel could adopt its flexible and decentralized command and control system earlier to absorption of various PGM systems.

In summary, it would appear that in the time range discussed, the possibility of a change in the military balance favoring, in a critical way, the Arab side is very unlikely. This observation is important in the assessment of the possible initiatives for war and also in the military outcomes of such wars.

13 Patterns of Middle East Politics in the Coming Decade

Ian Smart

It goes without saying that the final chapter in this section should be "futuristic." The interdependent variables are so numerous and sensitive that, within such a short space,there must be an implicit choice of those particular values which are subjective, even capricious. This, moreover, is futurism on an appallingly wide canvas.

I do not know what will happen in the politics of the Middle East, the wider politics of OPEC, the equally extensive politics of the OECD world, or the relations to occur between those groups. If I did, I might become richer—I would already be happier. The fact is, available evidence equally supports an indefinite range of scenarios, including scenarios which are directly contradictory. The rate and timing of economic recovery in the industrial countries, the partly associated evolution of the world demand for Arab, Middle East, or OPEC oil, the interaction between oil prices and the rate of investment in alternative energy sources, and the future path of Arab-Israel relations are all matters of necessary uncertainty, just as all are central to any prediction of the situation in which we shall find ourselves, God willing, in 1985.

Confronted by such uncertainties, I can only offer an outline of how my instinct, rather than my evidence, prompts me to think politics may move in the decade ahead. I shall begin with the domestic politics of the major oil-exporting states in the Middle East, especially of Saudi Arabia, Iran, Iraq, Kuwayt, the United Arab Amirates (UAA), and the smaller producers of the Gulf. I shall then turn to the future of political relations among the principal Middle East members of OPEC and, briefly, between oil exporters and the oil-consuming countries of the OECD. My instinctive expectation in each of these cases is relatively moderate; I doubt the imminence of either Armageddon or Utopia. And if I am asked whether I feel absolutely certain that my expectation of moderate outcomes is plausible, I am forced to reply, like the monks of Shangri-la, that I feel only moderately certain.

The Oil Producers

The impact of events since October 1973 upon politics within the Middle East oil-exporting states may have been less urgent than their impact on politics in the oil-importing world, but, in the final analysis, they were unlikely to be less traumatic. Within a few months, a group of countries with enormous territory, in the aggregate, but a comparatively tiny population has been catapulted into a new economic era. Even countries like Iraq or Iran, whose populations are relatively large and whose external balance of payments may soon be in deficit, have accumulated surpluses. Their confident expectations of future income mean that, for the moment at least, the traditional constraint upon economic development imposed by the available investment capital has ceased to dominate planning. With the contraction of world demand for oil since 1973, some must resort to borrowing (in which the problem of collateral security is unlikely to be serious) and some will have to trim or defer particular development projects. The fact remains that their current ability to buy the essentials of economic development, if not all the luxuries, is effectively unconstrained. During the period 1974-76, as an indication, the member states of OPEC, after paying for their enormously increased imports, will have accumulated a surplus income from oil sales of some $146 billion. That surplus is distributed very unevenly; Algeria and Ecuador, for example, are expected to spend more on imports in 1976 than they earn from oil. Nevertheless, it is clear most oil exporters, especially those in the Gulf, have a substantial financial reserve already built up. This reserve can be drawn upon in the future to support their continued development even if their earning power should diminish.

That is not to say that no serious obstacles will stand in the way of the economic development of Middle East oil-exporting states. There will be large obstacles in the shape of deficiencies of human and mechanical infrastructure: the shortcomings of administration, the lack of manpower—especially skilled manpower—and the absence of adequate fixed assets such as port or overland transport facilities. In almost all cases, it will take years to overcome these obstacles. For the remainder of the 1970s, however, delay will not be caused by lack of money.

It is easy to be over-persuaded by those who advertise limitations upon the shorter-term ability of oil-exporters to absorb their current incomes domestically or those who argue that the full domestic effect of OPEC members' apparent increase in earning power will await a transfer to them of "real" wealth from the industrial countries in the 1980s. In the first place, the ability of the OPEC countries to expand their imports of goods and services is considerably greater than was initially expected; the collective OPEC import bill reached $36.3 billion in 1974, climbed to $56.1 billion in 1975, and is expected to exceed $65 billion in 1976. In the second place, the difficulty some oil exporters face in converting all new foreign exchange earnings instantly into productive investment has, if anything, encouraged the direct import of consumer goods—including luxuries which have a more immediate, if superficial, impact on the life-style of the countries concerned. In the third place, either the expectation of imminent prosperity or the frustration associated with its delay may have as powerful a political effect as prosperity itself (as British politics in anticipation of North Sea earnings amply illustrate). Conversely, it may also be dangerously easy to assume that, whatever their shorter-term difficulties, all OPEC states face an indefinitely golden future in the 1980s and 1990s.

The intrinsic assets of individual OPEC countries are very different; some, such as Algeria and Iran, have only limited reserves of oil and must expect to see their production declining by the mid-1980s. In addition, all must suffer from the sharp rise in the cost of their manufactured imports, which is partly provoked by the increases in the price of their own oil and which, whatever effect it has on future oil prices, seems likely to erode the value of their accumulated financial reserves. Finally, in the long term, all must face the challenge presented by the substitution of other energy sources, again encouraged by higher oil prices. This last point may be crucial. It is not impossible that some OPEC countries over a term of, say, twenty years, will have to endure a double trauma: the traumatic experience of sudden affluence, followed by the even more traumatic experience of having to curtail their economic growth as their oil earnings decline. However, that, if it occurs, is for the much longer term. There is no chance whatever that the world demand for OPEC oil will collapse by 1980 or 1985. Indeed, a strengthening of demand is much more likely as the industrial world climbs out of its recession. Thus the overwhelming probability is that OPEC oil exporters will have earned a very great deal of money by 1980, spending a much higher proportion of it than most people thought possible, and looking forward with whetted appetites to earning and spending even more. It is by no means too early, therefore, to weigh the likely political effects of their new wealth—actual and prospective—upon the domestic politics of the oil exporters and upon the domestic politics of the Middle East oil producers in particular.

Three levels of effect can reasonably be distinguished. The first is the effect upon the governmental, administrative, and decision-making systems of the countries concerned. The second is the effect upon the political process at large of greatly accelerated plans for economic development. The third is that of the more diffuse effect of new wealth, or the confident anticipation of new wealth, upon political attitudes within the societies of those countries.

The first of these levels is easy, but dangerous, to overlook. New earning power imposes new demands upon governments, para-governmental organizations, and private business. In all the countries to be considered, those demands are multiplied by another factor coincidental with the achievement of new earning power: the assumption of far greater responsibility for the management of oil production itself. In this connection the course of events leading through stages of "participation" to national control of oil production (and oil pricing) is as important as the sequence of events generated by the dramatic increase in the price of OPEC oil. In the face of these pressures, the governments involved have no choice but to become more complex and more variously competent entities. In the great majority of cases (Iran and Kuwayt being partial exceptions), they face serious shortages of adequately trained administrative manpower. They must nevertheless assume the role which they have seized or had thrust upon them. At the same time, they must undergo substantial change and expansion. That process will inevitably offer more scope for political competition and potentially more routes to political power, especially as it will entail diffusion of substantial responsibility beyond the limits of the familial or inter-familial elites in which it was formerly concentrated. As the small supply of highly competent administrative manpower is spread more thinly over an expanding governmental machine, the bureaucratic efficiency of particular components of the machine will decline. A tension will become more apparent between the expansive tendency of governmental institutions in the aggregate and the urge to centralize real administrative authority in the hands of the few persons whose loyalty is unquestioned and whose capabilities and status are outstanding. One result will be to impose an ever-growing personal strain upon members of that small group; the incidence of coronary failure may well become a political problem in its own right.

The second level, the effect of accelerating economic development on the political process at large, is more familiar ground to students of development. Few general comments are needed. There are, however, some points that demand emphasis. All the countries concerned will, for example, face a well-known need to strike some balance, on political as well as economic grounds, between the long-term gains to be expected from large-scale industrial development and the more immediately available benefits of developing social services and public utilities. Some countries will find that more difficult than others. A relatively small diversion of resources will provide a social welfare system in Kuwayt, where the process is already well advanced or in, say, Qatar or Abu Dhabi, where population is small and territory less than vast. A much larger diversion will be needed in countries like Saudi Arabia and 'Uman, because of territorial area, or Iran and Iraq, because of population size. Unless some overall consistency is maintained in this context, the failure of some governments to keep up with others in the provision of social services may become a political issue. Countries will also differ widely in their need to import labor for development purposes. All will have to import highly skilled technicians and managers—even if Iran and, possibly, Iraq will be less subject than others to that pressure. Many, including Saudi Arabia, Qatar, 'Uman, and members of the UAA, will also have to import more or less large quantities of unskilled or semi-skilled labor. The potential domestic political significance of such imports needs no elaboration. The point is that, in all the oil-producing states of the area, foreign presence, in one form or another, is likely to become paradoxically more rather than less obtrusive as an indirect result of the elimination of foreign control over the oil industry.

A more general point is relevant to this second level of effect. The process of development, and especially of longer-term industrial development, entails the reinforcement and proliferation of vested interests in the maintenance of the process itself. The number of groups and individuals directly or indirectly in debt to the development process will steadily increase—as will the opportunity for influence or profit to which individuals or groups may aspire. On the one hand, the development process constitutes a new and rich field for competition, between both "insiders" and "outsiders." On the other hand, it creates a new level of long-term interest in stability among those who have obtained a stake in the process itself. The two are inevitably countervailing. My own view is that, in most of the countries here considered, the interest in stability will come to be of prevailing importance for the governments and for political and social elites. I suspect that the much-advertised "conservatism" of regimes in countries such as Saudi Arabia or 'Uman has often been misinterpreted. It has not, on the whole, been conservatism as we know it in the West, where conservatism derives from a desire to maintain the existing distribution of immovable property, but rather a conservatism which reflects a desire to preserve the political power of particular groups but has been combined with considerable flexibility in regard to property and policy. In part, this may have been because so much of the property adjoined to power in the "desert" Arab states was itself, in the past, movable and personal. It could readily be abandoned or exchanged. This will change rapidly as a function of economic development. Property and power will come to be linked in new ways for the regimes concerned and will become largely dependent upon the continued implementation of long-term plans. I suspect the result in all these countries, not excluding Iraq or Kuwayt, will be a new form of "conservatism"—the conservative aspects of capitalism in its Western sense—and that the set of values which it implies will divorce members of elites from some of their traditional social values while attaching them more firmly to the maintenance of the political status quo.

Even if the ruling elites in these states do, in fact, obtain a stronger interest in the maintenance of the existing political system through the continuation of the economic development process to which it is linked, that does not mean that elites will always be united by recognition of that common interest. There will remain ample scope for disagreement, even conflict, between "insiders" whether over the exact distribution of authority, the detailed design or implementation of policy, or the pace at which a generally agreed policy is to be pursued. Even within the most homogeneous groups, the Saudi royal family for example, it is entirely possible that there will be disagreement between generationally divided factions: the older generation, almost exclusively educated at home and strongly attached to a traditional rhythm of change, and the younger generation, largely educated abroad and probably more impatient. More generally, the very fact that there will be a rapid growth in the size and variety of the elite groups which share responsibility and power means that the scope for dissent among insiders must also increase. And that scope will not be limited indefinitely to the bounds of the public sector. Although the development of a private entrepreneurial class is still, in most of these states (other than Iran and Kuwayt) at an early stage, the process, even in Saudi Arabia, has already begun. One result will be the progressive emergence of new groups outside government but competing eagerly and with increasing effect for a share of power to match their share of property. Even then, however, I would expect my general projection of a new conservatism among elite groups to hold good. The competition, in fact, will not be to destroy or change the system but to join it.

The third level of effect, involving the diffuse impact of new wealth upon political attitudes, is obviously touched by that last remark. But it is only a small part of the story. The larger part is again, in a sense, familiar. Rapid development will involve the rapid expansion of higher and technical education in the countries affected; industry and government will need their graduates, their accountants, and their engineers to cope with development demands. Simultaneously, a major social and political revolution will be taking place as large numbers of women, especially in Saudi Arabia, are emancipated and trained in skills formerly reserved for men. At the same time, the aggregate of wealth fueling and arising from development will increase sharply. So will familiarity with the rewards that such wealth can obtain—in terms of power and property. However, there is no chance that the diffusion of new wealth through the whole of society will proceed at the same pace. Nor is there any chance of real power being diffused so swiftly; indeed, the need for rapid decisions by a small number of people may actually provoke a recentralization of authority. We shall thus see the familiar picture of the economic differential within societies widening as the corporate wealth of those societies grows. Meanwhile, more and more members of the societies, women as well as men, will be acquiring new qualifications and skills and witnessing from a distance the fruits of a prosperity to which those qualifications seem to entitle them but from which the "system" seems to be separating them yet further. Simultaneously, the elite groups which run the system will be acquiring a stronger interest in the maintenance of the political status quo. If the picture seems over-familiar, even hackneyed, I make no apology.

Into this soup of general effects, there must be injected the factor of specific psychology. If I refer to an "Arab" psychology, it is neither because I am insensitive to the frailty of such generalization nor because I have any claim to special knowledge. There are certain attitudes arguably characteristic of Arab—and especially Arabian—society which seem relevant. One characteristic attitude is a high regard for intellectual achievements and literacy or legal learning, exceeding any regard for manipulative or supervisory skills. It will be surprising if this does not affect the bias of aspiration in the field of higher education, making it much easier to find ready candidates for training as doctors, lawyers, economic analysts, and scientists than to find those who must emerge as foremen, shop floor managers, or skilled technicians.

Another characteristic attitude is pride in individualism. Not only does this make it difficult to attain effective coordination of effort in a collective cause, it also implies a preference for achievement in the private, rather than the public, sector (the current predominance of the public sector notwithstanding). In a country such as Saudi Arabia, one problem appears to be a high proportion of younger men trained at the state's expense, largely abroad, in administrative and analytical skills who prefer to devote those skills to private enterprise rather than governmental service.

A third characteristic attitude is the inclination to measure success in terms of personal authority rather than participation in a collective authority and, as a result, to perceive personal ambition as something to be pursued through the acquisition of rights, including a right to command, rather than through labor. It has sometimes been common to speak of the "Puritanism" of the Bedu. In any sense other than that of a religious or moral fervor, nothing could be more misleading. If some paradigm must be found in English history, it should perhaps be not the Roundhead but the Cavalier: individually more than corporately proud, tightly bound by rules of cultural convention, preferring intellectual prowess and artistic sophistication to the joys of productive labor in the common cause, persuaded of a rightful hierarchy but extraordinarily mobile in social relationships, aspiring to command but not to belong.

All of this I have said in more or less general terms. Obviously, the utility of such generalizations is limited. The countries and societies under examination are, in many respects, extraordinarily varied. Yet it seems that some generalizations may still be useful. I do, for example, believe that while the intractable individualism of Arab—and, indeed, Iranian—society will always leave open the possibility of an extraordinary figure such as Qaddafi seizing control, the general tendency among regimes and elites in the oil-exporting countries of the Middle East, as they become more deeply implicated in long-term economic development, will be toward a new conservatism founded in a widening consensus in favor of the political status quo. I also believe there will be a general tendency for the gaps between rich and poor and between powerful and powerless to widen, just as the stakes in the competition which that implies will increase. In one form or another, I expect that all the countries concerned will face increasingly difficult problems of infrastructural deficiency as they pursue their economic development plans and that the deficiency of middle-level executive and technical manpower will be the most serious of all such problems. Finally, I believe that the inevitable expansion and elaboration of decision-making structures in these countries will multiply the apparent routes to personal authority and greatly extend the field for personal and inter-group competition for political power.

The implication of this general vision is reasonably obvious. I think it likely, in fact, that we will witness a considerable increase in domestic ferment and civil disquiet within many of the countries I have mentioned. It will, moreover, be a rather different sort of ferment from that which many Middle East states have experienced in the past. Most of the successful and unsuccessful revolutions and coups in the area since the 1940s have reflected efforts to make some more or less radical change in the character of the national political system (and/or international political alignments) rather than a competition over who will control the existing system. In the future, however, it is the latter type of competition that seems likely to become of dominant importance. The concern of those who will promote civil dissent—sometimes, I suspect, by violent means—will be the control, rather than the radical re-distribution, of the national cake. To put it crudely, the Middle East may turn out to be importing not only a new version of capitalist conservatism from the industrial West but also a new version of domestic unrest from Latin America.

Such phenomena will clearly take on a different guise in different countries, if only because the various pressures will bear differently upon them. In the thinly populated states of the Arabian Peninsula and the lower Gulf I would expect the agonizing choice to be between accepting manpower shortage, a decisive constraint on economic development, and inviting a possibly uncontrollable increase in immigration, which would be particularly disruptive, just as I would expect a growing danger of "palace revolutions," ostensibly over policy but actually over the control of the existing system. In the more thickly populated Arab oil-producing states of the area (Iraq and probably Kuwayt), I would expect the more serious danger to lie in the obtrusiveness of economic differentials and the over-elaboration of decision-making structures, leading to a much higher risk of broadly-based social and political dissent. (Outside the Gulf, the case of Libya may resemble the former model, while that of Algeria may resemble the latter.) As to Iran, the pattern may recall that of the more thickly populated Arab states, but there may be more resilience in the face of such pressures simply because of the longer Iranian experience of ambitious development plans. Against this, Iran may become more exposed than any of the Arab oil-producers (except possibly Iraq) to the activity of radical groups frustrated by the increasingly strong orientation of the existing regime toward maintenance of the political status quo and disappointed by the probable curtailment of excessively ambitious development plans.

I do not mean to paint too black a picture. I see no reason why the pressure of domestic ferment should not be contained and, in the longer term, dissipated in most of the countries concerned. Meanwhile, I expect some reduction in the level of international conflict in the region. The fact remains that I foresee a rising domestic turbulence within many of these countries, just as I expect an increasing conservatism in the formal domestic and external policies of their governments.

International Relations

The acquisition of greater wealth and the embarkation upon more ambitious development plans is likely to strengthen the forces of nationalism in the Middle East oil-producing states. Certainly, I would be surprised to see any rapid progress toward political integration in the area or any politically effective resurrection of pan-Arab (still less pan-Islamic) ideas. On the other hand, the mutuality of interest in economic development and the recognition of the extent to which "producer solidarity" in OPEC and OAPEC is a pre-condition of that process will militate against the exacerbation of conflict between oil-exporting countries. OPEC is a reason, rather than a mechanism, for containing political conflicts between its members; it is no less effective for that.

None of this means that the traditional rivalries and underlying conflicts of the region will be definitively resolved. Iran and Saudi Arabia will continue to watch each other with some apprehension, as will Iran and Iraq and Iraq and Kuwayt. In the future, however, I would expect active conflict between such near neighbors to occur rarely, if at all. The general inclination, as more attention is demanded by domestic development and, perhaps, domestic dissent, will be to live and let live internationally. Two warnings must nevertheless be entered.

The first is that the acceleration of economic progress in the oil-rich states may excite new envy and renewed enmity on the part of some without oil of their own. Hitherto, the oil-rich have dispelled such emotions by guarded promises to finance the large-scale development of their poorer neighbors. Saudi Arabia, with others imitating it, has also contrived to avert criticism by publishing a national development budget so large ($144.5 billion over five years) that it purports to absorb a large part even of Saudi income, despite the fact that only a fraction of the indicated amount is likely to be spent. Eventually, however, the chickens may come home to roost. The actual expenditure of Gulf oil-producing states on development prospects outside their own territories has so far been extremely limited. At the same time, their territorial allocations of income to indigenous development have often been implausibly high. As those considerations—unless they alter—become more apparent, the latent jealousy of the poorer countries of the region may well revive. I am skeptical about this leading, for example, to a renewal of Saudi-Egyptian conflict, but I am less skeptical about the possibility of renewed conflicts between Egypt and Libya or between Syria and Iraq.

The second warning is that the difficulty into which some oil-producing states may run in sustaining their own economic development programs may create some risk of the refurbishment of old ambitions. Two cases stand out: Algeria and Iran, both of which may find their oil production tapering off by 1985. In the former case, an Algerian government, facing rising domestic expectations but potentially declining income, has already been tempted to look enviously toward the dominance which Morocco has been establishing over the Sahara phosphates. In the latter case, an Iranian government in similar straits would hardly seek to bid for the resources of Iraq, but might well adopt a more aggressive policy toward the exploitation of off-shore resources in the Gulf itself. Either case may, in other words, represent a possibility of conflict provoked by a threat of disappointed expectations.

Particular cases of potential envy or desperation aside, the idea that oil-producers will remain at least reciprocally tolerant may seem to ignore the prospect that world demand for OPEC oil will decline in the late 1970s and remain at lower than the current level during the first half of the 1980s. It is that prospect, after all, which has supported anticipatory advertisements of serious stress within OPEC during that period, involving conflicting and competitive tendencies to raise real prices (to maintain revenue) or to reduce them (to increase market share) in a falling market.[1] It is not, of course, impossible that that may happen. As I have already indicated, the thesis is based upon premises concerning demand restraint and the rate of alternative supply development which I consider personally to be implausible. Without being able to argue the case in detail here, I can only state that I expect a slow increase in world demand for OPEC oil from 1976, reaching a level in the early 1980s somewhat above that of 1973, and generating pressure to minimize, but not reverse, the gradual fall in the real price. In those circumstances, there will be little, if any, general pressure for OPEC countries to compete more viciously for market shares.

As that indicates, I suspect, in the context of the 1980s, OPEC is here to stay. In such circumstances, the economic arguments in favor of reciprocal restraint and common action between oil-exporting countries will dominate any political divergencies deriving from the reinforcement of nationalisms. In other words, Middle East oil-producing countries are unlikely to feel much sense of political community but will become increasingly conscious of economic interdependence. The hope is that the same thing will apply to the relations between those countries and their customers, especially in the developed world. There is every reason why it should. As I have argued elsewhere, the oil-producers, in as far as they attach importance to their own economic development, have no choice but to convert the dependence of the industrial countries on their oil into a reciprocal dependence in which they rely on industrial countries (and other developing resource-exporters) to facilitate and sustain their own industrialization.[2]

Whether relations between the exporters and importers of oil will evolve in that rational manner is still uncertain. Several dangers threaten the prognosis. One is the continuing inclination of some in the industrial world to regard the economic aspirations of oil exporters or the operational solidarity of OPEC as a threat to their prosperity and a challenge to their virility. I am depressed, for example, as much by tone as by content, when I read a sentence such as:

> It is in the interest of the industrial countries—indeed of all consuming countries—that conditions be created in which OPEC loses and cannot subsequently regain the power to set oil prices at artificially high levels.[3]

For one thing, the word "artificially" is surely meaningless in this connection unless, through a system of administered prices and coherently restricted production within an integrated economy, some seller is being forced to sell, or some buyer to buy, against his will. For another thing, it is by no means obvious that a situation of uncoordinated pricing, with all it might imply about international competition for preferential access, potential effects on energy usage and development, or economic welfare in particular producing and particular consuming countries, would be "better." For a third thing, such assertions are calculated to inhibit the emergence of a sense of genuine economic interdependence between oil-exporters and oil-importers, on which "the interest of the industrial countries" is far more likely to depend.

Even if slogans of divergent interest, on both sides of the oil equation, fade away, there will remain an even more pathetic threat to the prognosis of relative international harmony. I refer to the Arab-Israel conflict. This essay hardly provides the scope to consider that circumstance in detail. I must at least admit, however, that I see little prospect of the Arab-Israel conflict being finally resolved or of it being totally divorced from the issue of oil supply.

It follows from this that the threat of a new OAPEC embargo on supplies to Western customers will persist. Personally, I expect it to diminish as the 1980s grow older. One reason is that, whether or not there is renewed fighting on Israel's borders, I think it likely that the tendency toward progressive interstate accommodation which began in 1973 will continue and grow stronger. Another reason is that the focus will shift, as it has already begun shifting, from the hostility between states to the problem of the Palestinians, on whose account OAPEC members, rhetoric notwithstanding, may be less likely to employ the "oil weapon" in its 1973 form. A third reason is implicit in my optimistic expectation of greater economic interdependence between OAPEC countries and their industrial customers. In 1973, OAPEC had, as it were, a "free shot"; little, if anything, was lost in cutting off supplies or expropriating Western assets. By 1980, and even before, as industrialization proceeds and as OAPEC states become more dependent on Western technology, Western capital goods, and, ultimately, Western markets, a great deal will stand to be lost. That will not invalidate the "oil weapon." It will, however, tend to convert it, in Arab eyes, from a weapon of compellance to one of ultimate deterrence, less likely to be used to prevent a direct Western intervention on Israel's behalf.

None of these arguments persuades me that a new embargo is impossible. The possibility will remain as one limit upon the extent of Arab-OECD shared interests. For that reason and others, the relationship will, at best, be one of qualified harmony, founded upon a recognition of reciprocal economic advantage but insufficiently substantial to resist all political imperatives.

That last remark applies not only to relations between Western industrial countries and OAPEC states but also to those between the former and Iran. There is no persuasive indication that Iran would, in fact, join a supply embargo in the context of the Arab-Israel conflict; politics aside, the growing pressure to maximize the country's income militates against it. Nor is there a substantial probability that Iran will seek a closer alignment with the West, in political or strategic terms, than it has at present. Partly because of the possible international repercussions (vis-à-vis the Soviet Union and/or Iraq) but also because of domestic considerations, it seems unlikely that the Shah will place his country's naval or military capabilities at the disposal of Western strategy—and still less likely that he will accept more specific association with British, French, US, Australian, and even South African forces which have been mooted.[4]

One of the few factors which might significantly alter Iranian calculations would be a marked change in Soviet policy or in the character of US-Soviet relations. The strategic imminence of the Soviet Union remains the primary preoccupation of the Iranian government. If the Soviet Union were to revert to a policy of more active hostility, toward the West in general or toward Iran in particular, the Shah might seek a closer involvement with the West and especially the United States. Short of that contingency, he is likely to keep a polite distance.

The possibility of a radical change in Soviet policy aside, the interest of the Soviet Union in the Middle East must represent another of the doubts about the moderately optimistic prognosis outlined earlier. Again, the subject is too large to explore. Once more, however, I am inclined to expect a moderate outcome: neither a more sympathetic Soviet attitude to Western interests in the Middle East nor a more determined effort to undermine them. Something may, of course, depend on the emergence of more direct Soviet interest in Middle East oil. Recent research has demonstrated convincingly that the Soviet Union, far from becoming a larger supplier of oil to Western markets, is likely to find more of its production required within Comecon between now and 1980 and may actually have to become a more active purchaser of Middle East oil. The volume, however, is likely to be relatively small—possibly only 1 million barrels per day at the peak. In the first instance, the Soviet government would, no doubt, seek to obtain this on preferential barter terms from Iraq, and especially from North Rumaylah. If, as I suspect, the Iraqi regime has by then become more conventional and conservative in its attitudes and more detached in its relations with Moscow, the Soviet Union will probably be happy enough to buy its oil on market terms—incidentally contributing to the maintenance of overall demand for OPEC oil in the process. All in all, my personal view is that Soviet interests and policies, provided there is no radical change of Soviet international purpose, are likely to shadow, but not modify, the general prognosis.

* * * *

The arbitrary and instinctive projection which I promised has been moderate: moderate turmoil within oil-exporting countries, moderate restraint between them, moderate reciprocity in relations with the West. I have not touched upon the third side of that international triangle: the relations between the oil-importing countries of the OECD. There, I am sometimes less optimistic that moderation will prevail. In particular, I am deeply troubled by the possibility that attempts to defeat the policies of OPEC and OAPEC, rather than to adapt in order to moderate them, will disturb relations with producers and enormously exacerbate friction between consumers whose interests would be sharply divergent. That, however, is a different subject. In this context, I adhere to my moderate view. I do so, nevertheless, in the full knowledge that one or another accident is overwhelmingly likely to subvert it, at least in part. If I were forced to select the accidents whose possibility, however remote, concerns me most, the list would include a new OAPEC embargo on supply (especially in the earlier part of the eighties), a radical outburst in Iran (or possibly Iraq), a collapse into political factionalism and conflict in Saudi Arabia, a violent Syrian-Iraqi conflict, and, I fear, an epidemic of folly in the industrial world. None of these is impossible. All of them we should contemplate. Each of them is more likely to be averted by prayer than by analysis.

IV

Future Challenge

14 *Mixing Oil and Money*

Benjamin J. Cohen

The energy crisis has posed a fundamental challenge to the ability and will of the countries of the industrial world to act together in response to common problems. All dimensions of relations—economic, political, and military—among the North Atlantic countries and Japan have been affected by the oil-price increases that have occurred since the October War of 1973. This chapter focuses on one aspect of economic relations, the aspect of monetary relations, treating it as a case study of industrial-country relations in general. The questions asked: How have the industrial countries reacted to the impact of higher oil prices? Have they met the test tional cooperation? The answer, I shall argue, is: No, so far, they far, they have failed to meet the test.

* * * *

The story of the oil price increases since late 1973 is, of course, well known.[1] "The era of cheap oil for the industrialized world is finished," said the Shah of Iran in a memorable understatement. He need hardly have added: the era of higher revenues for oil producers has begun. From a level of $15 billion in 1972 and $25 billion in 1973, the revenues of the Organization of Petroleum Exporting Countries (OPEC) soared to $95 billion in 1974 and to $98 billion in 1975; in 1976, earnings were expected to top $111 billion and to go even higher in subsequent years.[2] Arab states would account for well over half of the total, and Iran for about a fifth.

The world has never before been confronted with such an immense transfer of wealth. In aggregate terms, the situation is unprecedented. As Winston Churchill said in another context, never before have so many owed so much to so few. The massive shift of the international terms of trade in OPEC's favor means that consuming countries must necessarily give up more goods, services, and assets in exchange for each barrel of oil they import. The effect is like a giant excise tax. The higher revenues of oil producers raise prices in consuming countries, both directly, through their impact on the price of all forms of energy, and indirectly, through their impact on wage demands and other cost elements in the production structure, while at the same time reducing demand through the withdrawal of active purchasing power. The result is a relative lowering of living standards in consuming countries.

The transfer of wealth to OPEC had both "real" and monetary implications. On the real side, a considerable reallocation of resources in consuming countries was required to the extent that OPEC's higher revenues were returned to consumers in the form of increased demand for their goods and services. Inevitably, there would be severe dislocations in many non-OPEC economies as their production structures were redirected to generate a greater net volume of exports. Some countries, with economies at or near full capacity, would find it difficult to curtail internal demand in order to make room for additional exports; some countries would simply have little or no potential to expand exports at all in the future. (This was especially likely to be true of many less-developed countries.) In addition, further resource reallocations in consuming countries would be dictated by the differential impact of increased energy costs on the comparative efficiency and profitability of various domestic industries. Energy-using industries (e.g., automobiles) would be under pressure either to adjust their product mix or to release resources to energy-saving industries (e.g., mass transit).

On the monetary side, problems arose to the extent that OPEC's higher revenues were returned to consumers not in the form of increased demand for their exports, but rather in the form of increased demand for their assets. It was well known that the "absorptive capacity" of some of the biggest oil producers was limited: they simply were unable to increase their imports of goods and services at the same rate as their revenues. This was less true of such countries as Algeria, Iraq, and the non-Arab members of OPEC. These countries were relatively densely populated with more attractive development prospects, diversified natural resources, and trained administrative capacity; each had the capacity to absorb virtually all of their higher incomes, even in the comparatively short term. But these countries did not account for even half of the total oil exports. The bulk of oil revenues accrued to Saudi Arabia, Kuwayt, the smaller Persian Gulf states, and Libya—thinly populated, largely barren countries that for a long time to come could reasonably be expected to spend only a small part of their higher income on foreign goods and services. The remainder—the "investable surplus"—would perforce be invested in foreign assets or otherwise lent back to consuming countries as a group.

Oil consumers, therefore, as a group must anticipate extremely large current-account deficits in their future relations with the oil producers. In 1974 alone, OPEC's surplus amounted to approximately $60 billion (as compared with $6 billion in 1973); another surplus of $42 billion was recorded in 1975, and further financial accumulations were expected for 1976 and thereafter, at least until 1978-80.[3] Estimates differ concerning the prospective magnitude of the cumulative building of OPEC assets. As Table 1 indicates (p. 198), projections of OPEC's investable surplus made since the energy crisis broke have differed greatly, from an early World Bank suggestion of some $650 billion (current dollars) in 1980 to later calculations running as low as $165-190 billion. The wide range of variation among these projections reflects their high degree of sensitivity to the assumptions that were made regarding *inter alia* the absorptive capacity of producing countries, the price and income elasticity of oil demand, and the prospects for expansion of alternative sources of energy supply. But even the figures at the lower end of the range, it must be admitted, represent a not negligible sum of money. OPEC's growing financial accumulations manifestly create serious problems for international monetary relations.

Some observers attempted to belittle the monetary implications of the energy crisis. Fred Bergsten, for example, wrote:

> There are indeed extremely serious consequences of the oil crisis. . . . But the international monetary situation adds relatively little to the problem. No industrial country will go bankrupt. The monetary system will not collapse. . . . The prophets of doom confuse the balance of trade and the balance of payments. They ignore the simple but central fact that the oil exporters must invest in the industrial world any of their increased earnings that they do not spend. The Arabs will not bury the money in the ground. Thus, there can be no deficit in the balance of payments of the industrial world as a whole.[4]

Such arguments were, at the very least, simplistic. Certainly it was true that there could be no deficit in the balance of payments of oil consumers as a group. (Note that this included more than just the industrial world.) The combined current-account deficits of non-OPEC countries must, by definition, be offset by aggregate capital-account surpluses. But one does not have to be a prophet of doom to

Table 1

ALTERNATIVE PROJECTIONS OF OPEC's INVESTABLE SURPLUS IN 1980
(in billions of dollars)

	Current dollars	Constant dollars (1974)
(1) IBRD (July 1974)	653	400[a]
(2) Chenery (January 1975)	495[b]	300
(3) Levy (June 1975)	449	286
(4) Willett (January 1975)	330-413[b]	200-250
(5) OECD (July 1975)	330-413[b]	200-250
(6) IBRD (April 1975)	330-371[b]	200-225
(7) Fried (1974)	251[b]	152.3[a]
(8) Irving Trust Co. (March 1975)	248	148.8[c]
(9) Deutsche Bank (May 1975)	220	132[c]
(10) U.S. Treasury (September 1975)	195	117[c]
(11) First National City Bank (June 1975)	189	113.4[c]
(12) Morgan Guaranty Trust Co. (Jan. 1975)	179	107.4[c]
(13) Deutsche Bank (October 1975)	164	98.4[c]

a) Conversion to constant 1974 dollars was done by Willett, b) conversions to current dollars and (c) to constant dollars were done by using World Bank price forecasts quoted by Committee for Economic Development (see source No. 6 below).

Sources:

(1) IBRD, "Prospects for the Developing Countries," Report of the Energy Task Force, 8 July 1974, p. 31.

(2) H. B. Chenery, "Restructuring the World Economy," Foreign Affairs, 53, (January 1975), p. 254.

(3) W. J. Levy Consultants Corporation, Future OPEC Accumulation of Oil Money: A New Look at a Critical Problem (New York, June 1975).

(4) T. D. Willett, "The Oil Transfer Problem," Department of the Treasury News, 30 January 1975.

(5) OECD, Economic Outlook, No. 17 (Paris, July 1975), p. 78.

(6) IBRD, a revised projection quoted in CED, International Economic Consequences of Higher-Priced Energy (New York, 1975), p. 17.

(7) E. Fried, "Financial Implications", in J. A. Yager and E. B. Steinberg, eds., Energy and U.S. Foreign Policy (Cambridge: Ballinger, 1974), p. 290.

(8) Irving Trust Co., The Economic View from One Wall Street, 20 March 1975.

(9) Deutsche Bank, OPEC: Facts, Figures and Analyses (Frankfurt, May 1975).

(10) Quoted in The International Herald Tribune, 11 September 1975.

(11) First National City Bank, Monthly Economic Letter, June 1975.

(12) Morgan Guaranty Trust Company, World Financial Markets, 21 January 1975.

(13) Deutsche Bank, OPEC: Facts, Figures and Analyses, revised after the conference in Vienna in September 1975 (Frankfurt, October 1975).

see signs of danger in this prospect of huge, sustained capital movements between producing and consuming countries. At least four specific problems for international monetary relations may be distinguished analytically.

First, there was the problem of how to maintain full employment in the consuming countries. I have said that the transfer of wealth to OPEC countries was like a giant excise tax, reducing demand through a withdrawal of active purchasing power. Coupled with the limited absorptive capacity of the biggest oil producers, this may be thought of as a net outward shift of the world's savings schedule: global spending on goods and services were reduced and global investment in financial assets (savings) were increased. A sudden increase of thrift could generate a circular contraction of incomes if real capital formation was not perfectly responsive to the greater availability of savings. From the point of view of oil consumers, the problem was to translate the financial savings of oil producers into productive job-creating activities. These savings must find their counterpart in additional real investment in the non-OPEC world or in a reduction of savings there. Otherwise, consuming countries would experience a sustained increase of resource unemployment and retardation of economic growth.

Second, there was the problem of how to distribute the current-account deficits of oil consumers. The aggregate surplus of oil producers must be reflected in a pattern of current-account deficits that was acceptable to the individual countries concerned. (An alternative way to express this: since current-account deficits must be financed, OPEC's financial accumulations must be reflected in a pattern of increased debt and equity claims that was acceptable to the individual countries concerned.) In the absence of an understanding regarding the allocation of these deficits, consumers could pursue inconsistent payments policies. Such competitive policies were bound to be mutually frustrating, since in the face of the limited absorptive capacity of OPEC countries, any single consuming country could reduce its own trade deficit only by increasing the trade deficits of others. If such policies were generally followed, the net result could well be a serious misallocation of resources and a destructive contraction of effective demand and world trade.

Third, there was the problem of how to finance the desirable pattern of current-account deficits among consuming countries. This was the problem of petrodollar recycling. I have said that the combined current deficits of consumers must, by definition, be offset by capital-account surpluses. But what was true for consumers as a group was not necessarily true for each consumer individually. (That is the fallacy of composition.) Reflows of funds from OPEC countries did not tend to match up with the distribution of current deficits among consumers. OPEC countries did not invest in consuming countries in proportion to their current deficits: some countries were simply more attractive than others as places to invest. Consequently, some consuming countries enjoyed relatively healthy external accounts after the energy crisis broke, while others found themselves in serious over-all payments difficulties. From the point of view of oil consumers, the problem was to ensure that countries that did have over-all payments deficits would somehow be able to finance them by borrowing at reasonable terms. This required flows of capital among the non-OPEC countries to channel oil revenues from consumers who benefited disproportionately from OPEC investments to those who were most in need of them—in other words, a recycling of OPEC's surplus revenues. In the absence of adequate petrodollar recycling facilities, some countries found it impossible to borrow at any terms at all. The danger of international bankruptcy could not be lightly dismissed.

Fourth, there was the problem of the disposition of OPEC's surplus revenues. Although OPEC countries were already beginning to diversify a portion of their investments, geographically and in terms of asset structure in 1974–75, it was evident that for a long time a large proportion would undoubtedly continue (given the high liquidity preference of the biggest oil producers) to be concentrated in short-maturity assets (bank deposits, etc.). By mid-1975, the official monetary reserves of the oil producers as a group had risen to $55 billion—one quarter of the world total. By the end of the decade, given their prospective surplus earnings, OPEC countries might accumulate reserves in excess of $100 billion, most of which will be concentrated in the hands of four Persian Gulf states and Libya. It is not at all clear that an international monetary order can remain stable when such a large proportion of the world's liquidity is unilaterally controlled by such a small number of countries, especially when those countries have a record for economic and political volatility. The argument may be made that in the interest of assuring monetary stability, some kind of action would be desirable to ensure that these funds were not shifted about in a chaotic and irresponsible fashion—in effect, to induce OPEC countries to treat their surpluses as long-term savings rather than as short-term investments.

Of these four problems, the first two, the problem of maintaining full employment and that of distributing current deficits among consuming countries, are closely related analytically. The level of domestic demand is one of the principal determinants of a country's trade balance, and a country's trade balance is one of the principal constraints on policies for controlling domestic demand. The two problems really collapse into the single issue of current macroeconomic management within the parameters of the existing international monetary system and are best discussed as one. Similarly, the problems of recycling and of the disposition of OPEC's surplus revenues are closely related analytically, though these are more concerned with changing the parameters of the existing monetary system. Each involves considerations not just of current macroeconomic management but, more importantly, of institutional and structural reform. Analytically, these two problems blend into the broader issue of world monetary reform.

Thus, the monetary implications of the energy crisis encompass both the issue of current macroeconomic management and that of structural monetary reform. Owing to space limitations, this chapter will concentrate on just the former of these two issues.[5]

* * * *

Insofar as the issue of current macroeconomic management was concerned, a radical reordering of the traditional payments objectives of industrial countries was called for as a result of the raising of oil prices. Traditionally, most industrial countries have aimed for surpluses in their current account—partly for old-fashioned mercantilist reasons and partly to facilitate net acquisitions of assets overseas. These same countries (together with other oil consumers) must plan for large current-account deficits vis-à-vis the oil producers, at least until the end of the decade. It is a cliché that the biggest payments-adjustment problem generated by higher oil prices were among the consuming countries themselves, rather than between consumers and producers. The test for the industrial countries in this connection is how well they were able to share out the potential burdens of this adjustment problem.

There were two burdens in particular to worry about. One consisted of the increased debt and equity claims implied by the present and prospective current deficits of oil consumers. If consumers collectively were successful in maintaining full employment, current deficits per se could not be regarded as undesirable. Quite the contrary, the deficits meant a delay in the required net outward transfer of resources to oil producers, in effect postponing the relative lowering of living standards in consuming countries. The problem, however, was that current deficits must be financed: consumers must either give up external assets or incur additional liabilities. In a full-employment world, the burden of adjusting to OPEC's current surpluses was the burden of increased debt.

The second potential burden reflected the possibility that consumers collectively might not be successful in maintaining full employment. Some countries were unwilling or unable to incur increased debt, and they might be tempted to try to reduce their current deficits by domestic deflation, by exchange depreciation, or by trade and capital controls. Domestic deflation would mainly depress the level of employment at home; depreciation or controls would mainly have the effect of depressing the level of employment abroad (unless offset by expansionary policies in countries willing to incur additional external debt). Such competitive policies were bound to be mutually frustrating and ultimately destructive. The burden in this event was the greater amount of output foregone in consuming countries.

If this second burden was to be minimized, an understanding had to be reached regarding allocation of the first burden (i.e., the burden of increased debt). The test for industrial countries, therefore, had been to coordinate their macroeconomic and external payments policies in such a way as to achieve an acceptable distribution of current-account deficits.

Coordination could be based on a variety of criteria.[6] There is no single measure of optimality in burden-sharing. Deficits could be allocated:

1. In inverse proportion to the ability of consuming countries to curtail internal demand in order to make room for additional exports. This would presumably mean larger deficits for the poorest consuming countries, which would benefit most from a delay in the required transfer of wealth to OPEC.

2. In direct proportion to the ability of countries to incur increased debt. This would presumably mean larger deficits for richer countries.

3. In direct proportion to the marginal rate of social return on capital in consuming countries (the marginal efficiency of investment). This would presumably mean larger deficits for rich and/or rapidly growing countries.

4. In direct proportion to the potential in different consuming countries for producing substitutes for OPEC oil (on the ground that development of substitute sources of energy would require considerable outlays for investment in coming years). This would presumably mean larger deficits for such countries as the United States, Canada, and Great Britain.

5. In direct proportion to some notion of "normal" current balances of consuming countries; for example, pre-1974 surpluses or deficits adjusted for net "oil deficits" (i.e., increased imports of OPEC oil less increased exports to OPEC). This would presumably mean larger deficits for the biggest consumers of imported oil, such as the United States and Japan. (This measure was a relatively narrow definition of oil-induced current deficits. A broader definition might take into account the shift in international competitiveness of individual national industries with varying degrees of dependence on imported oil.

What was the reaction of the industrial countries? The answer is that they failed to meet the test. Coordination of macroeconomic and external payments policies has so far been negligible; there was little consultation and no public agreement at all on the distribution of current-account deficits. Instead, the situation was every man for himself and the devil take the hindmost.

Consider Table 2 (p. 204), which shows the net changes of current balances that were experienced by Organization of Economic Cooperation and Development (OECD) countries in 1974, the first full year of the energy crisis. It is difficult to find any coherent pattern in these figures. Were the increased deficits allocated in proportion to ability to curtail internal demand? Then how does one explain the relatively small declines in the current accounts of some of the poorest OECD countries, such as Greece, Iceland, Portugal, and

Table 2

CURRENT BALANCES OF OECD COUNTRIES, 1973-1974
(in billions of dollars)

	1973	1974	Change from 1973 to 1974
Australia	+ 0.56	- 2.60	- 3.16
Austria	- 0.37	- 0.50	- 0.13
Belgium-Luxembourg	+ 1.29	+ 0.66	- 0.63
Canada	+ 0.02	- 1.68	- 1.70
Denmark	- 0.50	- 0.99	- 0.49
Finland	- 0.43	- 1.20	- 0.77
France	- 0.69	- 5.90	- 5.21
Germany	+ 4.31	+ 9.34	+ 5.03
Greece	- 1.19	- 1.22	- 0.03
Iceland	- 0.04	- 0.20	- 0.16
Ireland	- 0.21	- 0.68	- 0.47
Italy	- 2.67	- 7.92	- 5.25
Japan	- 0.14	- 4.69	- 4.55
Netherlands	+ 1.77	+ 1.61	- 0.16
New Zealand	+ 0.17	- 1.68	- 1.85
Norway	- 0.35	- 1.01	- 0.66
Portugal	+ 0.55	- 0.50	- 1.05
Spain	+ 0.56	- 3.15	- 3.71
Sweden	+ 1.13	- 0.99	- 2.12
Switzerland	+ 0.28	+ 1.00	+ 0.72
Turkey	+ 0.47	- 0.70	- 1.17
United Kingdom	- 2.88	- 9.00	- 6.12
United States	+ 0.34	- 0.87	- 1.21
	+ 1.98	-32.87	-34.85

Source:
OECD, Economic Outlook, No. 17 (July 1975), pp. 57-58.

Turkey? Were the deficits allocated in proportion to ability to incur debt? Then how does this explain the net improvement in the current balances of Germany and Switzerland? Deficits certainly were not allocated by such sophisticated criteria as the marginal efficiency of investment or the potential for producing substitutes for OPEC oil. And in relation to the criterion of normal surpluses adjusted for net oil deficits, current deficits in 1974 were actually distributed in a strikingly perverse fashion, as Table 3 demonstrates. The six biggest OECD countries together managed to improve their current balances, net of increased oil deficits, by some $30 billion. (The Big Three—the United States, Germany, and Japan—alone accounted for nearly all this improvement.) All other oil consumers as a group (including non-OECD consumers) were forced to accept a deterioration of their current balances, over and above their net oil deficits, by a similar amount.

Table 3

CURRENT BALANCES, ADJUSTED FOR NET OIL DEFICITS, OF THE SIX BIGGEST OECD COUNTRIES, 1974

(in billions of dollars)

	Net change of current account	Net increase of oil imports (-)	Net increase of exports to OPEC (+)	Net change of current account adjusted for net oil deficit
	(1)	(2)	(3)	(4)=(1) - [(2)+(3)]
France	- 5.21	- 7.36[a]	+ 1.00	+ 1.15
Germany	+ 5.03	- 6.78	+ 1.75	+10.06
Italy	- 5.25	- 6.71[a]	+ 1.00	+ 0.46
Japan	- 4.55	-14.45	+ 2.75	+ 7.15
United Kingdom	- 6.12	- 6.49	+ 1.00	- 0.63
United States	- 1.21	-16.59	+ 3.25	+12.13
	-17.31	-58.38	+10.75	+30.32

a) Includes small amounts of other mineral fuels.

Sources:

Column (1) from Table 2.

Column (2) from Committee for Economic Development, International Economic Consequences of High Priced Energy, Appendix A.

Column (3) from OECD, Economic Outlook, No. 17 (July 1975) Table 45.

In effect, therefore, smaller countries as a group bore the burden not just of their own higher-priced oil imports but also of the biggest consuming countries. Ex post, such a pattern of deficits could perhaps be justified in terms of the criterion of ability to curtail internal demand, the smaller countries benefiting most from the delay in the required transfer of wealth to OPEC. But ex ante, such a pattern was justifiable only if, in addition, adequate recycling facilities were made available to the smaller countries to finance their current deficits on a sustained basis. In fact, however, this was simply not the case. The biggest countries did not accept the responsibility of helping the smaller countries to bear up under the burden of their increased debt,[7] even while forcing that increased debt upon them. In terms of burden-sharing, the contribution of the biggest countries was actually heavily negative.

Why was such a situation tolerated by the smaller countries? In part it was because, in 1974 at least, most were still able to finance their current deficits by borrowing at more or less reasonable terms; some had fairly ample foreign exchange reserves that they could run down for a time. But mainly it was because they had little choice in the face of the superior market power of the biggest countries. Some observers have called this "muddling through."[8] I would call it "power economics." In the absence of effective collaboration among sovereign states, what determines the outcome in a competitive situation such as this is power: the ability to manipulate the particular situation to advantage. The biggest countries had this ability owing to their sheer weight in the world economy as markets and sources of supply. The outcome did not require deliberate trade measures on their part. Quite the contrary, all of them joined in formal pledges in the OECD and the International Monetary Fund (IMF) *not* to resort to protectionist policy devices for balance-of-payments purposes. Such measures were unnecessary because the big countries already enjoyed overwhelming monopolistic and monopsonistic power in international trade. Through the free play of inherently unequal market forces, they had the ability to manipulate the situation to advantage by means of private economic choices. They were able to increase their export values sharply, both to oil producers and consumers, and to reduce the value of their non-oil imports. They were thus able to minimize the burden of increased debt for themselves by shifting it onto others.

In fact, what occurred in 1974 was a cascading of the burden of adjustment among consuming countries, from the more powerful to the least powerful—with the weakest being forced to bear the greatest burden of all (in relation to their ability to incur increased debt). We can think of three groups of consumers: the six biggest OECD countries (the Big Six); the remaining eighteen members of OECD (the Middle 18); and the non-oil developing countries (popularly known as the Fourth World). For the Big Six as a group, the adjusted current balance improved by $30 billion. For the Middle 18, there was only a relatively moderate deterioration in their adjusted current balance. (The OECD reports that about half of the observed $17.5 billion decline of the aggregate current balance of this group was accounted for by higher payments for oil; at the same time, the Middle 18 increased exports to OPEC by $1.75 billion.)[9] For the Fourth World, virtually all primary producers, adjusted current balances deteriorated sharply by almost $18 billion (an observed change of $27.8 billion adjusted for a net oil deficit with OPEC reported in the vicinity of $10 billion).[10] In effect, it was really the Fourth World that had to bear the largest share of the burden of adjustment. The Middle 18 were saddled with some of it by the Big Six, but the major portion was successfully transferred onward. It is an old adage in political science that in any collectivity of diverse interests, there is always an inherent tendency to reconcile conflicts among their separate ambitions, as much as possible, at the expense of outsiders. This is apparently what the collectivity of industrial countries did in 1974.

In fact, fully 80 percent of the combined current-account deficit of oil consumers in 1974 was borne by primary producing countries, including primary producers in the periphery of Europe and in Australasia.[11] The main reason was the precipitous drop in the terms of trade of primary producers—some 15 percent between 1973 and early 1975.[12] This was due in part to the high rate of inflation in industrial countries, as well as to the oil-price increases, which raised the prices of their imports; but mainly it was due to the severity of the recession in industrial countries, which sharply reduced the prices of their exports. Recession in the industrial world was the principal means by which the burden of increased debt was transferred to primary producers. The corresponding burden of unemployment in industrial countries was considered acceptable on the grounds that it was an essential part of the fight against inflation.

These trends persisted, in some respects even intensified, in 1975. As the preliminary data collected in Table 4 (p. 208) testify, the Big Six

Table 4

CURRENT BALANCES OF THE BIG SIX, 1974-1975
(in billions of dollars)

	1974	1975	Change from 1974 to 1975
France	- 5.90	+ 0.02	+ 5.92
Germany	+ 9.34	+ 3.57	- 5.77
Italy	- 7.92	+ 0.20[b]	+ 8.12
Japan	- 4.69	- 0.73	+ 3.96
United Kingdom	- 9.00	- 3.40[b]	+ 6.60
United States (a)	- 2.34	+11.05	+13.39

a) Trade balance only.

b) Estimate.

Source:

Various publications.

(Germany excepted) continued to improve their current balances awesomely. The United States reported its greatest trade surplus ever; Germany, despite the drop from 1974, enjoyed its second largest surplus on record; and Japan, its third largest. The Fourth World, meanwhile, experienced another sharp deterioration in its current-account deficit, this time to an estimated $35 billion.[13] (The Middle 18 approximately held their own on current account.) As a result, the share of the combined current deficit of oil consumers borne by primary-producing countries rose above the 80 percent mark set in 1974.

* * * *

Are these trends likely to persist in 1976 and beyond? *Can* they persist? It is always hazardous to indulge in prediction, particularly in situations such as this which are so fraught with economic and political unknowns. Yet a few remarks about the future are not out of order. One can imagine a variety of possible scenarios developing out of the present events.

At one extreme, one can imagine a total breakdown of the world trading system, owing to the excessive weight of the increased debt burden pressing down on primary-producing countries (and on some industrial countries as well). Another aggregate deficit of $31 billion had been projected for the Fourth World in 1976, continuing the pattern set in 1974-75,[14] though some of these countries were already finding it difficult to obtain external financing at reasonable terms. A few clearly reached the limit of their borrowing capacity; and, for most, foreign-exchange reserves were simply too low to take up much of the remaining slack.[15] It might not be very long before some were forced to take serious action to cut their deficits, most likely by depreciation or trade and capital controls. The alternative, a substantial belt-tightening at home, could cause widespread starvation and would probably be politically disastrous.

Similar problems existed in some of the industrial countries, where workers were becoming increasingly restive about prevailing high levels of unemployment. To promote domestic recovery while avoiding deterioration of their current accounts, a few industrial countries might be tempted to resort to competitive exchange depreciation or to trade and capital controls of their own (IMF and OECD pledges to the contrary notwithstanding). The British government, for example, imposed emergency restrictions on a variety of import items.[16] The Italian government, which had used such controls once, could soon feel obliged to use them again. And relations between the United States and the European Community (EC) have been considerably strained since 1974 by a running series of trade disputes. Isolated incidents of this kind could easily escalate into genuine economic warfare leading to a collapse of the trading order. The risk of disruption, even chaos, is real, as Tom Willett has noted:

> Attempts by individual countries to adjust could degenerate into beggar-thy-neighbor policies that would cause economic damage over and above the damage caused directly by the oil-price increases.
>
> Thus, all the countries of the system have a collective interest in encouraging each individual country to avoid taking adjustment measures that would exceed some "fair share" of the total scope for adjustment available to the group.[17]

A "fair share" approach would represent the opposite extreme of the range of possible scenarios. One could imagine the industrial countries, apprehensive of the risk of disruption and chaos, coming together to reach an understanding on a more acceptable distribution of current-account deficits. Alternative criteria for burden-sharing have already been outlined. Adequate institutional forums for ensuring consistency of national macroeconomic and payments policies through close and frequent consultations already exist in the IMF and the OECD. All that was required was sufficient political will on the part of the industrial countries to accept the necessary reordering of their traditional payments objectives.

Such political will, however, was precisely what had been lacking. The fair share approach may be in the collective interest of all oil consumers as a group. It was not in the felt interest of the industrial countries alone—not as long as they have the primary-producing countries to bear much of the adjustment burden for them. Criteria for burden-sharing are inherently difficult to agree upon and implement. Reordering priorities is distasteful to some, perhaps even painful for others. It was much more appealing to leave the outcome to impersonal market forces—to "power economics"—that could be relied upon to reconcile potential conflicts mainly at the expense of outsiders. It is no accident that this was the approach that the industrial countries followed. It was also the most likely scenario to emerge in 1976 and beyond. Most probably, Fourth World countries would continue to be weighed down by an increasing burden of foreign debt; undoubtedly, they would continue to receive just enough financial assistance from the rich to stop them short of really serious beggar-thy-neighbor policies. The industrial countries had no interest in provoking genuine economic warfare. But neither did they have much interest in bearing any more of the burden of adjustment than they could possibly avoid.

* * * *

The North Atlantic countries and Japan like to think of themselves as a loose sort of community, sharing certain interests and purposes that set them off from the rest of the world's countries. One test of this claim of community was the ability to act in harmony at times of severe crisis. One of the (few) benefits of the energy crisis was that it exposed the hollowness of this claim. The industrial countries did not act together as a community in response to their common monetary problems. In fact, their behavior was in flat contradiction of even the weakest standards of international cooperation. They failed utterly to coordinate their macroeconomic and payments policies to achieve an acceptable distribution of current-account deficits. Instead, economic nationalism reared its ugly head, each country doing as much as possible to avoid the burdens of adjustment. Power economics, not cooperation, prevailed. That this did not completely rupture relations among the industrial countries was because most of the burdens of adjustment could be shifted onto others, namely the poor countries of the Fourth World. It is these countries which really paid the price for the failure of the industrial world to act as a community.

Can this conclusion be generalized to other dimensions of relations among the industrial countries? In my opinion, yes. At the rhetorical level, governments paid lip service to the ideals of international cooperation; they even endorsed and joined together in new institutional initiatives, such as the International Energy Agency (IEA) and the Financial Support Fund. But at the practical level, their priorities were quite different—with national interests always leading the list by a very wide margin. This was as true in the political and military sphere as in economic relations. The situation was inherently unstable; it might not always be possible to reconcile conflicts at the expense of outsiders. Would the industrial countries then be able to prevent the game from becoming negative-sum?

15 *Resource Transfers to the Developing World*

Guy F. Erb and Helen C. Low

The non-oil developing countries have been severely buffeted by world economic events since October 1973. Assistance to help tide them over the crisis has been made available in a variety of ways by both OECD and OPEC countries. This chapter will examine the channels used to help them finance their unprecedented deficits, and will discuss the broader context in which the issue of resource transfers has been placed by these events.

The importance of resource transfers from the Organization of Petroleum Exporting Countries (OPEC) to developing countries derives not from the funds it has loaned or granted—these have been small in comparison with the burden which higher priced oil has imposed on these countries—but from the opening up for discussion of the whole balance sheet of the world economic system. OPEC has used its leverage in a variety of settings, most notably that of the Conference on International Economic Cooperation (CIEC). Led by Algeria, Iran, and Venezuela, OPEC has tied the energy concerns of the industrial world to the development concerns of the Third World, setting in motion a dialogue on a restructuring of the international economic order.

OPEC has acted as a catalyst to bring the CIEC into being in Paris and as a prime—but far from sole—actor in mobilizing the developing world stance. The developing countries have thus far rallied behind OPEC leadership despite the damage to their economies the stiff oil "tax" has caused.

The outcome of this venture is still to be played out. Several potential hazards threaten the solidarity between OPEC and other countries of the developing world. Potential rifts lie in the differences in interests between the oil-sufficient and the oil-dependent countries and between the semi-developed countries of the Third World and the near-stagnant poorest countries. Basic divergences of opinion and circumstance threaten the cohesion of OPEC itself. Nonetheless, a strong impetus to a concerted effort arises from widespread deep resentment of the framework the industrial countries imposed on world economic systems and the vicarious satisfaction which the non-oil countries have derived from the success of OPEC.

Repercussions of Recent Events

Neither incremental aid from the Development Assistance Committee (DAC) countries nor OPEC aid fully compensated the non-oil developing countries for the multiple calamities which befell them in 1974 and 1975. The oil price increases in 1974 added about $11 billion to the 1973 oil import bill of $7 billion, despite substantial curtailment of oil imports. Food shortages and crop shortfalls in all the major grain-producing regions of the world drove up prices at a time when developing countries needed increased grain and fertilizer imports of $3.5 billion. Recession in the industrial world, which gathered momentum through 1974 and 1975, had a double-barreled impact on the developing countries through a decrease in demand for their products, both primary commodities and manufactures, and through a decline in commodity prices which turned the terms of trade sharply against them. The terms of trade were worsened also through inflation in the prices of industrial goods. While the food picture improved significantly in 1975, OPEC notched oil prices higher and the industrial world recession deepened further, raising the overall deficit of the developing countries by a further $8-12 billion.

Payment through exports for the increased outlays for fuel, grain, and higher priced industrial goods was frustrated by sagging markets in the industrial countries. The net effect was a shifting from the industrial world onto the primary producers of the brunt of the foreign exchange burden resulting from the higher oil prices. This was concentrated more fully on the developing world members of that group as time elapsed. Viewed from the other side, to the extent that the developing countries borrowed to sustain their imports from the industrial countries, they cushioned the industrial world's slump—and facilitated the transfer of the payments burden.

The Internal Impact

The impact fell with varying degrees of severity on the developing countries, reflecting their degree of economic development, their dependence on imported oil and grain, and the reserve position in which they found themselves at the onset of the crisis. For the poorer countries, excepting only those whose principal exports had initially provided them with a cushioned reserve position and a few which had little trade with the outside world, the shock was immediate and severe. For the low-income countries designated by the United Nations as "most seriously affected" (MSA) by the crisis, the payments gap which had to be met by emergency measures amounted to over $3.1 billion in 1974. By mid-1975 the original group of thirty-two had been increased to forty-two and would have been still larger if a cut-off level of $400 per capita income had not applied. The shortfall in 1975 beyond their regular capital inflows was estimated at $4.4 billion, of which emergency assistance covered $1.5 billion. These countries were forced to cut imports sharply, draw down their limited reserves, and borrow funds as best they could.

At the other end of the spectrum were a group of semi-industrial countries which had been prospering in the years immediately preceding the crisis. A number of them had experienced impressive rates of economic growth and had built up a substantial reserve position. Some of them attempted to straddle the recession, borrowing heavily to tide themselves over the lull in order to sustain their pace of growth. This was a calculated risk, dependent for its success in large measure on the length and depth of the recession. These countries continued their imports of industrial goods and fuel, although with mounting restraint as the months passed. As 1975 progressed, it became increasingly difficult to maintain this posture and by the end of the year virtually all had been forced to retrench.

One measure of the profound effect of the events of 1974 and 1975 on the oil-dependent developing countries was the consequence for internal growth. For the poorer countries, already struggling with stagnant economies before the crisis began, the doldrums deepened. For the middle and upper income groups of developing countries, the momentum of growth was halted and temporarily reversed. The World Bank estimated aggregate negative growth rates of 0.7 percent in the per capita incomes of the poorest countries (per capita income under $200) and 1.2 percent in the other developing countries in 1975.

Financing the Deficit

The repercussions of the crisis on the external financial position of the oil-dependent developing countries were dramatic. From an aggregate current account deficit of $9 billion in 1973, a measure of the net inflow of resources in that year, they rolled up a $27-billion shortfall in 1974 and reached a level conservatively estimated at $35 billion in 1975. If scheduled debt repayments were included in the picture, the gross financial position of this group of countries would show a deficit of $44 billion for 1975. Analysis of the manner in which the 1975 net deficit was financed attributes $17 billion to development assistance and direct investment, $3 billion to the drawing down of international reserves by the deficit countries, drawings of $2 billion from the International Monetary Fund (IMF), and $14 billion borrowed from private commercial banks.

With the increasing reluctance of private sources to lend funds on the scale reached in 1974 and 1975, it was widely expected that the current account deficit would, perforce, be somewhat lower in 1976. This would entail the cutting back of imports even further than in 1975, perhaps by another 4-5 percent in real terms. The extent to which exports would expand, the key variable in the balance-of-payments picture, depended on the pace and quality of recovery in the industrial world. While the banking world looked to increments in flows of official funds to soften the effects on the developing countries of private credit contraction, the US Treasury, noting the mood of Congress, anticipated a stringent limit to public fund extension. Hence the US government tended to look to the private sector to provide the needed incremental funds. Consequently, unless the industrial economies revive considerably, 1976 may prove to be a difficult year for much of the developing world. Neither private nor public sources of external assistance can be counted on to provide resources adequate to regain and sustain reasonable rates of growth.

The Legacy of Indebtedness

While recovery of activity in the industrial world could considerably ease further stress on the external accounts of the non-OPEC developing countries, it would not suffice to dissipate the overhang of indebtedness which they had built up during these critical years. Much of their current account deficit was financed by extensive borrowing from commercial sources. Such borrowing met about 45 percent of gross financial requirements in 1975. It was estimated that the level of the disbursed external debt (government and government-guaranteed) of more than one year duration owed by the non-oil developing countries increased from just over $60 billion at the end of 1973 to about $90 billion two years later. The trend also was toward shorter term lending and at higher rates. While this manner of shifting the problem to the future averted an acute immediate crisis, it exacted the price of an increased external levy on the future production of these developing economies. The full impact of increased debt service will be felt around 1978-79.

In assessing the significance of enlarged external debt, wide differences in the position of individual countries is again notable. Some countries were encountering difficulty in servicing debt prior to 1974. Others continued to be able to handle sizable debt payments but relied heavily on foreign capital to finance their development; these explicitly geared their policies to maintaining creditworthiness. Between the two extremes were a spectrum of countries saddled with potentially severe payments problems by the exigencies of the crisis years. Among these, some, such as the copper producers, were maintaining a precarious balance in meeting their external obligations. While a chain reaction of defaults was considered unlikely and avoidable, concern was expressed for stabilizing the conditions of debt service for a substantial number of developing countries.

It was with that group of countries in mind that the Group of 77, meeting in Manila in January 1976, proposed a sorting out of the external debt of interested debtor countries. Three categories of debt were laid out for separate treatment: cancellation of official debt for the category of countries designated by the United Nations as least developed (LLDC)— and other land-locked and island developing countries —and cancellation or postponement of debt service payment for MSA countries; assurance for multilateral development institutions that they will provide each debtor country with program assistance adequate to cover its debt service to that institution; and a rescheduling of commercial debt over a twenty-five-year period. The fourth UN Conference on Trade and Development (UNCTAD IV) was asked to consider this proposal with a view to convening a debtor/creditor conference.

The legacy of external indebtedness created during the crisis years was only one facet of the longer-term picture of structural adjustment by the developing world economies to the changed post-1973 world economy. This process was far from being accomplished. For many countries it had hardly begun. It involved not only adjustment to the changed price of oil, that is, to the substantially increased costs of energy use in the economy, but also the recapturing of lost growth momentum. To bring about such adjustments required increased external funds—resource transfers—on a significant scale. Whether and on what terms such resources could be obtained were the questions being addressed in the Paris dialogue of producers and consumers of energy and other raw materials.

Resource Transfer Patterns

To meet their needs for external resources over and above their foreign earnings, developing countries have traditionally relied on the bilateral assistance programs and export credits of the Organization of Economic Cooperation and Development (OECD) and the Socialist countries; on private capital markets; on direct foreign investments; and, increasingly, on loans from multilateral agencies. The assistance programs and other transfers of OPEC members have joined these main sources of financial flows.

After the dramatic rise in petroleum, food, and fertilizer prices and their effect on developing countries, a welter of proposals surfaced for new mechanisms to transfer additional resources to them. While the responses of OECD and OPEC countries permitted them to accumulate a deficit of over $35 billion on current account, thereby financing a significant portion of the short-run disequilibrium, the longer run problems of adjustment to the changed conditions have yet to be resolved. Therefore, the development assistance policies of both the "old rich" and the "new rich" were part of the competition between them for influence in the Third World.

The OECD Countries

The pattern of resource transfers to the developing world on which the OPEC price increases were superimposed in late 1973 was largely the product of historical connections between donor/creditors and recipient/debtors. The vast bulk of the resources came from the members of the Development Assistance Committee (DAC) of the OECD , almost $25 billion in net flows to the developing world in 1973 out of a total of $35 billion from all sources. The trend of the early 1970s was toward higher total flows, caused chiefly by increased resources from the private sector. Concessional transfers, while rising, were not keeping pace with the growth of GNP in donor countries. In response to the acute problems of developing countries, this downward trend was arrested and reversed in 1974, the aggregate share of DAC GNP allocated to concessional assistance rose to 0.33 percent. This amounted to $11.3 billion, of which about $3 billion was channeled through multilateral institutions. Net private flows also increased appreciably to $14.1 billion. In 1975, concessional flows increased by a further $1.1 billion; projections for 1976 anticipated a slightly increased flow of concessional resources but a substantially diminished transfer of private funds.

The Socialist Countries

Resource transfers from the centrally planned economies have remained relatively static, unaffected by recent developments on the world economic scene. They amounted to a net flow of about $1.4 billion in 1974, virtually all provided on concessional terms. Almost all of the aid was distributed bilaterally and was concentrated on a few countries. The increasing Chinese share accounted for over one-third of the total in 1974.

OPEC Assistance

Resource transfers from OPEC members, which had amounted to less than $1 billion in 1973, rose to a level estimated between $4.7 billion (DAC calculations) and $5.2 billion (UNCTAD calculations) in 1974. (See Table 1, p. 219.) According to the DAC Secretariat figures, a little less than half of this was disbursed on concessional

Table 1

Estimated Financial Flows of OPEC Members to Developing Countries in 1974

(US $ Million)

	Non-Concessional			Concessional				
							As % of	
Donor Country	Bilateral	Multi-lateral	Total	Bilateral	Multi-lateral	Total	Oil revenues	GNP
Middle Eastern:								
Algeria	-	5	5	3	32	35	0.9	0.3
Iran	20	289	309	378	23	401	2.0	0.9
Iraq	-	-	-	210	27	237	3.3	1.8
Kuwait	180	66	246	328	56	384	4.6	3.1
Libya	25	7	32	73	24	97	1.4	0.8
Qatar	2	25	27	42	9	51	2.8	2.6
Saudi Arabia	30	963	993	710	100	810	2.7	2.3
UAE	40	129	169	107	30	137	2.6	1.8
Subtotal	297	1,484	1,781	1,851	301	2,152	...	...
Other:								
Nigeria	-	240	240	2	9	11	0.1	0.1
Venezuela	-	445	445	20	41	61	0.6	0.2
TOTAL	297	2,169	2,466	1,873	351	2,224	2.4	1.4

Note: Figures are subject to revision. In particular, some of the bilateral disbursements estimates are highly tentative. Oil revenue figures are Secretariat estimates (except for Iran). GNP figures are based on latest IBRD estimates (June, 1975). Nigeria was omitting in computing disbursements as a percentage of oil revenue and GNP for these countries as a group.

Source: Maurice J. Williams, DAC Chairman, in 1975 Review: Development Co-operation, Efforts and Policies of the Members of the Development Assistance Committee, Organization for Economic Co-operation and Development, Paris, France, November 1975.

terms, most of which was distributed bilaterally since few of the multilateral institutions set up by the Arab members to handle such lending had begun operation. The aid was heavily concentrated on a few nations: three-fourths of it went to Egypt, Syria, and Jordan; nine-tenths of the total was allotted to Arab and Muslim countries. Calculated in a manner as comparable as possible to that used to assess DAC data, OPEC assistance carried a grant element of about 65 percent, compared with 87 percent for DAC countries. Such transfers amounted to 1.4 percent of the GNP of major OPEC members in 1974 and 2.4 percent of their oil income. OPEC nonconcessional flows mainly went toward the purchase of bonds from multilateral institutions, chiefly the World Bank. (The $3.2 billion which OPEC countries placed at the disposal of the IMF Oil Facility are not included in that total because these sums did not constitute an outflow from the subscribing countries.)

In 1975, overall OPEC disbursements were estimated at over $6 billion, with concessional transfers accounting for $4.5 billion. The OPEC total was projected to increase by a further $1 billion in 1976.

The trend of OPEC aid can reasonably be expected to reflect changes in the external financial situation of the oil-exporting countries. Their aggregate surplus decreased from a $67-billion high in 1974 to a level variously estimated at $25 billion to $46 billion in 1975. Projections for 1976 are similarly varied. Surpluses from oil revenues are generally expected to decline, with the countries of the Arabian peninsula receiving most of the surpluses that are realized. Therefore, total concessional transfers will probably dwindle. With the expected diminution of the role of Iran and Venezuela, the countries chiefly responsible for much of the present diversification of recipients, the breadth of OPEC transfers in the future is likely to depend on the extent to which the Middle East oil-exporting countries channel funds to the activities of the existing multilateral lending institutions.

Eurocurrencies

Eurocurrency loans to non-OPEC developing countries of Africa, Asia, and Latin America amounted to about $6.7 billion in 1974 and $7.2 billion in 1975. (See Table 2, p. 221). As the global level of Eurocurrency lending decreased in 1975, the share of funds borrowed by

TABLE 2 BILATERAL CONCESSIONAL ASSISTANCE COMMITMENTS BY OPEC COUNTRIES IN 1974

$ *million.*

Countries	Algeria	Iran	Iraq	Kuwait	Libya	Nigeria	Qatar	Saudi Arabia	UAE	Vene-zuela	Total	Share of recipient in total *(Per cent)*
Afghanistan*		10.0	10.0					65.2			85.2	2.2
Bahrain+ *				11.2				7.9	50.1		69.2	1.8
Bangladesh*	1.0		51.0	20.0	1.0		1.5		76.2		150.7	3.9
Burundi					1.0						1.0	×
Chad*			n.a.		7.6		1.9				9.5	0.2
Egypt+ *		350.0		81.8	16.9		5.0	400.0	12.6		866.3[1]	22.6
Egypt/Syria+ +				125.0				143.0			268.0	7.0
Equat. Guinea					1.0						1.0	×
Ethiopia					1.0						1.0	×
Gambia					1.4						1.4	×
Guinea				15.0	10.1						25.1	0.7
Guyana										15.0	15.0	0.4
Honduras										5.0	5.0	0.1
India		133.0	143.9								276.9	7.2
Jordan+ *		8.0		42.0			16.8	47.7	14.2		128.7	3.4
Lebanon+ *		45.5	27.5	3.0				6.0	2.0		84	2.2
Lesotho		1.0			0.5						1.5	×
Mali*	1.2										1.2	×
Malta								5.0			5.0	0.1
Mauritania+ *			2.5		5.1		9.9	20.2	15.0		52.7	1.4
Morocco+ *		30.0		13.1				50.0			93.1	2.4
Niger*				0.4	0.2	0.8					1.4	×
Oman+ *				3.4							3.4	0.1
Pakistan*		587.1			50.0		10.0		100.0		747.1	19.5
Sahel*	0.3								6.0		6.3	0.2
Senegal*		13.5									13.5	0.4
Senegal River Development*								10.0			10.0	0.3
Somalia+ *			17.5	7.0	9.6	0.4	14.0	30.0	19.5		98.0	2.6
Sri Lanka			20.0								20.0	0.5
Sudan+ *		64.0	10.0	15.6			14.0	14.4	2.0		120.0	3.1
Syria+ *			50.0	183.5	41.9			100.0	18.5		393.9[1]	10.3
Thailand								40.0			40.0	1.0
Togo					1.2						1.2	×
Tunisia+ *		4.5		16.6	0.6		10.0	18.6	30.1		80.4	2.1
Uganda					14.9						14.9	0.4
Yemen A.R.+ *			9.5	17.6	11.1			36.8	4.0		79	2.1
Yemen PDR+ *			5.0	19.6	6.7						31.3	0.8
Zaïre									26.0		26	0.7
Zambia	0.8					0.8					1.6	×
Total	3.3	1,246.6	346.9	574.8	181.8	2.0	83.1	994.8	376.2	20.0	3,829.5	100.0
of which: to Islamic countries	2.5	1,112.6	183.0	559.8	160.8	1.2	83.1	949.8	350.2	—	3,403.0	88.9
to Arab countries	—	502.0	122.0	539.4	91.9	0.4	69.7	874.6	168.0	—	2,365.1	61.8

1. Not including amounts shown under "Egypt/Syria" for which no breakdown is available.
+ Denotes Arab countries as defined by membership in the Arab League.
* Denotes Islamic countries as defined by membership in the Islamic Development Bank plus Afghanistan, Syria, Yemen PDR.

Source: Maurice J. Williams, DAC Chairman, in 1975 Review: Development Co-operation, Efforts and Policies of the Members of the Development Assistance Committee, Organization for Economic Co-operation and Development, Paris, France, November 1975.

this group rose from 22 percent to 31 percent. While it was not possible to attribute country of origin to such funds, it was estimated that about $24 billion of OPEC funds were utilized in the Eurocurrency market in 1974, about three-fourths of the total. OPEC members appear to have committed a much smaller amount to this use in 1975, and some were in fact themselves returning to the Eurocurrency market as net borrowers.

Multilateral Channels

Multilateral development agencies transferred a total of $4.3 billion to developing countries in 1974 and $5.2 billion in 1975, roughly 10 percent of total net resource flows. Over two-fifths of this was transferred on concessional terms, primarily to the poorest countries. The DAC countries had initiated and traditionally funded these institutions and continued, in 1974, to increase the level of grants and capital subscriptions to them. The purchase, in that year, by OPEC members of over $2 billion worth of those institutions' bonds substantially broadened their base of support.

The World Bank almost doubled its borrowing in fiscal 1975, primarily through direct placements, and expanded its loan commitments by more than $1 billion—to over $4 billion. Forty percent of the borrowed funds were supplied by OPEC, $1,041 million from Iran and Saudi Arabia. While it has traditionally made project loans, it lent $500 million in 1975 to finance needed imports. Plans are underway to increase the World Bank's capital base since it has been approaching the limits of its lending capacity under present legal requirements for capital backing. At the projected rate of lending, further capitalization of $30 billion will be needed under existing rules.

A quintupling of the capital base of the International Finance Corporation (IFC) to $500 million has also been under discussion. Gross commitments of the IFC increased by almost 40 percent in 1974, but only 4 percent in 1975. One of the expanded functions envisaged for this institution, which was set up to promote private enterprise in developing countries, was the encouragement of the development of raw materials, especially minerals.

The International Development Association (IDA), which lends funds for fifty years with carrying charges of 0.75 percent, began to commit funds from its fourth replenishment of $4.5 billion in early 1975. While only Kuwayt has contributed to IDA in the past, several OPEC members have been participating in discussions for the fifth replenishment. Backers hoped to achieve a doubling of the current level of resources in IDA-V. But this pace of replenishment threatened to outrun the willingness of its principal contributor. Congress authorized the spread of the $1.5-billion US contribution to IDA-V over four years instead of the targeted three, which put the United States two years out of phase with the projected start of IDA-V. A further stretchout was threatened in March 1976 when the House voted to appropriate only $320 million of the $375 million expected.

A Third Window of the World Bank was designed to make up to an additional $1 billion of concessional funds available to middle-income countries by subsidizing interest payments on regular bank lending. Contributions now in sight from nine donors, including Saudi Arabia, Kuwayt, and Qatar, will permit loans of about $600 million with an interest rate subsidy of 4 percent applied to the bank's regular rate (now about 8 percent). Third Window operations will be devoted chiefly to countries with per capita incomes under $375.

The regional development banks increased their lending programs significantly and were stretching the limits of expansion possible within existing capitalization. The Inter-American Development Bank and the Asian Development Bank were projecting expansion of their capital base and were discussing with donors a substantially increased replenishment of their soft-loan operations.

OPEC Proposals for Multilateral Channels

OPEC members designated multilateral channels for 27 percent of their concessional assistance commitments in 1974, about the same proportion as did the DAC countries but largely through new institutions set up under their control. At the Rome Food Conference in November 1974, OPEC countries, headed by Saudi Arabia, proposed an International Fund for Agricultural Development (IFAD) to be funded initially at a level of $1 billion with contributions provided equally by OPEC and OECD countries. An integral part of the proposal was that control be shared equitably by the contributors and the recipients. IFAD was endorsed by OPEC and the US Congress.

A desire to have a voice in the functioning of institutions to which they contributed their funds counted heavily with the OPEC countries. Partly for this reason they set up a number of aid and lending institutions of their own, some of which began operations in 1974. The largest commitments were made to the Islamic Bank and the Arab Bank for Economic Development in Africa, neither of which was in operation in late 1975. A development fund to provide interest-free loans for program and project assistance, proposed by Iran and Venezuela, was whittled down from a $5 billion level to about $1 billion. This was to be based on a ten-cents-a-barrel levy on oil production in 1976. After vigorous debate in January 1976, the fund was further modified by the OPEC finance ministers; it was to consist of specific contributions from member states totaling $800 million.

OPEC members have also pressed for increased representation in the International Monetary Fund (IMF) and the World Bank. At the Jamaica meeting of the IMF in January 1976, a decision was made to raise the OPEC countries' share of increased IMF quotas from 5 percent to 10 percent. At the same time, it was agreed that OPEC countries with surplus currencies would follow the same rules of availability for the IMF as did industrial countries with currencies in surplus. The OPEC share in the capital of the World Bank, and hence in voting power, was also in the process of being increased.

The International Monetary Fund

Designed to provide temporary balance of payments assistance to its members, on terms requiring them to take internal steps to redress the imbalance, the IMF was in a position to handle only a limited portion of the deficits of developing countries in 1974 and 1975. To meet the extraordinary circumstances of that era, an Oil Facility was set up under IMF supervision but operating outside its usual procedures. When the 1975 Facility completes its operations, 6.9 billion in Special Drawing Rights (SDR) will have been provided, of which OPEC members will have made available SDR 5.0 billion (SDR 4.0 billion from its Middle East members). It was expected that about 40 percent of it would be utilized by over thirty developing countries. A related Subsidy Account was also established in the IMF to lower the rates of interest on borrowings from the 1975 Oil Facility by the category of countries designated as most seriously affected (MSA). Contributions received from OPEC and some OECD members made possible about half of the planned reduction in interest rates.

Another mechanism outside the usual IMF framework was a Trust Fund set up to provide concessionary balance of payments assistance to countries whose 1973 per capita incomes were less than SDR 300. Resources for this fund would comprise profits from the sale of about 17.5 million ounces of IMF gold. This was expected to provide a maximum of $400 million over each of the next four years. Provision was also made for voluntary contributions to the Trust Fund. A further 7.5 million ounces of IMF gold was to be sold and its profits distributed directly to all developing countries according to their quotas. The rationale behind this allocation of gold-sale profits to the Trust Fund and developing countries was to lessen the overall windfall to the industrial countries resulting from their preponderant share of the IMF gold holdings.

In addition to these special mechanisms, the IMF took account of the inflated level of international monetary transactions, through increased quotas, and the problem of swings in the export earnings of primary commodities, through changes in its Compensatory Financing Facility. The IMF Interim Committee decided at its Jamaica meeting to increase global quotas by almost one-third to a level of SDR 39 billion. During the eighteen-month period required for members to approve this change, quotas would be temporarily increased by 45 percent: each of the four credit *tranches* was enlarged to 36.25 percent of quotas. (The developing countries had lobbied for a temporary quota increase to be available entirely on the more liberal conditions of the first credit *tranche*.) The additional use of fund credit through this change in the rules provided about $1.5 billion to the developing countries for 1976.

The Compensatory Financing Facility, established in 1963 to help members bridge temporary shortfalls in export earnings, has been significantly expanded. The overall amount which can be drawn was increased to 75 percent of a member's quota; 50 percent of the quota would be available over a twelve-month period, and an escape clause provided exceptions for major emergencies. Provision was made to utilize the Facility at an earlier stage of a shortfall than had been previously possible, a shortcoming which limited the Facility's usefulness in the recent period of inflation. Moreover, in calculating the shortfall, provision had been made for a "judgmental forecast" if the formula produced a computation which the Fund considered not reasonable. While it was anticipated that these changes would increase developing-country use of Fund credit by about $1 billion in 1976, heavier use would now be possible. Drawings of SDR 1.5 billion in a twelve-month period would trigger a review of the formula and consideration of additional changes.

Aid and Influence

The magnitude of the current account deficits of the developing countries and the limitations of the responses from the industrial world, through bilateral and multilateral channels, have caused many developing countries to turn toward OPEC as a potential source of finance. The liquid wealth of the oil producers was euphorically regarded in 1973-74 as a possible source not only of financial assistance but of funds which might support buffer stocks and other trade related measures.

The Third World Response to OPEC

The OPEC price action struck a chord in many developing countries which shared with OPEC members a sense of grievance against the developed world, the legacy of the colonial era. Many governments of developing countries were well disposed to express their solidarity with the oil exporters. Moreover, the harsh US political responses to OPEC during 1973-74, the limited direct contribution by the developed countries to meeting the increased oil, food, and fertilizer requirements of the poor ones, and the apparent possibility of receiving financial support from OPEC members strengthened the bonds between them and other countries of Africa, Asia, and Latin America.

The cohesion of the developing countries with OPEC was strongest during early 1974. It reached a peak during the Sixth Special Session of the UN General Assembly, whose concluding resolution of 1 May

1974 called for a new international economic order. The same identification of interests resulted in the breakdown of the April 1975 Paris talks between oil producers and consumers over the question of whether energy problems should be treated alone or other development issues be included in the bargaining agenda.

The events between April 1974 and April 1975 and the increasing isolation of the United States from Europe and Japan on Third World issues caused a reassessment of American policies toward OPEC and the developing countries. While that process was going on in late 1974 and early 1975, the developing countries, in particular many African countries, began to question the benefits to them from solidarity with OPEC. As we have seen, OPEC transfers have been highly concentrated and have not proved adequate to cover the increased oil payments by oil importing developing countries. The challenge to OPEC from within the group of developing countries, with the possibility of a positive developed-country response to Third World initiatives, combined with the repercussions of the industrial world's recession, led to the ascendance of a "moderate" group of developing-country representatives in the United Nations. They took the lead in responding constructively to the US initiatives made at the Seventh Special Session of the General Assembly in September 1975. The confrontational line taken by Algeria, which had dominated the alliance between the oil exporters and other developing countries, was replaced by a dialogue with the developed countries on specific measures to improve the export earnings and the growth prospects of developing countries. Shortly thereafter, agreement was reached to reconvene the producer/consumer forum as the Conference on International Economic Cooperation (CIEC). Guidelines for negotiations in this forum on energy, commodity policy, and development issues, and related financial questions between "North and South" were hammered out in Paris in mid-December 1975, a meeting which had echoes of the confrontation of 1974 and the conciliation of 1975.

The 10 percent rise in oil prices announced by OPEC in September 1975 was accommodated to by developed-country oil consumers grudgingly. Many developing countries expressed bitter dissatisfaction with the price rise and the restricted distribution of OPEC assistance. It was probably in reaction to this criticism that the OPEC countries decided to establish a fund to provide interest-free loans, an idea which had been proposed earlier. Almost $700 million of the $800-million total was pledged by Middle East members, with contributions ranging from Iran's $210 million to Qatar's $18 million. The fund would be used to replenish monetary reserves and to finance specific development projects.

US Initiatives

In the United States, Secretary of State Henry Kissinger's speech to the Seventh Special Session was presented by some administration figures as a form of low-cost international cooperation involving little budgetary allocations or adjustments in American trade policies or industrial structure. While acceptance, by the moderates among the group of developing countries, of the Kissinger initiatives as a basis for future talks may have given an impression that such a low-cost option would suffice to separate OPEC from other developing countries, and perhaps even divide the low-income from middle-income developing countries, that assumption was questionable at best. Divisions between OPEC and other Third World countries did not occur during the December CIEC discussions or at the Kingston IMF meeting in January 1976. Nor did they disrupt the Manila meeting of the Group of 77. Moreover, US positions which were interpreted as seeking to induce dissension proved counterproductive. Given the difficulties of implementing even modest US proposals, US capacity to use aid or trade policy initiatives to foster such a split is doubtful. Opposition within the United States to concessions on commodity policy and on other trade and investment issues, for example, would hamper efforts to pursue commodity-by-commodity negotiations. The US administration's intent to join the Tin Agreement faced opposition within the industry and within Congress. Failure by American negotiators to achieve US objectives in the Cocoa Agreement negotiations was caused in large part by inter-agency disputes which delayed formulation of US proposals.

Despite its halting progress toward a positive approach to the Third World, the United States finds itself in a leadership position among the developed countries as they deal with "North-South" issues. The weight of the US economy in the world system, the difficulties faced by the members of the European Communities in reaching common negotiating positions, and the reluctance of Japan to make proposals for multilateral action make it unlikely that significant accommodation of developed and developing-country positions can be effected without active US participation. European or Japanese initiatives, such as the Lomé Convention (which linked the European Community with forty-six African, Caribbean, and Pacific countries through a package of trade, aid, and technical assistance), may occur but they will remain limited in geographic and financial scope. Thus it remains to be seen whether the aid and trade measures promulgated by the developed countries will prove adequate to deliver on the promise of cooperation held out at the conclusion of the Seventh Special Session.

The Conference for International Economic Cooperation

This is the backdrop against which the current dialogue on resource transfers was taking place: a year of small incremental increases in funds from official sources with substantial cutbacks predicted from private flows; a heavily increased level of external indebtedness which could in many cases prove burdensome if export markets were not expansive and/or if funds to facilitate rollovers were limited; and lowered imports into the developing countries and interrupted rates of growth which could seriously impede the necessary process of adjustment to the changed energy picture.

It was not surprising that with problems looming on that scale the developing countries appeared unwilling to settle readily for marginal changes or minor adjustments of the existing structure. The scope of resource transfer which the developing world was bringing up for serious consideration goes far beyond the question of mobilizing 0.7 percent of the GNP of industrial countries to finance development projects. It cut across the established patterns of trade restriction, of technology transfer, of commodity pricing. It visualized change not as increased handouts but as a restructuring of the rules of the game. The developing countries were demanding equality of opportunity in the international economic arena.

Whether the Conference on International Economic Cooperation can move beyond dialogue to action in a larger framework remains to be seen. The role of OPEC in this process will depend on its own cohesion and on continued support by the non-oil developing world if it should again raise oil prices. It depends also on the extent to which OPEC oil can continue to exert leverage on the industrial world. The Third World reaffirmed its intention to use that leverage for all it is worth. As Venezuelan Minister for International Economic Affairs Manuel Perez Guerrero, who heads the developing-country side of the CIEC talks, put it:

> . . . we are going to use our energy bargaining power to obtain concessions from the west impossible until now. If the bridge we are building at the conference turns out to be made of words and delusions, we will not fall into the river alone, and the major countries have more to lose than we do.[1]

Whatever may lie in store in this arena, no amount of rhetoric or stonewalling was likely to lower the pressure for serious negotiations that the OPEC and other developing countries initiated. Nor would it be possible to return the world economy to its pre-OPEC structure. A process of adaptation to change began in the international system. The main questions have become for whom the changes will be made—for what countries, for which segments of their population—and over what period of time.

16 Changing Financial Institutions in the Arab Oil States

T. R. McHale

The Arab oil states are newcomers to the center of the international stage. Until well after World War II, Kuwayt, the United Arab Amirates, Qatar, Algeria, Iraq, and Libya were subject or client states of England and France with narrowly focused concern for independence. Following the October War, these states, along with the richest oil state, Saudi Arabia, collectively emerged as a major world financial power. Divided on many issues by ideological, confessional, and political values and often by local quarrels, the Arab oil states found unity in a shared Arab-Islamic identity and a common adversary relationship with major industrial oil-consuming states. Individually they also have a high vulnerability to external pressures and, with the exception of Kuwayt, low levels of material and social development.

The quantum jump in oil revenues accruing to the Arab oil states rapidly enlarged the available options in domestic, regional, and world politics and greatly enlarged the potential influence of existing governments. As an initial response to the new wealth, the individual Arab oil states committed massive sums to domestic development. Coincidentally, the conservative regimes of the Arab Gulf states undertook significant forward obligations of funds to stabilize or enhance their regional positions. Iraq stepped up its war against the separatist Kurdish minority, and Libya took to political adventure by financing multiplying radical groups and causes in many parts of the world.

Most dramatic and sustained was the intervention of the Arab Gulf states into the quarrel with Israel. As early as the summer of 1967, after the disaster in the June War, Saudi Arabia and Kuwayt pledged annual subventions to Egypt, Jordan, and Syria toward their postwar rehabilitation and to diplomatic efforts to regain possession of their lost territories. In fact, Egypt and Syria might never have been able to organize and pay for the October War without

Saudi monetary and diplomatic support. After the war the two oil states, joined by others, proved generous on an unprecedented scale. Nor had it been happenstance that the Palestine Resistance Movement originated in Kuwayt, where by the late 1950s the Palestine community was already firmly ensconced. Their numbers continued multiplying until by the mid-1970s they constituted probably more than one-fifth of the population. The oil-state support of Arab causes was not always coordinated. In Lebanon, the competition of the oil aiders reflected rival ideologies, to the organic impairment of the most sophisticated Arab state and the emergent financial capital of the Arab world.

The use of financial resources by the Arab oil states to support or promote political objectives seemed likely to spread. Their growing financing activities in Africa represented the first collective Arab move in this direction, and reflected the rise of financial power in the oil states and the erosion of European political and economic influence in postcolonial Africa. It also suggested a tentative financial strategy aimed at securing support among LDCs of the Fourth World for broad Arab objectives including, but not limited to, the Israel question.

The mounting wealth of the Arab oil states speedily gave rise to a proliferation of Arab-financed and controlled banks, funds, and foreign aid programs since 1973. The multiplying Arab financial institutions, however, were accompanied by overlapping functions and areas of interest, particularly in foreign aid where national and multinational Arab programs and projects were hastily framed with only scant knowledge of foreign operational environments. Major differences in short-term objectives among the Arab oil states also became apparent. Nevertheless, "Arabizing" the financial intermediaries through which the rapidly expanding wealth passed became a major long-term objective in all Arab states. Arab leaders came to recognize more and more that the identity of basic "shared goals" of the nascent institutions had to precede effective use of the latent power of Arab oil revenues.

The importance of financial institution building in the Arab states in the mid-1970s could be appreciated when placed in historical perspective. Until the end of World War II, the Arab world, with the exception of Saudi Arabia and Yemen, remained under imperial rule or political dominance. Economically poor and underdeveloped, the Arab countries, it was generally assumed in 1945, would continue as they had, serving as economic and political outposts of

European metropolises. At the same time, American-European ownership and development of the oil industry in the Arab states remained largely unchallenged. The concerned Arab countries had no voice in fixing world oil prices or the pace of oil exploration, field development, or production within their boundaries. This yielded dualistic economic development in most Arab oil areas, with dynamic Western owned and managed enclaves largely insulated against the traditional and slowly changing social and economic conditions of the local population.

As the Arab world progressively won political independence, significant shifts in internal economic policies and external relations followed. The effectiveness of the new policies varied from country to country as diverse ideologies, personalities, and aspirations competed for regional attention. But regardless of national purposes, all Arab states focused a growing attention on internal economic development and welfare. Simultaneously, they sought to enlarge their income from oil by bargaining individually and collectively for higher prices, as the companies expanded their oil output, in absolute terms and as a share of total world production.

The policies of the Arab oil states, aimed at economic growth to satisfy rising aspirations for material rewards, proved a necessary base for rapid development. Internal political unrest in several countries and financial constraints in most, inadequate planning, and a shortage of essential skills slowed down the pace of change. Yet the shift among Arab oil governments from a passive custodial role to a more active promotional role in domestic economic development became manifest by the early 1960s; the question of development was progressively focused on time frames rather than basic goals.

The relative importance of oil and oil income in the Arab world grew steadily in the 1960s after the rise of the Organization of Petroleum Exporting Countries (OPEC) and the Organization of Arab Petroleum Exporting Countries (OAPEC) as major bargaining entities. OPEC, formed in 1960, and OAPEC, in 1968, wrested more and more leverage in the international oil markets. By the end of the decade, oil had become the dominant source of government revenue and national income in Saudi Arabia, Kuwayt, the Trucial States (the United Arab Amirates from 1971), Iraq, Libya, and Qatar. No less important was the fact that the Arab oil states no longer depended on Western capital for exploration and development of their oil resources as increasing export earnings provided more than ample capital for new production facilities and exploration and development programs.

* * * *

Kuwayt played a unique role in the development of Arab financial institutions by initiating a variety of new financial intermediaries. It also provided examples of locally owned banks and funds which were effective at home and others which provided regional and international political leverage.

Kuwayt's leadership could be traced to historical circumstances. Kuwayt became sovereign in 1961 at a time when oil-generated income already exceeded the economy's limited absorptive capacity for domestic investment. With massive funds left over from domestic development, capital exports and foreign-aid programs constituted unplanned effects of sovereignty. Thus, the creation of the Kuwayt Fund for Arab Economic Development (KFAED) shortly after independence, manifested the financial capacity of Kuwayt to establish an aid program and the practical recognition that development aid could serve Kuwayt's political interests.

The growing potential of oil income as an influential factor in international politics was suggested in the Arab-Israel war of June 1967 by the first large-scale direct grant aid program for Egypt, Syria, and Jordan underwritten by Kuwayt, Saudi Arabia, and other Arab states. Publicly described as compensation for war damages and loss of revenue caused by the closure of the Suez Canal, the aid actually provided a major and widely recognized point of political leverage for the donors and diminished the influence of the concerned major powers.

Despite the expanding financial means and the new attitudes, the magnitude of funds, other than direct grants, moving from the Arab oil states through Arab institutions remained modest into the 1970s. The reason was obvious: most Arab states lacked national banking systems with domestically managed banks of issue or central banks and none had strong, domestically oriented, investment, merchant, and commercial banking structures. As a result, surplus investable funds from private and public sectors tended to flow to or through the American and European-dominated banks and other financial intermediaries to the established European-American financial markets. Although Iraq, Algeria, and Libya had nationalized their banking systems, they preserved external financial relationships with the same European-American financial institutions. This directed the flow of more and more funds into the Western dominated financial system.

Historical factors combined with the minuscule number of Arab financial intermediaries to handle the growing domestic wealth in the Arab oil states and to curtail Arab international economic influence. A long period of political and ideological fragmentation had left the Arab world a disparate group of states lacking a sense of cohesion on many key international issues and without a perception of collective Arab power. Internal economic development programs in the several Arab states moved slowly and without any serious attempts to rationalize or integrate such programs on the basis of common Arab aspirations. Cooperation within the Arab world was also inhibited by endemic suspicions fueled by widely recognized ideological, political, and confessional cleavages.

The relative efficiency of the Western banks and intermediaries in handling the financial needs and objectives of individual Arab oil states with despatch and confidentiality should also be mentioned. Over many years, the leadership in the oil-rich Arab states had developed close relationships with Western banks and depended on such banks in the complex area of international finance.

* * * *

The jump in oil prices in 1974 led to five-fold increases in Arab oil-state incomes. It also brought about the expectation of massive investable surpluses in the future and a dramatically changed view of the collective power position of the Arab oil states vis-à-vis the rest of the world.

The recognition by Arab governments that oil and oil income in 1974 represented a critically important international power lever was sudden; but the limits of oil weaponry without control of oil markets and without requisite financial institutions became apparent almost immediately. The role of appropriate institutions in the oil states was particularly clear in internal development where the restricted absorptive capacity proved as effective a deterrent as had lack of funds. The realization spread that money alone, even in unprecedentedly large amounts, could not secure the internal development and external leverage sought by the Arab states. The desire to translate latent influence into real influence stimulated the search for new appropriate financial intermediaries which might use the Arab resources for the perceived best interest of the Arab states. It also induced changes in existing Arab financial organizations.

As noted, internal economic development in non-oil sectors in the oil states was limited in size and location before 1974. The oil governments became preoccupied with military budgets and modest commitments to plan implementation, even where plans had already been framed. Several oil states created development funds, banks, or corporations to service internal requirements, but with a few exceptions they lacked the necessary staff, skills, leadership, and funding to play a primary role in the development process.

Suddenly awash with funds, the Arab oil governments discovered that their own peoples had speedily cultivated exaggerated expectations for rapid internal development at all levels. To meet the new set of circumstances, a number of new domestic banks and funds aimed at accelerating domestic investments soon emerged. At the same time, the government and the financial leaders adapted the goals and plans of existing development organizations to the new realities. The Saudi government, for example, greatly enlarged its Public Investment Fund and its potential scope of financing, with official capital commitments equal to the total value of existing industries at the time. It also formed new organizations and redirected existing ones. Of particular interest, it quickened internal development through the private sector by making available, for the first time, long-term investment capital.

The Public Investment Fund apart, domestic development in Saudi Arabia by 1976 was being supported or promoted by an increasing range of functionally specific government-financed development funds or banks. These included:

1. The Saudi Industrial Development Fund: Started in 1974, it had an initial capitalization of 500 million Saudi riyals (US $150 million), with immediate access to additional funds from the government as needed. The fund sought to encourage private sector development by offering medium or longer term interest-free loans to Saudi enterprises for opening or expanding business firms. Its charter also permitted loans to joint foreign-Saudi enterprises so long as Saudi participation exceeded 25 percent.

2. The Contractors Financing Program: Also begun in 1974, the program furnished interest-free medium-term loans to Saudi contractors to cover the cost of buying construction machinery and equipment. The capital resources of the program came from direct government budgetary allotments as required.

3. The Real Estate Development Fund: Set up in 1974, this fund issued interest-free loans to Saudis up to 70 percent of the cost of land and building for personal occupancy. It also financed, on the same terms, up to 50 percent of the cost of buildings used as investments. Essentially, the fund made available to every Saudi the money to build a new home and to move into the development of investment properties.

4. The Saudi Arabia Agricultural Bank: Created in 1962, the bank was authorized to offer or guarantee loans from other sources in all aspects of agricultural financing within the kingdom. The capital of the bank was quickly enlarged to meet the needs of any Saudi agricultural operation with full access to credit for any legitimate requirement.

The Saudi Arab pattern of institutionalizing internal development financing by the creation of a growing range of new specialized organizations had parallels in the other Arab oil states. The differences for the most part related to size or forms appropriate to the ideology of the government. Coincident with the move to institutionalization after 1973, the Arab oil states also expanded their direct budgetary commitments to roads, ports, education, hospitals, and social services. Most observers felt that such infrastructural commitments erred on the side of duplication rather than undercommitment of funds.

The changing organizational approaches of the Arab oil governments for the handling of funds for internal development after the 1973 war was paralleled by a major attempt to institutionalize external development aid. The Kuwayt Fund for Arab Economic Development (KFAED) which had operated quietly but effectively since its creation in 1961, was relatively unknown outside the Middle East and parts of Africa. Two years after the October War, the number and size of the Arab development aid institutions had expanded to a position of major international importance. The growth in the size of Arab development aid funds and the shifting focus of such aid has taken many forms.

In 1974 the Kuwayt National Assembly increased KFAED's capitalization five-fold to US $3.5 billion. The Assembly also amended the functions of the fund to encompass the entire less developed world. By early 1975, KFAED was lending to a growing number of non-Arab states on the basis of concessionary loan policies including longer maturities, long periods of grace on repayments, and low-interest levels. The fund also began to assimilate the cost of feasibility studies.

Other Arab oil states followed Kuwayt's example in finding funds for channeling development aid abroad. The largest, as one might expect, was the Saudi Development Fund. Organized in 1974 with an initial capitalization of 10.0 billion Saudi riyals (US $2.9 billion), the Saudi Development Fund had access to capital increases as needed to finance development projects in the Fourth World. Development aid was to be given on the basis of flexible conditions which were expected to be highly concessionary. Among the other Arab external development funds were the Abu Dhabi Fund for Arab Economic Development, the Iraq Fund for External Development, and the Libyan Arab Foreign Bank. Varying in scope and resources, the funds share the common objective of promoting development in the LDCs through long-term, low-interest rate lending. Oil-dry Arab countries were the principal beneficiaries, followed by Islamic states, and finally the remaining LDCs.

Shortages of skills and experience hampered most aid organizations, and many of the new Arab banks and funds were struggling with recruitment and building problems. Nevertheless, a beginning was made. Such funds have financed major projects, including the Suez-Mediterranean oil pipeline in Egypt, hotels and roads in Jordan, power plants and factories in Syria, sugar mills in Sudan, irrigation projects in Yemen, textile plants in Morocco, and agricultural equipment factories in Bangladesh. A wider range of projects in Africa and Asia has been under review.

The Arab oil states also participated in multinational Arab financial organizations. Most of these were area or functionally specific and represented a new dimension of financial power with a political and economic potential of major proportions. In 1971, on the recommendation of Kuwayt, the formation of an Arab Funds for Economic and Social Development (AFESD) was initiated. Operations of the fund, patterned after the KFESD, began in 1973 with an initial capitalization of US $338 million contributed by sixteen Arab states. Kuwayt, Saudi Arabia, and the United Arab Amirates furnished over half the fund's initial capital; early in 1976 they took the lead in expanding the capital base to $1.38 billion.

As shown in Table 1 (p. 240), the AFESD granted loans to eighteen projects in nine Arab countries with aggregate commitments of $321.5 million by the end of 1975. Of particular significance in 1975 was the negotiation of two major loan commitments. By the use of international co-financing and loan guarantees for the Talkha II fertilizer project in Egypt and the new Arzew port development project in Algeria, the fund organized credit many times its own direct contribution. The AFESD expected to double its loan commitments in 1976 and possibly expand its activities to several non-Arab states in Africa and Asia. It also hoped to use its resources as seed money wherever possible.

Another multinational investment firm, formed in Saudi Arabia in 1974, was the Arab Investment Company (AIC). Initially capitalized at US $200 million, later enlarged to US $250 million, the company's founding members included Saudi Arabia, Kuwayt, Abu Dhabi, Qatar, and Bahrayn. The first three states put up most of the capital; Syria, Iraq, and Jordan joined the consortium in 1975. In its first year, AIC issued loans in Sudan, Jordan, and Syria. The most significant characteristic of the Arab Investment Company was a profit-oriented, private sector focus despite exclusive government funding. The Gulf International Bank, established in 1975, was yet another multinational Arab bank. Founded by Kuwayt, Saudi Arabia, Bahrayn, Qatar, the United Arab Amirates, and 'Uman under Kuwayt's leadership, the bank avowed the objectives of replacing non-Arab financial intermediaries in the area whenever possible. The Gulf Bank planned to operate in the merchant banking field and to service private as well as public-sector Arab interests. The founding governments furnished the initial subscribed capitalization of US $102 million.

Also set up in 1975, after more than a year of study and discussion, was the Arab Petroleum Investment Company (APIC). With an authorized capitalization of US $1,014 million, APIC was financed by all the members of OAPEC, but with 51 percent of the capitalization coming from Saudi Arabia, Kuwayt, and the United Arab Amirates. Headquartered in Damman, Saudi Arabia, APIC was

Table 1

AFESD PROJECT LOANS TO DATE
(million Kuwayti Dinars)

Country	Project	Project Cost	Amount of Loan	Date of Agreement	Type of Loan*	Interest Rate
South Yemen	Mukalla Multipurpose	5.1	3.2	7 Feb. 1974	Special	4%
Syria	Fuel Storage Tanks	10.6	2.0	"	Standard	6%
Tunisia	Electric Power	2.7	2.0	"	"	6%
Egypt	Talkha II Fertilizer Plant	37.9	6.5	13 April 1974	"	6%
Algeria	New Arzaw Port	84.4	6.0	"	"	6%
Sudan	Gadaref-Kassala Highway	15.0	8.0	"	Special	4%
North Yemen	Electric Power	6.0	4.0	12 Dec. 1974	"	4%
Syria	Ghab Cattle Breeding	10.7	5.4	22 Dec. 1974	Standard	6%
Sudan	Telecommunications	7.7	4.8	28 Jan. 1975	Special	4%
Algeria-Morocco	Telecommunications	7.2	3.3	"	Standard	6%
Egypt	Turah Cement	27.7	6.7	13 April 1975	"	6%
Jordan	'Amman Northern Approach	8.0	5.0	14 Aug. 1975	"	6%
North Yemen	Hudaydah Water and Sewerage	9.2	6.0	"	Special	4%
South Yemen	Aden Port Rehabilitation	5.0	3.9	"	"	4%
Sudan	al-Rahad Roads	6.7	4.4	13 Nov. 1975	"	4%
Tunisia	al-Borma Gas	6.4	4.0	"	Standard	6%
Egypt	Fustat Water Supply (Cairo)	23.5	9.7	31 Dec. 1975	"	6%
Egypt	Hilwan Sewerage (Cairo)	18.3	8.3	"	"	6%
	Total	292.1	93.2			

* The allocation of development assistance funds and interest rates are based on a country's need, per capita income, national priorities, and national and regional impact. Standard concessionary loans a 6% interest, with 5 years' grace and 15-year repayment period. Special concessionary loans carry a 4% interest, with 5 years' grace and a 15-year repayment period.

Source:
Middle East Economic Survey, 6 February 1976

designed to function as a full service investment bank for all the Arab oil producers.

Perhaps the most interesting multinational financial intermediary in the Arabian oil states is the Islamic Development Bank. Formed in 1974 with an authorized capital of US $2.4 billion, the bank has, as its objective, the fostering of economic and social progress in the twenty-seven Muslim states making up its membership and in other areas where there are established Muslim communities. The main office of the bank is located in Saudi Arabia; it was financed primarily by Saudi Arabia and other Arab oil states.

* * * *

The Arab oil states, for many reasons, have shown particular interest in Black Africa. Oil politics was exemplified in this area as early as the end of the 1960s when an increasing number of African states broke relations with Israel for reasons not unrelated to promises of financial aid. The first Arab financial institution to center its activities in Africa was the Afro-Arab Company for Investment and International Trade (AFARCO), a subsidiary of the government-owned Kuwayt Foreign Trading, Contracting, and Investment Company (KFTCIC). Started in 1972, AFARCO created a branch office in Nairobi. AFARCO invests in the public and private sectors in the form of equity participation or direct loans. Where capital was not forthcoming for projects deemed worthwhile, AFARCO sought concessionary funds, usually through the Arab-African Bank, the Libyan-Arab Foreign Bank, or from its parent, the Kuwayt Foreign Trading, Contracting, and Investment Company. The scope of AFARCO financing may be seen in a list of projects for which it had provided or committed at least partial financing up to January 1975 (Table 2, p. 242).

On the outbreak of the 1973 war, promises of oil supplies and financial assistance for development were key considerations in the severance of diplomatic relations between almost all members of the Organization of African Unity and the state of Israel; the expectations of favorable treatment of African states were openly discussed in an Afro-Arab meeting early in 1974. The conferees explored two-tier oil pricing to permit African states to buy oil at a large discount or receive oil at nominal prices but with long-term credits and an acceleration of development aid. No agreements were recorded, but general promises were made to work through three organizations which had been proposed in an Arab Summit meeting in Algeria immediately preceding the Afro-Arab meetings.

Table 2

LIST OF PROJECTS SUPPORTED BY AFARCO, 1972-JANUARY 1975

Country	Project	AFARCO Direct Contribution	
Chad	General Assembly Building	KD.	237,500
Uganda	Tannery Factory	U.S. $	600,000
Mauritania	Housing Project	£ Sterling	600,000
Cameroon	Timber	U.S. $	500,000
Gabon	Construction	U.S. $	2 million in principal
Senegal	Construction	KD.	200,000
Togo	Fertilizer Project	U.S. $	30,000

Source:
Middle East Economic Survey, 6 February 1976

The first of the new agencies was the Arab Fund for Loans to African Countries (AFLAC). AFLAC's stated purpose was to "finance oil imports, develop indigenous oil resources in Africa, and to compensate African countries for economic losses suffered as a result of breaking relations with Israel." Saudi Arabia, Kuwayt, Iraq, the United Arab Amirates, Qatar, and 'Uman provided the initial US $200-million financing for the fund. The announced terms of loans were highly concessionary: 1 percent interest repayable in twenty-five years with a ten-year grace period. By early 1975, nineteen African countries had availed themselves of the loan facilities (Table 3) and capital commitments to the fund were to be doubled to ensure continued operations. The Arab Bank for Economic Development in Africa, based in Khartum, was financed by Saudi Arabia, Kuwayt, Algeria, the United Arab Amirates, and Qatar with an initial capital of US $231 million. The bank's exclusive aim was announced as development assistance to those African countries which had provided political support for the "Arab cause." Yet another was the Arab Fund for Technical Aid to Africa, initially capitalized at US $25 million and administered by the secretariat of the Arab League. Financed primarily by OAPEC, the fund finances technical training in preparation for large-scale social or educational projects in African countries friendly to the Arab cause.

We have so far examined changes in financial institutions as they relate to internal development and external aid. However, direct commitments of funds have also played significant roles in these

Table 3

DISBURSEMENTS BY AFLAC, 13 OCTOBER 1974 - 25 JANUARY 1975
(US $ million)

Country	Date (First Instalment)	Amount	Date (Second Instalment)	Amount
Uganda	13 October 1974	5.65	20 January 1975	5.65
Liberia	17 October 1974	1.8		1.8
Tanzania	17 October 1974	7.1		7.1
Gambia	24 October 1974	0.35		0.35
Mali	28 October 1974	3.9		3.9
Rwanda	3 November 1974	1.0		1.0
Chad	6 November 1974	4.4		4.4
Equatorial Guinea	10 November 1974	0.25		0.25
Madagascar	18 November 1974	2.4		2.4
Central Africa Rep.	20 November 1974	1.2	25 January 1975	1.2
Guinea Bisau	2 December 1974	0.25		0.25
Burundi	3 December 1974	1.0		1.0
Sierra Leone	7 December 1974	1.8		1.8
Lesotho	17 December 1974	1.4		1.4
Dahomey	17 December 1974	1.2		1.2
Zambia	28 December 1974	6.35		6.35
Senegal	15 January 1975	3.75		3.75
Kenya	23 January 1975	1.8		1.8
Ethiopia	25 January 1975	7.1		7.1

Source:
Frank A. Mwine. Arab Economic Aid to Africa. Kuwayt: Fund for Arab Economic Development, 1975

areas. The vast expansion of budgetary commitments to internal development has already been noted. Direct aid grants and loans from Saudi Arabia, Kuwayt, the United Arab Amirates, and other Arab oil states were known to have been massive, but the nature and specific recipients of military or paramilitary support were frequently unclear. Specific nonmilitary direct grants have also been made from time to time, but usually to fellow Arab countries or those in nearby Africa. 'Uman, Yemen, Chad, Sudan, Mauritania, and Uganda have been among the recipients.

The rapid growth of Arab financial influence has been derived from the growing wealth of the Arab oil states, each with its own internal politics and external perception of the rest of the world. In a move to integrate the Arabization of financial and political influence in the Arab world, the initial steps toward the establishment of an Arab Monetary Fund (AMF) were taken. The sponsors of the fund expect it to become operational by 1977. The idea of the Arab Monetary Fund originated in a meeting of the governors of Arab central banks in Casablanca, Morocco, in 1974. At a second meeting in November 1975, also in Casablanca, a formal resolution endorsed articles of agreement for an Arab Monetary Fund. A later meeting in Damascus in December approved the articles. The immediate objectives of the Arab Monetary Fund as set forth in the articles were: (1) the adjustment of the disequilibrium in the balance of payments of member Arab countries; (2) the establishment of a common Arab position on international monetary and economic problems; and (3) the "political" placement of reserves of member countries with the view of preserving or increasing their real value.

In the long term, AMF sought to: (1) integrate on a sound basis the monetary bases of complementary economies and ensure equal development of member countries; (2) stabilize the external value of the currency of member countries so as to maintain convertibility; (3) work toward the abolition of all laws and regulations which prevent the free movement of capital between Arab countries; and (4) harmonize Arab state monetary policies toward the rest of the world.

The AMF was expected to grant short and medium credit facilities to member countries on advantageous terms for the accomplishment of its objectives. It was also intended to coordinate development objectives in the Arab countries and furnish guidance to aid programs sponsored by Arab institutions in other parts of the world. The initial size and the individual subscriptions of the member Arab countries have not yet been decided, but it was clear that the Arab oil states would make available the bulk of its operating capital and that with potential massive resources it was likely to have a major influence on the world monetary order.

The increasing wealth of the oil states after October 1973 has dramatically altered the relations among the Arab states and between them as a group and the rest of the world. These have been changes in form and substance, but the long-term political dimensions, largely untested by a major crisis, remain unclear. What was uncontested was the attempt to build Arab institutions, or Arabize existing ones, as a means of securing more effective use of the large financial resources available to the Arab world.

Institutions cannot be created overnight, and much of what happened in the flush of the oil bonanza was greater in promise than in immediate impact. Yet, the Arab financial framework being erected should make possible major shifts in internal and external economic relations, and it should provide a major new point of political leverage in the world. The monumental sums committed to internal development and external aid was of particular significance. In Saudi Arabia, for example, proposed annual "development" expenditures were over five times the kingdom's entire GNP in the early 1970s; the same magnitude of internal development committed may also be found in the United Arab Amirates. In external aid, the committed capital resources of several Arab funds were significantly larger than those of such major international development institutions as the Asian Development Bank, the Inter-American Development Bank, and the Banque Africaine de Développement. And, in the aggregate, Arab international development institutions exceed the original $10-billion authorized capitalization of the World Bank. A direct comparison of the capitalization alone is meaningless, but the size of Arab commitments and its potential are basic facts of international finance and international relations.

17 The International Energy Agency: The Political Context

Wilfrid L. Kohl

Following a period of Western alliance disarray and nationalistic policy responses in the wake of the 1973 Arab oil embargo, the industrial oil-consuming countries pulled themselves together and agreed to establish what was essentially a new "Atlantic" organization, the International Energy Agency (IEA). According to its proponents, the IEA was an act of creative American leadership, perhaps equivalent to the Marshall Plan, aimed at reshaping Western energy policies, reducing dependence on OPEC, and preventing the spread of economic dislocations in the West. Critics contended, on the other hand, that the IEA was mainly a political device to exploit a new area of West European vulnerability and perpetuate American hegemony on the Continent through the creation of a kind of "economic NATO." Moreover, many have seen it as a counter-cartel or confrontational bloc, reducing rather than increasing the chances of future agreements between consumer and producer countries on oil prices and access to supplies.

This chapter attempts to throw light on this controversy. It will first review the international political context of 1973-74 from which the IEA emerged. The purposes and achievements of the new agency will be examined and assessed against a background of changes in the North-South context of the IEA since 1974 and in West European views. Finally, it will seek to probe the effects of the energy issue in general and the IEA in particular on US-West European relations.

Origins of the IEA—an American Initiative

The months immediately following the October 1973 Middle East war and Arab oil embargo were characterized by a breakdown of the European Economic Community (EEC) and Western Alliance cooperation.[1] Moved by their considerable dependence on external, especially Middle East, oil supplies, which made them highly vulnerable to Arab control of supplies and price increases, the key West European countries resorted to nationalistic, bilateral diplomacy—a *sauve qui peut* approach—to shore up their situation. The Netherlands, the one European country subjected to an embargo, appealed to the European Community to share available oil equitably among all member countries but received no help. France and Great Britain dispatched a series of bilateral missions to the Middle East to cultivate relations with the Arabs and swap arms and industrial products for oil. The one common action the EC countries did take, the signing of the pro-Arab resolution of 6 November calling on Israel to give up its occupied territories, severely irritated the United States, which had not been consulted and whose secretary of state was deeply engaged in efforts to try to mediate the Arab-Israel dispute and prevent any further extension of Soviet influence in the area. Transatlantic tension also resulted when the United States, fearing Soviet intervention in the Middle East, informed but did not consult its European NATO allies of a global US military alert in October and subsequently took steps to resupply Israel from European (especially West German) NATO bases.

Haunted by the specter of Western alliance disintegration, a possible West European "tilt" toward the Arabs, and the need to deal with the embargo and increasing oil prices, Secretary of State Henry Kissinger in his speech to the Pilgrims Society in London in December 1973 proposed that the countries of North America, Europe, and Japan form an Energy Action Group and develop plans for collaboration in all areas of the energy problem with the objective of assuring required energy supplies at reasonable cost. A short time later, in February 1974, the United States convened the Washington Energy Conference of consumer countries, which produced an ambitious communiqué calling for a comprehensive action program to conserve energy and develop new energy sources, prepare emergency oil allocation plans for future oil crises, and launch collaborative research and development efforts. There was also a pledge to avoid competitive depreciations or new trade restrictions and to seek new credit facilities to ease the balance of payments impact of higher oil prices. But the real accomplishment of the conference was the establishment of the Energy Coordinating Group (ECG) headed by senior officials from all key consumer countries (except France) to take steps to implement the action program. Working intensively through the spring and summer of 1974 under co-chairmen Thomas

Enders, US assistant secretary of state for economic affairs, and Vicomte Etienne Davignon, political director of the Belgian Foreign Office, the ECG produced in the early autumn the "Agreement on an International Energy Program." That document became the foundation of the new International Energy Agency, formed in November and linked to the OECD.

Just as the United States had convened the Washington Energy Conference, it also dominated the staff work of the ECG. Why did the United States, a country potentially almost self-sufficient in energy resources, take the lead in proposing a new international agency for energy cooperation against the threat of the OPEC cartel? It appears that the United States did so mainly in pursuit of a number of foreign policy or diplomatic goals. Secretary Kissinger wanted to prevent the West Europeans from taking sides with the Arabs, an eventuality that could have had serious negative consequences for his Middle East peace negotiations. Moreover, Kissinger saw the need to establish a consumer country solidarity and to take certain protective measures to reduce dependence on Middle East oil before trying to persuade or force OPEC to reduce oil prices. The Secretary was also worried about the disruptive effects of higher oil prices on Western economies, which might turn countries inward and threaten what was left of the postwar liberal international economic order. And finally, the energy issue came along just as the United States was having difficulty in reasserting its leadership in the "Year of Europe" exercise. Clearly exploiting Europe's new vulnerability and relative American strength, the United States saw an opportunity to revive Atlantic solidarity and reassert US influence through the IEA, which made America, in effect, a guarantor of Western Alliance economic security.

Western European attitudes toward the American initiative were mixed. At the Washington Energy Conference, France openly refused to participate in the ECG. Led by its outspoken Foreign Minister Michel Jobert, the French opposed the formation of a closed consumer bloc that might foster confrontation between oil-consuming and oil-producing countries. A number of its European partners were also wary on this point, but Jobert's principal concern seemed to be the rejection of what he saw as a new Atlantic structure designed to link French and European economic security to the United States, thus opening the way for renewed American hegemony over the Continent.

Recognizing that so far the EC had not produced an effective energy policy, the other members of the Community led by West Germany decided to join the American initiative. As Henri Simonet, the EC commission vice president, later explained:

> The political motive behind the decision of the member states of the Community to accede to the IEA lies in the realization of their predicament. Faced with the success of the organization of the oil-producing countries in establishing a cartel for a commodity, the vital character of which was forcibly demonstrated by the embargo and ensuing price boosts, they concluded that the only safe course was to rally behind the United States in the latter's bid to build up a countervailing power to OPEC. In doing this, they expressed their preference for the American strategy over the French strategy of shunning any formal agreement among the industrialized countries.[2]

However, a short time thereafter, the members of the EC called for an organized Euro-Arab dialogue as well.

What Is the International Energy Agency?

The IEA has a governing board chaired by Ambassador Etienne Davignon of Belgium and composed of ministers or their delegates from each of the eighteen member countries. Voting in the governing board takes place under a weighted voting scheme, taking into account a country's oil consumption. Neither the United States nor any other single country has veto power. A secretariat housed within the OECD in Paris is directed by Dr. Ulf Lantzke of West Germany. There is a management committee of senior representatives from each participating country and standing groups on each of the four areas of concern of the agency: emergency questions, the oil market, long term cooperation, and relations with producer and other consumer countries. Of the eighteen countries that signed the agreement, thirteen had taken the necessary formal steps to ratify it by early 1976. The other countries were expected to ratify shortly thereafter.

The heart of the IEA was an oil allocation scheme in case of a new oil embargo. Members were committed to stockpile oil supplies sufficient to sustain consumption for sixty days with no net oil imports (later increased to ninety days). They were also to prepare contingent oil demand restraint measures which could be activated in an emergency to reduce consumption. In the event of a cutoff of oil supplies to any one or more member countries, the other members agreed to share the burden. There was an automatic procedure under which emergency oil allocation and demand restraint measures would take effect whenever one or more of the members sustained, or was about to sustain, a 7 percent reduction in its oil supplies. If a country was affected, it must first reduce its own consumption by 7 percent. Any additional shortfall would be made up by the other members, according to a predetermined formula, from their own consumption or emergency reserves. If the cut in supplies becomes so severe as to use up half or more of the emergency reserves of the member countries, new measures would be proposed by the governing board. Emergency procedures were to be effected in cooperation with the oil companies.[3]

Other activities of the IEA included the gathering of information on and the monitoring of the international oil market within a framework of consultation with the oil companies. The IEA also developed a long term program of energy cooperation, including research and development, while seeking ways to foster cooperation with oil producers and with other oil consuming countries in the North-South dialogue.

France refused to join the IEA even under the government of President Valéry Giscard d'Estaing, although the latter agreed in his summit meeting with US President Gerald Ford in December 1974 at Martinique not to oppose the IEA, with which it would maintain some kind of liaison (a situation somewhat analagous to the French relationship with NATO), and to work with the United States and other consumer countries in the development of new energy sources. Since then, however, the members of the European Community have been consulting among themselves before taking positions within the IEA (i.e., on the floor price issue). The EC sits in the IEA as an observer, but with the right to state its views. Thus, through these mechanisms France has in effect been playing a role in IEA decisions. In early 1975 the French did join the IEA-related $25-billion safety net proposed by Secretary of State Kissinger to alleviate oil-payment deficits among the industrial countries.

Alongside the emergency oil sharing scheme, the second principal accomplishment of the IEA was the Long Term Energy Program adopted in January 1976. The purpose of this program was to encourage consumer countries to reduce excessive dependence on imported energy, thereby diminishing their vulnerability to a future OPEC embargo and price rises. The heart of the program was the Minimum Safeguard Price (MSP) for oil set at $7 a barrel FOB Persian Gulf (i.e., a price of about $7.60 for Rotterdam and $8.25 in the United States), which would protect investments in North Sea and North Alaskan slope oil and some conventional alternative energy sources such as coal and nuclear. Following a year of considerable debate and opposition by many of the energy-poor European countries, the MSP was supposed to protect against future OPEC oil dumping when the price declined. But in reality the price would likely remain well above that level until sometime in the 1980s.

The other parts of the Long Term Energy Program included a framework to facilitate joint investment projects in domestic energy sources and research and the development of alternative sources. The framework would permit the drawing together of technology, capital, and manpower from two or more IEA countries. There was also a commitment to develop non-discrimination procedures as regards access to energy technology, investment opportunities, and production, especially for countries taking part in joint development projects but also for other IEA countries. Targets and regular reviews were set for accelerated national energy production in the member countries. There was also a commitment to foster greater energy conservation efforts, including the setting of targets and the regularizing of the notion of an energy report card. This Long Term Energy Program took about a year to negotiate.[4] The way in which it was implemented would determine whether the IEA would have a real effect on the reshaping of domestic energy policies of the consumer countries.

Changes in the North-South Context and European Views of the IEA

In 1974 there was considerable difference of view between the United States and its West European allies, of which France was the most outspoken, on how to deal with the oil cartel. The United States, thinking that OPEC would soon break down, sought to apply maximum pressure; this was a major reason for forming the IEA. Washington wanted to postpone as long as possible any consumer-producer conference until a solid consumer bloc had been organized. Much more sanguine about OPEC's survival prospects, France and the other West Europeans resisted the notion of confrontation and supported the initiation of conciliatory consumer-producer dialogue. The Martinique compromise in December 1974, whereby the United States agreed to take part in an early consumer-producer conference if consuming countries coordinated their position in advance, set the stage for resolving the remaining differences in 1975. After the abortive Paris Preparatory Conference in April, the United States changed its position on OPEC and other North-South issues and essentially accepted the European analysis.[5]

The April Preparatory Conference failed to reach an agreement when, led by Algeria, the OPEC countries and several less developed countries insisted that the agenda be broadened to include, in addition to energy, other issues of concern to the Third World, such as raw materials and commodity prices, aid, technology transfer, and international monetary reform. What occurred was an intersection of the oil and energy issues with Third World demands for a New International Economic Order, as some OPEC countries attempted to assume the role of champions of the poorer countries. The industrial countries—led by the United States—refused to accept a broadened agenda, and the Preparatory Conference failed.

Shortly thereafter, the United States began to adopt a more conciliatory stance toward the Third World. Looking ahead to the Seventh Special Session of the United Nations General Assembly in the fall, Secretary Kissinger was persuaded that, in order to retain some moral leadership, the United States needed to change the tone and some of the substance of its policy on North-South issues.

Several factors explain the American willingness to participate in North-South dialogue. During early 1975, pressure was apparently exerted on the United States by a number of European countries. After the EC signed the Lomé Convention, which considerably liberalized its trading relations with the countries of Africa, the Caribbean, and the Pacific, France and Great Britain quietly told Washington that American policy toward the Third World was too obstructionist. Moreover, it was clear that the hard line American strategy had not succeeded in weakening or destroying OPEC, which remained an effective and more or less cohesive cartel. Thus, the way was open for a different, less confrontational approach. The arrival at the State Department of Undersecretary of State Charles Robinson, a man with views quite different from those of Thomas Enders, the architect of the earlier hard line strategy, coincided with the need for a new American approach. Robinson seized the initiative and played a major role in preparing Kissinger's September UN speech, which put forward new American proposals to grant trade preference to LDC tropical products and other commodities, to support the establishment of a special $10 billion IMF lending facility and an international investment trust under the World Bank, and to discuss the formation of international institutes for energy, technology, and industrial development for the LDCs.

Linked to the more positive American stance on North-South issues was a new American readiness to participate in a multilateral North-South conference. An American proposal that the conference set up three (later changed to four) commissions—on energy, raw materials, development, and finance—and a more successful preparatory meeting in October, opened the way for the convening of the Conference on International Economic Cooperation (CIEC) in Paris at the end of the year. Long urged by the West Europeans, the conference set up a framework for discussions and negotiations that could last for several years. With twenty-seven countries participating, it was hoped that the CIEC would provide a concrete forum for dialogue with the oil-producing countries on issues of oil prices and supply and for discussion with other Third World countries of concrete measures to improve their position in the international economic order. The United States was most interested in the energy commission, whose work would lead to more stable relationships between oil-consuming and oil-producing countries. But Washington also saw an opportunity in the CIEC for trying to divide the oil-producing countries from the poorer LDCs and to enlist more financial support from the oil countries for Third World development.

With the opening of the North-South dialogue on energy and other issues, the confrontational edge of the IEA, previously distasteful to many Europeans, had been removed. As the work of the four commissions of the CIEC got under way, the IEA was used as an important mechanism to coordinate the positions of the industrial countries, especially prior to the meetings of the Energy Commission. The IEA secretariat helped prepare the work of that commission, which the IEA had been invited to join as an observer. The stage was set for an institutionalized role for the IEA as the North-South dialogue unfolded.

This change in the North-South context was undoubtedly important in obtaining increased West European support for the IEA, especially its Long Term Program. After more than a year of controversy, it was notable that European IEA members agreed on the Minimum Safeguard Price and other issues. European countries were interested in different parts of the Long Term Program. For example, Great Britain vigorously supported the floor price to protect its future North Sea oil investments; Italy was most interested in access to American nuclear technology for its ambitious reactor program. If the IEA proves to be an effective mechanism for diplomatic coordination in the North-South dialogue, this factor may be expected to strengthen West European commitment to the implementation of the IEA Long Term Program.

It is important to note, however, that the European Community and several of its member states have hedged their bets in international energy policy, even though they have strengthened their support of the IEA. After a number of problems and false starts, notably what to do about the Palestine Liberation Organization (PLO), the Euro-Arab dialogue slowly began to get under way. The declared objective was West European technical assistance to help the Arab world industrialize and the forging of political links. It remains to be seen how much progress can be made within this framework or whether the talks will be stalemated by Arab requests for EC trade preferences or other political questions. On the bilateral level, there have been only a few agreements, notably by France and Italy, on oil access with the oil-producing states. But trade and investment relationships between the European and the producer countries have been growing. The EC Mediterranean policy reinforced this trend toward the formation of a European-Mediterranean-Middle East economic bloc, involving investments, technological assistance, and market access, which could not but help ensure future oil supplies.[6] Just how important this trend will be is as yet uncertain since the United States is also developing bilateral trade and investment relationships with oil producers, notably Iran and Saudi Arabia, and in many areas has more to offer than do the West Europeans.

The IEA and Its Impact on US-West European Relations: a Preliminary Assessment

In retrospect, there seems little doubt that as a foreign policy initiative the establishment of the IEA was an act of creative American leadership. As a framework for consumer cooperation and emergency oil sharing in case of a new embargo, the IEA is an element on the international scene which OPEC will have to take into account. Moreover, its formation helped to prevent Western alliance disintegration and economic nationalism in the wake of the oil crisis and helped to reinstate Atlantic solidarity around an important new project. Furthermore, the basis of the IEA, the "Agreement on an International Energy Program," was negotiated with considerable diplomatic skill and in a remarkably short time—less than a year. The initial confrontational aspect of the agency as a kind of counter cartel to pressure OPEC was less prudent and potentially dangerous. But this factor was modified with the change in the American position and the opening of a North-South dialogue in which the IEA was destined to play an important role.

As an international initiative in energy policy, on the other hand, the balance sheet of the IEA was less clear at this writing. On the positive side, the setting in place of an emergency oil sharing scheme was an important achievement, especially in an international context of continuing tension in the Middle East which could again erupt into open conflict, perhaps leading to another oil embargo. The oil allocation plan that would automatically go into effect does provide a kind of insurance policy to the Western consumer countries. But to be judged effective in helping to solve the remaining international energy problem, the IEA must meet the following two criteria: First, it must promote in concrete ways the revamping of the domestic energy policies of the consumer countries through increased conservation and the development of new energy sources, thereby reducing their dependence on imported oil. Second, the IEA will have to demonstrate diplomatic accomplishments in the North-South dialogue, leading eventually to a reduction in oil prices and / or accords on future access to oil supplies.

On both of these points the IEA has yet to prove its effectiveness. Its impact on the recasting of domestic energy policies has been limited, not the least in the case of the United States where, despite the passage of the Energy Policy and Conservation Act of 1975, much of the work of defining a national energy policy still lies ahead. The hopes of the IEA in this area are tied to the new Long Term Co-operation Program, a program which provides a promising framework for future cooperation on conservation and the development of new energy sources. But everything will depend on whether and how the program is implemented. As a mechanism for coordinating consumer country positions in the CIEC, the IEA has apparently made a reasonably good start. But only the future will tell whether the CIEC can yield concrete results.

What are the likely longer term effects of the "energy crisis" and the establishment of the International Energy Agency on the Western Alliance, i.e., on the US-West European relationship? It seems clear that the energy issue has underscored Western Europe's vulnerability, undermining any putative future power role for the European Community on the international scene. Unlike the United States, Western Europe cannot be self-sufficient—even potentially—in energy; it can only seek to reduce the level of its dependence. As a result, the structural asymmetry of the Atlantic relationship has been further unbalanced to the US advantage by the energy problem. Moreover, in military and diplomatic terms, America remains the only Western power apparently capable of using its influence to bring about a Middle East peace settlement, although the prospects for such a settlement seem remote.

Possibly counteracting this factor of structural asymmetry, however, may be the constantly growing American dependence on oil imports, approximately 40 percent of total oil consumption, coupled with the great difficulty the United States has been having in achieving a domestic consensus on energy policy. Although the European Community has also been having difficulty in forging a common energy policy, hampered by different member country energy endowments and different national approaches to regulating the oil market, there have been some signs that Western Europe may be making more rapid progress in this area than the United States. In 1974 the EC was able to establish a Community Loan System, and in 1976 it has been moving toward a Community accord on a minimum oil safeguard price to be linked with the IEA. Moreover, the Community has been negotiating more as a unit with the IEA and in the CIEC. And in a number of individual countries, national energy policies have made important significant gains, notably in the area of conservation.[7]

In conclusion, the European Community seems to be overcoming its initial paralysis instilled by the energy crisis of 1973-74 and may be on the brink of new steps to advance the integration process in the area of energy and related issues. The United States has not explicitly linked energy cooperation with Western Europe to cooperation in security or other issue areas. And the International Energy Agency has yet to prove its effectiveness in several fields beyond the initial emergency oil allocation scheme. So the creation of the IEA does not necessarily mean a new US hegemony over Europe. Nevertheless, the greater degree of potential American strength in energy resources, coupled with the vigorous US role so far in the IEA, does provide a potential future leverage point that might be used—explicitly or implicitly—to extend American influence in Europe and in the Western Alliance.

18 *Japan's Energy-Security Dilemma*

Kiichi Saeki

The October 1973 war and ensuing energy crisis forced upon Japan a dilemma, the foundations of which were almost certain to persist into the mid-1980s and quite possibly until the end of the century. These were Japan's dependence on Middle East oil for a crucial margin (80 percent) of its indispensable oil imports and an even broader dependence on the United States as supplier of a variety of essential imports including food, feed, raw materials, and high technology, as Japan's most important and profitable export market, and as the ultimate guarantor of Asian-Pacific peace and the military security of the Japanese homeland.

After October 1973, Japan faced the dilemma in foreign policy of steering a pragmatic course through the tangle of Middle East politics—especially in response to Arab political-economic pressures—as insurance against a repetition of the 1973 interruption of oil supplies, while at the same time cooperating with—or at worst, not undercutting—US Middle East and energy diplomacy in order to maintain Japan's close economic and political-security ties with the United States. Japan's underlying and historically too familiar dread was isolation from foreign sources of essential supplies, from export markets to finance the imports, and from the collective-security mechanism in which the US-Japan Treaty of Mutual Cooperation and Security has been the linchpin. Yet the politics of successfully managing this dilemma were not peculiar to Japan, but have proved troublesome to US allies in Western Europe.

* * * *

In April 1973, only six months before the outbreak of war and the oil crisis, Henry Kissinger, then national security adviser to President Nixon, broached a proposal for a new Atlantic Charter. The original charter, promulgated jointly by Winston Churchill and Franklin D. Roosevelt in a meeting at sea in August 1941, was a statement of Allied war aims, general principles which bound the Allies together in the face of a common threat. Dr. Kissinger's proposed new charter was intended to enunciate the principles binding the Atlantic allies and Japan together in the face of a diminishing cold-war threat through processes of détente and the emergence of a strong and autonomous Western Europe and Japan.

The Kissinger proposal, which resulted fourteen months later in a NATO Declaration on Atlantic Relations, proved overly optimistic about the future smooth prospect for détente and about the capacity of the allied democracies of Europe, North America, and Japan to accommodate their distinctive national interests in face of a common threat. The October War and the oil crisis brought the United States and the Soviet Union into hot-line confrontation over massive Soviet support to the Egyptian and Syrian war effort and overt Soviet encouragement of the Arab oil embargo. The Middle East eruption also split the Western Europeans among themselves, threatening the solidarity of the European Economic Community on the fundamental issue of energy policies, and raised recriminations between the United States and its European allies over the issue of the massive US resupply of Israel's arms needs and unilateral US handling of the brief US-Soviet confrontation.

The United States criticized its European allies, except Portugal, for their unwillingness to cooperate in military-supply transfers to Israel or in permitting overflight and transit services to the huge US military airlift to Israel. The Europeans responded with the complaint that the United States had conducted its diplomacy in the Middle East and with the Soviet Union without adequate consultation among its European allies and had placed its strategic forces on alert at the end of the October War without even advance notice to its allies.

In American eyes, the Western European countries and Japan were responding to the 1973 Middle East crisis on the basis of narrow and rival national interests. This lack of a coordinated front was jeopardizing the delicate diplomacy of the United States, which alone had the power to contain the military threat of either an Israeli collapse or a direct Soviet intervention and alone had the influence in the Arab and Israeli camps to promote and even lead negotiations on the political or the oil issues. In European eyes, and to some extent in Japan, the United States was admittedly conducting its Middle East diplomacy from a unique position of strength, but its priorities were not necessarily those of its allies. In particular, the apparent absolute

US commitment to Israel, the deep US preoccupation with détente, and the seeming US readiness to take a tough negotiating line with the Arab oil states added up to a strategy which, if it failed, would be disastrous to the interests of allies who were far more dependent than the United States on Middle East oil.

The Middle East crisis of 1973, in other words, challenged two of the most important objectives of the Nixon-Kissinger foreign policy: institutionalization of US-Soviet détente and revitalization of the alliance of industrial democracies.

* * * *

Japan was wholly unprepared, either in public opinion or in government contingency planning, to deal with the October crisis or its immediate and potential economic consequences for the Japanese economic security. Japan's overriding concern was restoration as quickly as possible of the interrupted oil supplies from the Arab Middle East. The remedy, realized through a series of diplomatic initiatives, invoked a progressive "clarification" of the Japanese position on Middle East affairs, to conform more closely to Arab views, including a call for Israel's total withdrawal from all Arab territories occupied in the June 1967 war.

Dr. Kissinger, by then US Secretary of State, expressed dissatisfaction with the momentary injury to the close Japanese-American relationship, indicating he firmly believed that Japan's participation was indispensable to a reorganization of the alliance of democracies. As he had pointed out in his April 1973 speech, "Japan has emerged as a major power center. In many fields, 'Atlantic' solutions to be viable must include Japan." The Japanese government leaned over backward in support of Kissinger's new Atlantic Charter proposal and his call for the creation of a new Energy Action Group to develop a common strategy on energy problems among the US and its allies. In fact, Japan was more forthcoming on both proposals than the Western Europeans and was the first country to accept the US invitation to join the new Energy Action Group.

European resistance on both counts was based in large measure on fears that US leadership was tantamount to US "domination" of Atlantic diplomacy in areas of the most vital interest to Europe, including the global problem of natural-resource diplomacy. Europe also appeared lukewarm to full partnership for Japan in what had traditionally been an Atlantic enterprise. This was a stumbling block which Columbia University's Professor Zbigniew Brzezinski had anticipated, alluding to the difficulties of integrating Japan into an essentially Western social structure. Yet, as Brzezinski had noted, the challenges of easing East-West tensions and of establishing a viable North-South "new order" required a framework of effective cooperation in which Japan, the United States, and Europe could, from the beginning, participate as equal partners, even though such a framework might take time to realize.

In any event, the US-proposed OECD-related International Energy Agency (IEA) took concrete form in November 1974, as the United States, Japan, and fifteen other leading oil-importing states, including all EEC members except France, reconciled their differences in the face of common need to develop cooperatively a long-term energy strategy. In the process, the United States proved more flexible than some had anticipated, and France, though holding out from formal IEA membership, became involved indirectly through the EEC and OECD. Japan, through its IEA participation, accepted responsibility for stockpiling oil against possible future emergencies and became party to agreements to restrict demand in an emergency, insuring stable and rational consumption for a considerable time through use and sharing of reserves. IEA membership also entailed cooperation in promoting energy conservation and development of new and substitute forms of energy. Moreover, in order to rectify international payments imbalances which accompanied the sharp rise in oil prices, an agreement in April 1974 offered OECD countries financial aid.

The original aim of IEA was to enhance the bargaining power of the participating states in the world oil market and to help them prevent boycotts and further large price boosts in the future. It seemed unlikely, however, that in time of crisis the machinery would work effectively.

* * * *

The October 1973 crisis was only one indicator that US-Japanese relations were undergoing change and adjustment. The Japanese people and government had already experienced the sobering effects of the Nixon Doctrine and the "Nixon shocks," recognizing that the partnership had reached a state where greater equality and mutuality were necessary. Further evidence of this need was found in the difficult textile negotiations (which were linked with the reversion of Okinawa to Japanese administration), the imbalance in US-

Japanese trade, the US embargo on soybean shipments to Japan, and other frictions of the late 1960s and early 1970s.

The oil crisis served to remind the Japanese people of their extreme vulnerability because of their almost total lack of natural resources, and thus helped them redefine their national "security" in economic and military terms. Hence it became clearer that their security relationship with the United States was not exclusively military, but encompassed as well a dependence on US foodstuffs and raw materials and on energy cooperation. Moreover, the Atlantic dimensions of the energy crisis and the North-South dimensions of the entire natural resource problem helped put US-Japanese relations in the broadest multilateral, rather than simply bilateral, perspective. The new challenge facing Japan and the United States was to adjust to a rapidly changing and increasingly complex and pluralistic world framework in which their common security was at stake.

There was also an Asian dimension to these changing Japanese perceptions. The tragic end to America's prolonged involvement in Vietnam, accompanied by rising tensions on the Korean peninsula, brought doubt and confusion to Japanese minds concerning the reliability of US commitments to Asian security. In addition, the heightened tensions on the Korean peninsula led to public reexamination of Japan's need to strengthen its own self-defense efforts, and, without discounting the large gap in capacities and geostrategic responsibilities of the two countries, greatly reinforced Japanese understanding of the absolute importance of sustaining US-Japanese mutual-security systems as the only reliable basis for Japan's security.

On such terms, the mutuality and genuine equality of the Japanese-American relationship appeared almost unreachable, if only because of the disparity in relative capabilities, relative vulnerabilities, and the constitutional and domestic-political limitations on how much and how fast Japan could contribute to mutual security. Whether the spirit of mutuality and equality was reachable probably depended on whether both governments (and peoples) would come to accept all the inherent disparities as the price for sustaining a relationship which was, in the broadest sense, basic to the security of both partners.

If mutual understanding and accommodation could be reached at this level, the Japanese contribution to mutual security might be substantially clarified on such terms as:

1. Guarantees to the United States of stable peacetime use of US military bases at Misawa, Yokota, Yokosuka, Iwakuni, and Kadena on the grounds that these five major bases were essential to Japanese security and to US regional security commitments. Secondary US bases would be merged or closed down.

2. Effectuation of defense cooperation in the event of an emergency under terms already agreed upon bilaterally, for "coordinated, effective operations" through creation of "a forum . . .for research and discussion concerning problems of US-Japanese cooperation," including "to what extent the arrangement of consultation is to be employed."

3. Clarification of degrees of cooperation appropriate, according to circumstances, should hostilities break out on the Korean peninsula. In this complex contingency, both governments needed to carefully explore the possible gradations of provocation and response, and the Japanese government had to consider the probable implications of domestic law and politics for any given situation. It is my personal opinion that, should it become clear that any hostilities result from an invasion by North Korea into South Korea, Japan, in the light of its own national interest, would have to be prepared to grant, in response to prior consultation with the United States, use of US military bases in Japan for purposes of conducting combat operations.

4. Continuing modernization and improvement of Japanese self-defense capabilities, as an obligation under the US-Japanese Security Treaty, within the limitations imposed by the Constitution. Yet Japan must continue to be the judge of the Constitutional and political limitations of this obligation. The minimum defense capability which was deemed adequate, and which should continue to be adequate for the future, was a small but high-quality capability costing about 1 percent of the GNP.

5. Strengthening the Japanese political consensus in support of US-Japanese security relationship as a top-priority objective of the Japanese government. In consideration of the changing global

security environment, and its impact on Japanese consciousness beyond political party and ideology, it should be possible to achieve such a consensus around the convictions expressed by American and Japanese leaders on the occasion of Prime Minister Takeo Miki's August 1975 visit to the United States: "The US-Japan Security Treaty is contributing substantially to the maintenance of peace and stability in the Far East. It is an indispensable element in the basic structure of international politics in Asia, and continued maintenance of the treaty is in the long-term interests of both nations."

* * * *

Japan's security in the broadest sense encompasses not merely its physical survival through military means (a function of the US-Japanse Security Treaty and Japan's own self-defense efforts) nor merely its assured access to essential fuels and other raw materials and to equally necessary export markets, but rather a combination of these and other considerations, including the obligation to participate purposefully in a rational restructuring of the world order. These considerations may differ in degree, but not in kind, with those Japan shares with the United States, the European democracies, and a substantial portion of the rest of mankind.

It was the growing understanding of these national-survival conditions which was rapidly drawing the Japanese people into a sense of more direct and more responsible participation in global affairs. The forced maturing of the Japanese-American relationship, the lodestone of postwar Japanese foreign policy, helped and so did the trauma of the energy crisis.

The frictions of the Nixon-shock era were overcome largely by cooperative Japanese responses to the causal circumstances—and by the accidental relative benefits to the US trade balance of the currency revaluations in the world recession which followed. It was possible also that the spectacle of Japan's helplessness in the oil crisis helped soften US fears of Japan's competitiveness, and that America's own sense of isolation in the aftermath of its withdrawal from Vietnam contributed to enhanced American expectations of Japan.

This does not necessarily mean, however, that the present "trouble-free era" in Japanese-American relations (as some have called it) is incorruptible. One of my American friends whom I highly respect has said that, if there is any problem which will cause future tension between the United States and Japan, it is that of conflicting positions on the Arab-Israel dispute. The abstention of Japan on the UN vote equating Zionism with "racism" was perceived by many Americans as abject Japanese submission to Arab political-economic pressure. Yet the realistic alternatives for Japan are not that clear under an imperfect IEA which has yet to offer, under foreseeable emergency conditions, a practical alternative to Japan's critical and continuing dependence on Middle East oil. In the absence of alternatives, Japan will no doubt continue to act from real weakness, rather than from imagined strength, on energy matters. At the same time, however, complying with all Arab demands would not solve Japan's security interests if, in the process, Japan sacrificed its cooperative and mutually dependent relations with the United States and Europe. More than any other advanced industrial country, Japan cannot survive in isolation.

This dilemma of Japanese foreign policy and the need to foster more sympathetic international understanding of the dilemma would probably continue to be a problem for another decade or more. There was a possibility that the world-market forces of supply and demand would independently regulate the price and supply of oil, thus alleviating short-term pressures on Japan and other importing states, while longer-term energy alternatives were pursued. It was also possible, and certainly to be hoped, that the creative US initiatives in the Middle East peace negotiations would reach a breakthrough stage and that a new flexibility on all sides, especially on the question of Palestinian self-determination, would be realized. Progress in this direction would deftly avoid any conflict of interests or policies between Japan and the United States in the Middle East. In the meantime, however, Japan's vital security interests required a diplomacy which sought to convert Japan's unilateral dependence on the Middle East oil-producing states into a bilateral interdependence, based on investments, aid, and trade, combined with a policy of deliberate diversification of oil-sourcing around the world.

19 *Energy and Economic Growth*

William D. Nordhaus

The energy crisis has been widely heralded as the first clarion call of doomsday; the beginning of an age of increasing scarcity and slow economic growth; the herald for massive changes in life-styles; a revolution in the international distribution of incomes and political power; the impetus to massive changes in the philosophical basis of Western life; and an end to consumerism as we have known it.

I do not believe these extreme views of the implications of the energy crisis; indeed, I am skeptical of even the milder versions which appear in the learned journals and glossy press. Rather, the energy crisis was simply the latest economic crisis, albeit a rather violent one. More whimsically, but more realistically, the Western countries were caught with their collective pants down, and perhaps they were temporarily confused about how to pull them back up. A few anatomical parts were even to get a little chilly in the ensuing winters; but the creaky democracies and oligopolies of the West eventually bent down and reached over a substantial midriff to pull up tweed pants which were perhaps a bit oversized. Then, by taking the belt in a notch or two, the West proceeded about its business at pretty much the pace it did before. And if a lesson was to be learned, the lesson was not that the West was too obese, that we were evolving a life-style au naturel, or that the world was running out of tweed, but simply that it was the better part of wisdom to keep one hand at all times on one's pants.

The Long-Run Energy Outlook

It is most fruitful to begin the examination of the relation between energy and economic growth by looking first at the long-run outlook. The distant future casts a long shadow in our direction—markets respond to perceived ultimate scarcity and (to a lesser degree) public opinion and public policies are shaped by long-run growth prospects. The most important change in the long-run outlook is the shift in perceptions about economic growth.

For a considerable part of its history, the American economy has functioned as a cowboy economy in the sense that there have been no important resource constraints on growth. This is not to say that land, minerals, and a clean environment have been freely available. Rather, agricultural land could be obtained at roughly constant costs; most essential minerals have been present at fairly high grade in considerable abundance; and the environment could be used as a sink without becoming fouled. However, our cropland stayed almost constant, some high-grade mineral deposits were exhausted, and the carrying capacity of our environment was strained.

The scarcity of resources led many to argue that the operating rules of our economy must change. Whereas in the cowboy economy we could afford to use our resources profligately, the new view of economic growth was that the closing of all our frontiers meant that we were operating in a spaceship economy where great attention must be paid to the sources of life and to the dumps where our refuse was piled. Things which have traditionally been treated as free goods—air, water, quiet, natural beauty—must be treated with the same care as other scarce goods.

It would seem difficult to question the observation that the world economy was progressing toward a closed system. Many have carried this observation further, describing a future imperiled by famine, depleted of essential materials, running out of energy, or choking in its own exhaust fumes. Behind these pessimistic visions was a deeper skepticism about the very fruits of economic growth.

Economists have for the most part ridiculed the new view of growth, arguing that it was merely Chicken Little run wild. I think the new view of growth must be taken seriously and analyzed carefully. What have we learned about the new view?

The first set of studies relate to theoretical investigations. (By theoretical I mean propositions based on largely untested assumptions about model structure—perhaps hypothetical would be a more accurate term.) In this category belong the celebrated writings sponsored by the Club of Rome as well as many offshoots of this work (the models of Forrester, Dennis H. Meadows, et al.) and less well-known descendants (the Mesarovich-Pestel and Bariloche models). These works have demonstrated that, under certain conditions involving technology, population, and resource availability, a sustained growth path for consumption is not possible. Interestingly enough, energy has generally not been the focus of concern in these models.

The conclusions of these works have not generally been accepted by economists because of the dubious nature of many of their assumptions. In particular, the assumptions regarding population growth and technology are quite unsatisfactory. Several authors have shown that the conclusions of these models are not robust to minor modifications in structure. Thus R. Boyd showed that introducing a new factor called "technology" in Forrester's *World Dynamics* model (a model which was the father of the better-known model in *The Limits to Growth*) would drastically alter the model's path. My work showed that any of three changes in model structure—ongoing technological progress, adequate factor substitution, or population decline—would lead to much more optimistic outcomes.

It should be stressed, however, that all of the debate about Club of Rome models has been theoretical. It has been demonstrated incontrovertibly that different world models paint drastically different pictures of future economic life. It is at this moment an open question as to which is the preferred model. Only careful empirical analysis can indicate which of the alternative models is closer to reality.

The theoretical models, then, are not much help in answering questions about the long-run relation between energy and economic growth. There have been a few empirical studies, and we now turn to these. Energy is in fact an excellent case study of the central propositions about the limits to growth. Unlike most mineral resources, energy is essential for many processes of production. In addition, energy resources are finite in supply, energy consumption is dissipative and leads to serious environmental problems.

Three important questions about energy resources are important for assessing future long-run growth. These concern resource availability, price, and environmental effects.

(One minor methodological point must be disposed of at the beginning. As I have no claim to clairvoyance, the statements in this chapter are guesses, albeit reasoned guesses, about future behavior. But they are only the subjective maximum likelihood guess; there is considerable uncertainty about future projections. Rather than burden every sentence with the proper qualification as to the exact uncertainty of the statement, I make such a blanket qualification at the outset.)

The first question is whether there are adequate energy resources to run the world's economy for an indefinite period of time. Unfortunately, a complete answer depends on the answers to the next two questions, but for a crude answer we can simply calculate the quantities of energy resources. Table 1 shows the ratio of resources to 1970 consumption under certain assumptions about the feasible technology.

Table 1

RESOURCE-CONSUMPTION RATIO FOR ENERGY, 1970

1.	Fossil fuels only	520 years
2.	Fossil fuels plus current nuclear technology	8,400 years
3.	Fossil fuels, current nuclear, and breeder technology	1,100,000 years
4.	Fossil fuels, current nuclear breeder, and fusion technology	53,000,000,000 years
5.	Fossil fuels and solar technology	4,000,000,000,000 years

Pretty clearly, the sheer adequacy of energy resources depends on whether certain future technologies will become available. Even with only the current technology (Table 1, line 2) there are resources for more than 8,000 years at the current rate of consumption. With breeder reactors, and more dramatically with a fusion or solar technology, there is virtually unlimited energy available.

The second question concerns the price at which energy resources will be available over the long run. The new view of growth sees a future in which energy resources become extremely expensive as mining turns to lower and lower grade energy resources. Thus it may well be that resources are available, but they are so expensive and so many are devoted to extraction that a dwindling amount of output is left for actual consumption.

I have considered the likelihood of this in another context. Starting with energy resources, with plausible demand paths and current estimates of the costs of extracting and processing energy resources, it is possible to calculate the results of a stimulated competitive market unfolding over time. In making this calculation, I assumed that the world's energy resources were efficiently allocated over time and space with an interest rate of 10 percent and that the supply of energy resource was that given by technological assumption 3 in Table 1 (that is, breeder reactors would be technically and environmentally feasible by the year 2010). Finally, assume that technological change proceeds at the same rate in the energy sector as in the nub of the economy.

The calculated path for energy prices was quite remarkable. The starting point in 1970 showed calculated energy prices very close to the actual. The efficient solution traced out a transition to the ultimate technology with the final nuclear-based technology ultimately taking over about 150 years out. The most interesting part was the price path. Over the first 50 years, the calculated price index of final energy products rose 2.2 percent annually relative to the general price level. The growth rate of energy prices relative to the general price level over the next 100 years was 1.3 percent annually—after which time energy prices were constant relative to the general price level.

Whether movements of relative prices of this magnitude become a drag on consumption depends on the future pattern of technological change. If productivity increases at its historical rate—output per man-hour has grown at about 2.5 percent over the last few decades—then a rise in energy prices of the order of magnitude cited above would mean that energy prices would continue to fall relative to labor's price and to average incomes. In this case, there would be no drag on consumption standards stemming from the gradual exhaustion of low cost fuels. Under the assumptions of the model, it thus appears that the long-run outlook for energy prices is favorable, although less favorable than over the last few decades. (The assumption of competitive behavior is clearly unrealistic. A cartel of oil producers would drive up the short-run price. But as Robert Solow has noted, monopolists are the conservationists' best friends: higher prices lead to lower consumption, a stretching out of finite resources, and possibly even lower prices in the future.)

The final problem that remains to be dealt with is the environmental aspects. Let me be clear on what I mean by environmental problems. Technically, these are "external diseconomies," or outputs of a process of production for which the buyers or sellers do not pay the full social costs. Thus if a mine has acid leach which fouls the water supply, if sulfur emissions lead to uncompensated health or property damage, or if oil spills spoil beaches—these are external economies, externalities for short.

The most important point about externalities is that if they are present there are good *theoretical* reasons to think that markets will lead to incorrect levels of production. This is quite different from the case of non-externality resources like oil and coal. For these non-externality goods, a market mechanism will tend toward the efficient allocation over time. But if externalities are present, the system is implicitly setting a zero price on water supplies, health, clean air, and clean beaches. No one would be surprised if, after setting the price of labor at zero, labor were used wastefully in many situations. And it is perfectly natural that if the price of clean air is zero, it will be heavily used and abused. Thus there is a clear presumption that if there are externalities, there will be overuse and misuse of environmental resources.

This brief diagnosis of the environmental disease suggests that the remedy is to put a realistic price tag on environmental goods. And of course this is just what we have been doing in a rather bumbling and chaotic way. The most clear-cut example of this approach was President Nixon's sulfur tax proposal in which he proposed that polluters pay a tax of $0.15 per pound of sulfur dioxide emitted, instead of the $0.00 per pound charged.

The question of guessing the importance of future environmental problems is compounded by two separate questions: What "price" will we charge on externalities? And what will be the technological response to the higher price; in particular, will emissions be considerably reduced?

I admit that I am worried about environment aspects of energy because of these questions. The cornerstone of a solution to environmental problems is a consensus on a technique for "pricing" the environment. We have, more or less, reached such a consensus for normal goods, and we use market prices as indicators. We cannot do this for the environment, so what can we do? I would propose that we use the technique of pricing emissions by pricing their effects on health and property. This has the advantage of being based on things which can be calculated and tested and have important efficiency properties.

An example of this kind of reasoning is the following paraphrase of a proposal for a radiation-emissions tax by a Harvard physicist:

> In examining nuclear radiation, it is usual to look at the produce of the dose times population, called the "man-rem." Since 1000 man-rems is a fatal dose, we set the price of 1,000 man-rems at the value of human life. If we are willing to pay $1 million to save a statistical life, this says the charge to a nuclear power plant should be $1,000 per man-rem.

I have hopes that such a rational technique for making environmental decisions will come into being. While I have hopes, I must admit that there are severe obstacles to this procedure. The common counter arguments are that it puts a price on human life, it sells licenses to pollute, and so forth. However, I believe that if we view the matter in a calm but humane way, we must consider the tradeoffs between length of life, quality of life, and environment. By putting explicit prices on the environment we can best implement our preferences and decisions about the relative values of these goods. Put slightly differently, critics of the effluent change appear uncomfortable with putting a price tag of, say, $1 million on human life. Are they more comfortable with current arrangements where a price of $0 is put on human life?

Looking forward, then, I divide the environmental energy problems into three classes: those where the data are good and the costs are small, those where the data are poor but the costs look small, and those which have potentially large effects.

For those problems where the costs are small, this means that with an appropriate control strategy (say the pollution taxes mentioned above), the externalities can be "internalized" at small costs, and the effect of environment as a constraint on economic growth is small. Four examples are ones where we have good data. One easily analyzed example is strip mining in favorable locations. It is estimated that reclamation expense in the order of $5,000 per acre is sufficient to put the land in better condition than it started; in most locations this adds about 1 percent to the market price of coal. Internalizing strip mining costs, therefore, would have a negligible effect upon the path of energy prices. A second example, alluded to above, is the routine emissions from nuclear power plants. If we take the current standards, then the $1,000 per man-rem leads to approximately .0006 cents per kilowatt hour, about two ten-thousandths (2/10000) of the current market price. Similar conclusions follow for electricity generation from other fossil fuels and emissions from automobiles.

A second category is where the data are less definitive but the costs appear to be small. The main uncertainties here are for accidents from nuclear reactors and storage of nuclear wastes. The estimates made by some groups (such as the Rasmussen report) gave rather modest estimates of the cost of accidents, but these data are not of the same quality as the first group, and many dispute their accuracy. A similar question is the strip mining of arid lands in the United States, which was recently reviewed by a committee of the US National Academy of Sciences. This group found that for certain arid and geologically unstable areas the risks of strip mining were probably low, but there are risks which cannot be judged.

A final group of environmental problems concern those which, in my estimation, are quite risky from a global point of view. The first of these is the diversion of nuclear material from peaceful purposes. Much careful diplomacy went into prevention of the spread of nuclear weapons since 1945, culminating in the Nuclear Non-proliferation Treaty in 1968. It is clear that with the spread of peaceful power reactors the cost of a government's becoming a nuclear power is much reduced; enough weapons-grade material is created in a light water reactor to make several dozen small bombs each year. In short, we are faced with a situation where the spread of a nuclear electrical generating industry around the world is almost certainly going to lead to the spread of the capability to build low-cost nuclear weapons, whether by official sources (as in the recent Indian case) or by unofficial terrorist groups (a case we have yet to witness).

There are techniques for inspection of the nuclear fuel cycle which significantly reduce the probability of successful diversion. These safeguards are under the aegis of the International Atomic Energy Agency in Vienna, which was formed as an adjunct to the Nuclear Non-proliferation Treaty. Recent analyses indicate that a complete inspection system could reduce the amounts diverted to very small levels if all countries agreed to take part in the inspection and if these inspections were more comprehensive. Recent analyses indicate that we are probably under-inspecting against diversion and over-investing against routine emissions. Unfortunately, there are strong externalities present in the inspection process, for while it would probably benefit all countries to set very strict inspection standards, it would pay any single country or group to cheat and develop a weapon while other countries were adhering to the agreement. This centrifugal tendency is particularly severe with a large number of countries.

The second set of environmental problems, which, in my opinion, is eventually going to be serious and costly, is the interaction between energy consumption and climate. In particular, it appears that emissions of carbon dioxide, particulate matter, and waste heat may lead to significant climatic modifications. Of these, it appears that carbon dioxide will probably be the first man-made emission to affect climate on a global scale, with a significant temperature increase by the end of the century.

A brief overview of the problem is as follows: combustion of fossil fuels leads to significant emissions of carbon dioxide into the atmosphere. The emissions slowly distribute themselves by natural processes into the oceans, the biosphere, and, at a very slow rate, back into fossils. Although this process is not completely understood, it is clear that the residence time of carbon dioxide in the atmosphere is extremely long, and approximately half of industrial carbon dioxide resides in the atmosphere. The ultimate distribution of carbon dioxide between the atmosphere and the other sinks is not known; estimates of the effect of man-made carbon dioxide remaining in the atmosphere range between about 3 and 50 percent.

The effects of the atmospheric buildup of carbon dioxide are not known with certainty, but there are thought to be two general effects. The first, and most highly publicized, is on the climate through the "greenhouse effect." Because of the selective filtering of radiation, the increased carbon dioxide is thought to lead to an increase in the surface temperature of the planet. Recent estimates range from 0.6° C. to 3.0° C. for the mean temperature increase due to a doubling of the atmospheric concentration. Recent experiments indicate, however, that the sensitivity of the temperature is much greater in the polar regions than in the lower latitudes.

According to most studies, uncontrolled paths will lead to significant increases in the average temperature by the year 2030, with increases in temperatures in high latitudes at about five times the mean. The major sensitive point in the short run is the floating arctic ice. With summer temperature anomalies of 4° C., the summer ice is predicted by Budyko to disappear in four years. According to most studies, an open Arctic Ocean would lead to a dramatic change in the temperature patterns, as well as precipitation patterns, with the most important changes occurring in the high latitudes of the Northern hemisphere.

Aside from this rather sharp and immediate result, the other effects of increased concentrations are either less discontinuous or act much more slowly. Budyko argues that a 50 percent increase in carbon dioxide would lead to melting of all land-borne ice, raising the level of the oceans up to 80 meters, and dramatically warming the global temperature—the eventual warming being in the order of 5° C. when all the feedback effects have taken place. This result is almost certain to be extremely slow, spread over a period of around 5,000 years, so that its possibility should probably be heavily discounted.

The consequence of these changes for human affairs are clouded in uncertainty. It is unlikely that any dramatic, global changes will be forthcoming before the end of the century. On the other hand, it is possible that a large redistribution of precipitation will occur within a relatively short period. Indeed, Bryson has argued that the drought in the semiarid region of Africa known as the Sahel is due to man-made changes in the global atmosphere, and dislocations like this will become more frequent.

Nevertheless, the problems associated with carbon dioxide buildup are neither inevitable nor necessarily costly. The pessimism associated with the global climate comes not because the solutions are costly—it can be shown that inexpensive technical solutions exist—

but rather that it takes a considerable act of faith to imagine that the needed steps will be taken. Whose fantasy envisages the UN General Assembly voting with great deliberation a carbon dioxide tax or a tax on export of nuclear materials after a repeal of the anti-Zionist resolution?

The Short-Run Outlook for the Energy Sector

Reasoning along these lines has convinced me that the problems of energy are not sheer resource adequacy. When we eventually make a transition to a new long-run equilibrium, the energy sector is likely to return to being a driving rather than a retarding force in the process of economic growth.

Having said this, I must now put in a major reservation to this conclusion: the transition to a new long-run equilibrium is surely going to be difficult, costly, long, and divisive. This is the short-run problem—the problem of transition.

It seems to me that in the transition there are two central uncertainties, or potential problems, which remain with us. These are problems of international energy relations and of timing.

First consider the question of international energy relations. In October 1973 the US officially entered the energy crisis with the imposition of the Arab oil boycott. This was accompanied by a dramatic price rise. These two measures made it abundantly clear that the United States and, even more so, other OECD countries, put themselves in a position of great dependency on unstable oil exporting countries. Shortly after, Project Independence was announced as an attempt to make the US self-sufficient in energy by 1980. Within a short time it was realized that this was impractical, and in the official report on Project Independence the target became reduction of instability by 1985.

Most observers agree that we can make great strides toward insulating ourselves from instability in a period of ten or so years. Many have questioned the exact strategy. First, it is clear that independence has its economic costs—estimates are in the range of $10-20 billion per year to attain complete independence. The costs come from turning to higher cost domestic fuels—and turning faster to these—than a dependent strategy. Weighing these costs, it seems unlikely that the economic gains are this large. Estimates of the cost of embargo are of the same order of magnitude, so if we are experiencing embargoes every fifth year the average benefit is only one-fifth of the cost. Second, one must have some reservation about moving to a system in which each country is setting up a wall of protective tariffs and taxes to increase its own national advantage, yet this is exactly what Project Independence does. This "protectionist model" of national economic policy is a subtle yet frightening reversal of the trend away from protectionism and toward free trade and international economic integration. This protectionist model has not spread much beyond energy, but the dangers and the political temptations are clearly present.

To summarize about Project Independence: for the United States, at least, this represents a temporary and rather special problem. There are no other obvious resources where the US is so dependent as oil and where the resource is so essential. Moreover, this is pretty clearly only a temporary stage, for at worst OPEC has limited resources and at best they will either break up or be replaced by substitutes. Thus, while the nightmare will be with us for one long night, it seems a good bet that this nightmare is not going to be a recurrent one over the life of our country.

The second uncertainty which we face, closely related to the first, is the timing of our resource deployment in the energy battlefield. One of the problems which has become very clear in the last couple of years, as we cope with the energy crisis, is the extraordinary lags in reaction and behavior. Is it really possible that two years after the embargo, and four years after the symptoms first started appearing, there is still no legislation dealing with the underlying causes of the energy crisis? This is just the most visible of the long lags. Is there any general reason for this?

In examining the problem of delays in reactions one must distinguish three different phases: a research lag, an acceptance lag, and a physical production lag. It will help to illustrate this if we examine a concrete example, such as the replacement of natural petroleum and gas with synthetic petroleum and gas. It is clear that one way of avoiding the twin difficulties of exhaustion of our resources and dependence on foreign sources is to turn to coal, tar sands, and oil shales for synthetic fuels. The resource bases of these fuels are perhaps 100 times as large as our domestic oil and gas; the synthetic fuel technology was proved when used by the Germans in World War II to replace imported petroleum.

Well, what are we waiting for? The problem is that there is little incentive for individual producers, even giant oil companies, to introduce the synthetic fuels technology given the risks and uncertainties of its outcome. Someone may bring along a better process, the oil countries might undercut the price, environmentalists might shut the factory down, and so on. Thus, many public and private groups are actively engaged in research on superior technologies, and public decision-makers are engaged in research on how best to get current technologies actually being built. There is no telling how long the research will last, but there is some evidence that large scale plants are actually going to be built in the near future.

The acceptance lag is yet another problem, though it is less severe for synthetic fuels than for nuclear power. A significant part of our electricity is generated with oil and gas, and this could be directly substituted away from by nuclear power if that were an alternative clearly acceptable to the public. But acceptance (as in the case of water fluoridation and chlorination) or rejection (as in the case of the SST) takes time; it is a learning process.

Finally, after research and acceptance have been completed there is the physical production lag. For accepted technologies (like coal mining or off-shore oil and gas drilling) the physical production lag is really the only thing standing between us and greater production. But the lags are sometimes quite long. For example, it is estimated that the effect of the crisis on oil and gas production will not show up until around 1978. New deep coal mines require at least five years as do fossil-fuel electrical generation plants. Nuclear generation plants currently are taking nearly ten years from plan to initial operation.

If we put all these lags together, what do we have? Table 2 (p. 279) illustrates the timing. First, we must conclude that in what I will call Phase I, a period of five to ten years, we must rely mainly on the capital equipment that was built and planned before the energy crisis hit us. The most promising policies for this short-run period are to use our capital stock more efficiently. A very important part of this short-run policy is rational pricing of energy, and it is probably wise to move with deliberate speed to energy prices which

Table 2

TIMING OF RESPONSE TO ENERGY CRISIS

Phase	Period	Constraints	Policies
I	up to 1985	Capital before energy crisis	Concentrate on efficiency + conservation
II	1985-2000	Only existing technology	Expand production with existing technology
III	2000-2025	Use current research	Expand production with currently researched technologies
IV	2025 and beyond	New technologies?	?

reflect the true social short-run scarcities. The 1975 energy bill had the merit of moving toward de-control of oil. The reduction of prices at the beginning served no useful economic purpose, but the political reasoning was clear.

In Phase II, for the balance of the century (1985–2000), we are in a position to expand production using currently proven technologies. This will include oil and gas drilling, on and off shore, a great expansion of coal and nuclear power, but probably relatively little new technology, such as synthetic hydrocarbons. In fact, only as we move into Phase III (2000–2025) do we see significant introduction of new technologies—that is technologies under study. Finally, as we move beyond the 2025 period, the uncertainties about new technologies are too great, and it is no longer possible even to guess the unfolding of events.

What to conclude about the timing? As one looks at Table 2, one cannot help but be struck by the incredible length of time needed to have the system respond fully. Yet the lessons of history as well as the predictions of computerized programming models clearly indicate that an ineluctible response will be forthcoming. It is even possible that the system will overrespond, in a cobweb cycle reminiscent of the years of glut and famine of agricultural markets. The combination of high prices restraining demand and inducing supply and new technologies could well lead to an energy glut. The sadist can even contemplate the consequences of this glut with sufficient pleasure to overcome his chills and pain.

Energy and Economic Growth

The first two sections of this paper constitute a long prologue to an analysis of the interaction of energy and economic growth. But they tell most of the story. To wrap it up, I will recapitulate what the outlook is.

1. In the short run, from 1973 to 1978 or so, the major effect on economic growth is the Keynesian effect upon aggregate demand. The rise in oil prices (and to a lesser extent the rise in other energy prices) constituted an excise tax increase of extraordinary proportions. The total "excise tax" increase for the OECD countries constituted in the order of $70 billion, and with the normal multipliers this would lead to a decrease in real GNP for OECD countries of about $150 billion, or 5 percent of OECD GNP.

In principle, appropriate macro-economic management could offset the unfavorable demand effect of the "excise tax," and this of course is the rationale for the $24-billion tax cut in the US and similar policies elsewhere. But a combination of confused economic management, concern with inflation, and reluctance to aggravate swollen balance-of-payments deficits led to a very sluggish response and the present worldwide recession.

How long the recession will last is a matter of some speculation. As of November 1975 most analysts saw a rapid recovery taking place and perhaps continuing over the next year, but continued slack would probably be on hand until 1980. The magnitude of the loss of output over the period 1973–80, assuming full recovery by 1980, is around $2,000 billion for all OECD countries. I have not seen a very careful quantification of the amount due to increased energy prices, but I would not be surprised if the demand effect was in the order of $500 to $700 billion for all OECD countries over the period to 1980.

Ironically, it appears that the most sizable effect of the energy crisis on economic growth will come from a source that was largely preventable.

2. The second short-run effect of the energy crisis is the slower rate of growth of national income and potential output. Potential output is the amount that an economy could produce at a given rate of resource utilization. Thus, the Keynesian demand effect comes not through the slow growth of potential output, but through the failure to produce our potential. In addition, there is an effect on potential output. Because of the higher price of imported energy, use of more expensive substitutes reduces the total output that the OECD economies can produce.

A very crude example will show the magnitude of the slowdown in potential output. In 1973 the US consumed about 12 billion barrels of oil equivalent, of which 2 billion were imported, all of these at the price of about $3 per barrel equivalent. The rise of prices to $10 per barrel leads to an increase in the value of imports of about $14 billion, this being the loss of real national income. If no substitution occurs, however, there is no change in real output—the real output flows (or real economic growth) are identical, but the distribution of that output is changed.

The only effect on potential output comes when substitution occurs, when the US desires to substitute away from high priced imports. For example, if domestic production increases to replace the 2 billion barrels of imports at a cost of $10 per barrel, the total output of the US decrease by $14 billion, this being about 1 percent of GNP. Thus, if this adjustment is spread over ten years, the rate of growth of potential would be about 0.1 percent slower than without the energy crisis.

For a more rigorous approach, it is necessary to build a complete model. In a paper by Gunning, Osterrieth, and Waelbroeck, following very similar reasoning to that used here, they estimated the growth of potential output in all OECD countries to be about 0.11 percent per annum slower over the 1973–85 period because of the oil price rise, down from 4.39 percent to 4.28 percent. The cumulative total loss of potential is $520 billion over the twelve-year period of 1973–85. This calculation assumes that OPEC stays intact and is able to maintain a constant real price.

3. In the longer run, say after 1985, the powerful forces of competition will probably start to gain the upper hand. If we use the simulations discussed above, however, we can get a rough idea of the effects of the depletion of energy resources on economic growth. Recall that we argued that, for the OECD, energy prices would be rising annually 1+ percent faster than the general price level as a result of depletion, assuming no differential technological change. Since energy consumption is projected to be around 6 percent of real OECD national income, this price rise constitutes a drag on economic growth of about 0.08 percent per annum. If technological change follows its historical patterns, with energy prices falling 1+ percent relative to the general price level, this would be reversed. In any case, once the system reaches long-run equilibrium again, and putting aside the environmental concerns discussed above, it seems unlikely that the energy system will be a significant drag upon economic growth.

To summarize the outlook for the effect of the energy crisis on economic growth, it is somewhat like a shock wave which dissipates itself as it is transmitted into the future. The initial reaction is the most severe in that the effects on demand through the excise tax effect will probably dominate till 1980. After that, the effect of moving prematurely to high cost substitutes for what are (from a global point of view) very cheap resources will be a smaller but still significant drag on economic growth. Finally, as the system moves toward a new long-run equilibrium, the drag on economic growth will be very small or even negative as new technologies come on line.

20 *The Pervasive Crisis*

J. C. Hurewitz

The energy crisis, as we have seen, encircled the globe. Not a single oil-importing state, no matter how small or remote or low its per capita income, could escape the impact of the steep rise in the price of oil late in 1973. The price rise reshaped overnight all major international economic conditions—trade, money, investment, aid, transfer of technology—and the rules for their political management. The existing noncommunist international economic system, which the United States and its allies had fashioned after World War II, was already collapsing before October 1973. The energy crisis quickened the pace of change, from the old system which was known, stable, and workable to an emerging system which was as yet unformed and whose final structure was still unknown.

The accompanying instability stirred the anxieties of political and economic leaders in the industrial states. More than two and one-half years after the October War, the resolution of the energy crisis as such—that is, the restored assurance of uninterrupted supplies of energy—still lay some distance in the future. Experts predicted little change in supply patterns before 1980. In the five years following, new non-OPEC oil and gas resources were expected to come on stream. But only after 1985, and perhaps not before the 1990s, or even the turn of the century, would oil substitutes begin to become commercially feasible.

The present book is based on the premise of variable national responses in the industrial countries to satisfy national interests. A stable adjustment to the evolving realities required the mutual recognition of these domestic considerations. The book rests on the further premise that beyond nationalism lies a common concern about diminishing the dependence of the industrial states on OPEC oil and their vulnerability to the political manipulation of supply. They thus shared an interest—but seemed only rarely to act on it—in supporting all measures that might conserve energy and yield new supplies outside the OPEC theater. Such supplies clearly could most easily come in the short run from stepping up, in all industrial states, new exploration and drilling on and off the shore, with due consideration to environmental protection.

In the long run, such fossil-fuel development could help tide over the transition to synthetics and conversion products and eventually to new forms of energy. For conservation as for research and development, the industrial allies looked to the United States for leadership. In both, however, the US was hobbled by domestic difficulties, as it was also in shifting back to coal for a larger proportion of its energy needs. The US, it is true, slowed down energy consumption in 1974-75. But that resulted, not from a deliberate policy, but from warm winters and from such market forces as recession and high prices. Research and development for conversion and for replacement energies proceeded fitfully. In every respect, the US was providing an erratic leadership.

Many factors fed into the world energy crisis. Energy consumption in the industrial states after World War II rose phenomenally. The annual average exceeded 5 percent, and the belief in a direct correlation between energy use and economic growth commonly went unquestioned. To satisfy expanding demands, the Nine, their West European neighbors, and Japan bought most of their oil from the Middle East. Until 1970, the international oil industry was characterized by a buyers' market, which helped keep prices down. A temporary tanker shortage, combined in 1970 with a reduction in Libyan output, began to create for the industry a sellers' market. The new condition was reinforced in that year when US production—for the time being, at least—peaked, as a result of more than a decade of mandatory oil import controls, which were lifted. The US became a primary importer as its reliance on foreign oil rose from 23.3 to 38.8 percent in three years. Neither the US nor any of its industrial allies, to say nothing of the OECD and the EEC, had yet adopted comprehensive energy plans. In a word, the US share of responsibility for the energy crisis, largely hidden from general view, should not be overlooked.

Meanwhile, OPEC's assertion of the right to regulate the flow of oil and its price at once changed the role of the vertically integrated oil MNCs. In the past they had owned comprehensive concessions which enabled them to command all operations from exploration and well-sinking in the concession zones to the gas pumps in filling stations everywhere in the world, with the notable exception of the communist countries. The inability of the companies and the failure of the industrial governments to challenge the unilateral actions enlarged the influence of the OPEC governments and emboldened them. They accelerated the process of nationalizing the major concessions and the companies' installations (wells, pipelines, and storage and loading facilities), but as late as mid-1976 had made only scattered moves to enter downstream operations. At the start, most industrial governments were overwhelmed by a sense of impending economic disaster or, at the very least, of economies twisting out of shape. In the event, their economies adjusted speedily and with surprisingly moderate long-range impact on structures, despite major changes in the conditions of external economic activities. Before October 1973, the company policies on the production and price of crude oil and its products were geared to the laws and fluctuating markets in the importing states. Thereafter, OPEC policymakers took decisions on their own criteria, showing little sensitivity to the needs of the importers. The MNCs, for their part, were squeezed between the governments in producing and importing countries. As the primary intermediaries in the international oil industry, the Big Seven and their smaller sisters still performed major functions, particularly in transportation, refining, and marketing. But as the roles changed, their relative importance declined.

The Soviet Union, for its part, remained on the periphery of the energy crisis. It owned no concessions in the Middle East and, even after starting in the late 1950s to pump oil beyond the communist pale, did not ever become a top participant in the international industry. The USSR, however, met all its energy demands from domestic sources, and continued delivering an overflow to its political allies. Its own position was thus not immediately periled. It also raised the price of oil piped to its communist customers. So long as the USSR clung to its energy autarky, it would enjoy greater flexibility than the US. From that circumstance and from the disarray of the industrial allies came the chief political benefit to the Soviet Union after 1973. But this gave it little manipulative influence, and the international impact of Soviet propaganda remained dubious. The policymakers in Moscow acted with caution, manifestly recognizing that Soviet interference with the movement of oil from the Persian Gulf to the OECD sphere could hardly fail to elicit a vigorous and unified response from the US and its allies. Thus, the threat to allied security arose, not because the Soviet Union had managed, or seemed likely, to lay its hand on the Persian Gulf oil tap, but because in the short run it was oil-autarkic at a time when the United States and its major industrial allies had come increasingly to rely on purchases from the OPEC area.

The paramount energy user, the United States, accounted for nearly one-third the world's total daily consumption. As part of its total energy package, the US consumed less oil and gas and therefore imported less than the other OECD countries. In absolute terms, however, its daily imports overtopped those of any of its allies. In 1975, the level of daily consumption of oil in the US averaged 16.7 million barrels, of which 6.5 million or 38.8 percent were imported. Before 1974, most of the imported oil came from Canada and Venezuela; thereafter, both progressively curtailed exports to the US, in Canada's case, as we have seen, as part of a larger program aimed at national autarky. Thus US imports from the Arab oil states in 1975 averaged 1.64 million barrels a day, or 25.2 percent of the import total, up from 14 percent a year earlier. Concerned Americans were beginning to reveal anxiety over the expanding Arab portion of OPEC sales to the US.

The US could make or break any cooperative program. Western Europe and Japan expected the United States to demonstrate the modes of self-discipline. A deliberate 10 percent cut in American consumption in 1975, for example, would have reduced imports by 26 percent and vulnerability correspondingly; and the loss of daily sales of more than 1.5 million barrels might also have given OPEC pause. The allies of the US understandably were dismayed over its continuing failure to enact bold conservation measures or to develop a viable program of exploration for new conventional supplies and of research and development in synthetics and conversion products and in new forms of energy. Instead of showing how to save the wasting resource, the US persisted in wasteful habits. The existing conspicuous guzzlers—automotive vehicles, temperature-controlled buildings, power stations, and industrial machinery—were the inefficient products of cheap energy and too numerous and widespread for prompt and inclusive control or early replacement. Initial standby measures of conservation—introduction of daylight-saving time, reduced speed limits on the highways, and the upgrading of efficiency standards for automobiles—were not followed by others with persistence or imagination.

Nor was an agreed long-range program, with incentives and restraints, put together, although the US did set up an Energy Research and Development Administration (ERDA) and inaugurated measures for accumulating a strategic reserve of one billion barrels of imported crude oil by 1982. Meanwhile, cooperation between the US and its industrial allies was impeded, as they moved in opposite directions in trying to cope with the effect of OPEC's price rises. The US artificially kept domestic oil prices low, while its allies made no effort to shield their domestic markets from external influences, allowing internal prices to soar beyond the already steep levels.

As the country with the most elaborate infrastructure for energy technology, the US should have vigorously pursued research and development for more efficient consumption of conventional resources and for alternative forms of energy. Instead, it was mired in indecisiveness and in unimaginative, slow-moving plans, even after ERDA came into being. Many blamed it on the Congressional President, the first in the country's history. Others blamed it on the singlemindedness of the conservationists and the environmentalists. Still others blamed it on the greed of the oil industry. But most of all, the constitutional controversy between the Congress and the Executive, in which energy issues had become entrapped, accounted for the American indecision.

In 1976, observers were much too easily ascribing the lack of positive action to the national elections. Undeniably, the elections were taking their toll. Yet even if the president chosen in November were to receive an unequivocal mandate, there was no assurance that he would be able in cooperation with the Congress to frame and win enactment of decisive legislation, since the national energy controversy did not divide along normal lines of political partisanship and economic ideology. Given the atomization of the groups taking part in the debate, it seemed unlikely that an early consensus could be reached on domestic exploration and production, research and development, conservation, and environmental protection, with generous consideration to the needs of the industrial allies of the United States and to the wants of the rest of the world. Such a program would at the very least have to promote the progressive movement from waste to efficiency, from high dependence on a rapidly depleting fuel to fuels in plentiful supply, and from a declining concern for the environment to a durable sensitivity to the maintenance of its balance. If these simple principles eluded the American reach, the explanation could be found in the country's deep divisions over energy issues. The divisions ran, not along party lines, but along interest-group lines, under a Constitution temporarily unhinged by Vietnam and Watergate. The Constitution's system of delicate checks and balances had given way to dominant checks and a vanishing balance. Domestic energy policymaking, in effect, stood still.

Despite the immobilism, the US government—or perhaps more accurately, Secretary of State Kissinger—contrived to bring about the diplomatic negotiations for the creation of an International Energy Agency, as a subsidiary of the OECD. Not an ideal agency that functioned resolutely, the IEA nevertheless did harness, if only loosely, most members of the OECD behind a clutch of virtuous objectives. The creation moved in the right direction. If the IEA proved to be a slow developer, it could be attributed to the inattention and inertia of its members, perhaps most of all to the distractions of the US and its failure—more aptly perhaps, its inability—to follow through.

Most European powers—the EEC included—and Japan acquiesced in American leadership in energy crisis management, not always, however, without resistance. In doing so, they tried to preserve their identities. France, which insisted on going it alone, opposed any international system that the United States might dominate, refusing formally to join the IEA, while accepting its benefits. Even within the EEC, France continued to uphold the Gaullist tradition of national identity first, Common Market second. Nevertheless, France served as a mediator between the industrial states and the oil-exporting states. The French initiative culminated in 1975 in meetings of representatives from the OECD and resource-rich members of the Group of 77 (whose ranks had grown to 112), as spokesman for the Third and Fourth worlds, to seek an accommodation on energy and raw materials. After a slow and uncertain start in the spring of 1975, the two groups assembled at the inaugural session of the Conference on International Economic Cooperation (CIEC) in Paris in December. Whether the institutionalized North-South exchanges in four continuous commissions, one each on development and finance as well as energy and raw materials, would linger into permanence or wither away, it was still too early to tell.

Much of the initial panic of the fall of 1973 among the OECD countries arose from the lack of information, preparation, and contingent policies. They were exercised, not over the energy crisis alone, but over its international economic and political spinoff—money, trade, aid, and investment. The combination explained the rush of West European countries and Japan for barter deals in competition with one another to their mutual disadvantage. It was OAPEC's production cutback in the October War that encouraged OPEC to double the price of oil; it was the scramble of the industrial states for oil deals that persuaded OPEC to redouble the price less than three months later.

One of the immediate effects of the energy crisis in the OECD area was to intensify the pressures for national solutions. The industrial oil producers—Canada and Norway as well as the US—promoted autarky, and Britain looked forward to it. The industrial nonproducers, among them Britain at the time, scrambled.

Also emphatically nationalist were the frantic efforts to promote the return flow, or recycling, of the massive oil revenues pouring into OPEC coffers. In the event, the recycling was brisk, including trade and investment, but the OPEC governments favored those strong OECD economies with the least risk (US, Germany, and Japan), that is, those with the least relative need. At the other end of the OECD economic scale, Britain suffered a major reverse. In view of the double-digit inflation and related economic ills in Britain, it would be overstating the case to attribute the abrupt decline in the value of sterling between November 1975 and June 1976 wholly to the fiscal assault on the British pound by the ministates of the Persian Gulf. Yet the timing of their policies hastened and aggravated the decline. As late as 1974, OPEC governments had accepted sterling in payment for as much as one-fifth of the oil sold to foreign countries. In 1975, sterling payments sank to less than 12 percent, and in the first quarter of 1976, to less than 6 percent. What the doomsday prophets for some time had been predicting was played out in Britain: first came the marked contraction of sterling payments to OPEC governments, followed by withdrawal of sterling accounts and ending in the replacement of sterling investments. On the positive side, the standby credit for $5.3 billion from ten other industrial states in June 1976 bought time for Britain to take remedial steps.

Crisis for OECD became opportunity for OPEC. The Middle East oil states were determined to use the bonanza for economic growth and diversification; for improvement of their status in the international organizations and enhancement of their political and economic influence in the world community; and for furtherance of the interests of the oil-dry nonindustrial states.

The common legacy of hostility and suspicion toward the OECD strengthened the ties between OPEC and the remaining nonindustrial countries. In their eyes, all members of the OECD were guilty by association with the former imperial powers, and unpopular OECD policies were indiscriminately labeled neocolonialism. This notion, the Soviet Union, Communist China, and their communist allies nurtured through the propaganda media. The oil-bereft countries thus experienced a vicarious thrill from OPEC's "victories." They too aspired to better their own economic condition, particularly those states with raw materials largely produced for OECD markets. The resource-rich states hoped to create cartels, comparable to OPEC, and supported its appeals for price indexation, and together with OPEC became the vocal delegates of the South in the CIEC. Although OPEC refused to establish preferential oil prices for the poor countries, its members compensated in part by low-interest loans and grants.

The sudden affluence yielded unplanned side effects: overheated economies and double-digit inflation, unbalanced growth at the infrastructural and productive levels, and clogged channels of distribution (ports, highways, mass transit, marketing facilities). In the meantime, the lack of trained manpower and institutions for initiating, implementing, and monitoring development plans impeded their efforts to use the new wealth as an effective instrument of policy toward the Fourth World. The combination of side effects threatened to overwhelm the oil states with delayed crises arising from hasty, ill-conceived opportunism instead of prudent use of the energy opportunity.

Furthermore, as in the OECD, nationalism at times also threatened to divide the OPEC. Its members, it is true, on occasion resolved long-standing disputes, as Iraq and Iran did in 1975 along their fractious boundary. Nevertheless, in the hierarchy of external aid, as we have seen, the oil-deprived Arab states come first; the first among these equals were those contiguous with Israel, replaced in mid-1976 by Lebanon. On the problems of Lebanon and Palestine at that time, the radical oil governments (Libya, Iraq, and Algeria) were working at cross-purposes with the conservative oil states (Saudi Arabia, Kuwayt, and the neighboring ministates). Relations between the Arab oil states in the Persian Gulf and non-Arab Iran grew verbally tense early in 1976 over proposals to create an Arabian Gulf News Agency and an Arabian Gulf Common Market. These developments suggested the possibility of future trouble within OPEC. From this subject many Western analysts shied away, because of the ample evidence of the continuing good health of the cartel as a price-fixer and because of the recognition that its members were not yet prepared to destroy, or even weaken, such an enviable money-maker.

Communications between OECD and OPEC were already jammed by enough static without need for further interference. Yet both sides persisted in their seeming preference for rhetoric over unambiguous language, often confusing their members as well as their adversaries. "Confrontation" found its way early into OEPC's vocabulary. The oil states could hardly be faulted if they preferred to deal with the major importers one by one, rather than as a group, so as to retain bargaining advantages. The French government also used the concept freely, as a means of suggesting identification with OPEC in its quarrel with the OECD. For example, OPEC labeled as confrontational the proposed creation of the IEA. Many Europeans agreed and, at first, resisted the American argument that establishing a voluntary international energy agency for members of the OECD would protect the importers' interest in negotiations with OPEC and the preparation of common and complementary energy programs.

American officials popularized "interdependence," at which some Europeans initially looked askance but which later most of their governments tended to accept uncritically as a useful concept. Interdependence in and of itself is a neutral condition that prevails between states which have become economic partners, whether in trade, aid, money, or investment. It may give rise to positive or negative effects or both. The OECD and the OPEC interdepended in crude oil. As long as low prices and free flow were the order of the day, the OECD viewed the condition as positive; the OPEC, increasingly as negative. The attitudes were reversed after the fall of 1973. Manifestly it is only the mutuality of interest and the recognition thereof that may be expected to yield positive results.

In the winter of 1973-74, the industrial importers of OPEC oil traded charges across the Atlantic over the resort to "bilateralism." The word was used to describe the scramble of the OECD members in the search for barter deals with individual oil states. In return, what American officials called "crisis management" during and after the October War, the Europeans often perceived as American bilateralism. A measure of bilateralism could be found in all US efforts at crisis management in the Middle East at that time, since a dividing line between the two could not be clearly fixed. At times, in American official usage, the bilateralism of West European countries and Japan bordered on immorality, since they were not cooperating in the common cause.

OPEC spokesmen on their part claimed that the massive transfer of monetary resources to the oil states was long overdue, since it was a mode of redistributing the world's wealth from the rich states to the poor. Superficially plausible, that contention, on close scrutiny, was no less rhetorical than most of the others. It did not require deep probing to ascertain that the sudden price rise resulted in the transfer of wealth to the OPEC sphere not from the rich First World alone, but even from the poorest of the poor Fourth World. Even if the OPEC governments had eagerly sought to draw up share-the-new-wealth programs for their less fortunate neighbors, none of the oil governments had in being the requisite bureaucratic and fiscal apparatus for the creation and prudent management of such programs. Moreover, the OPEC members, with few exceptions, seemed to draw an impassable line between interstate and intrastate redistribution. In most OPEC countries, the monumental revenues were widening the gap between the rich and the poor, the towns and the villages. As slowly and lopsidedly as the urban economy developed in the oil states, the pace of rural economic growth was even slower and more irregular. The suggestion about the redistribution of the world's wealth also aroused exaggerated aspirations in the Fourth World, especially among the resource-rich countries, which expected to receive help in organizing cartels so as to raise the prices of raw materials. Such cartels were not easy to establish, since, among other reasons, the production and sale of no other raw material could be organized on the model of OPEC.

Perhaps the most serious political consequence of the energy crisis was the globalization of the Arab-Israel dispute. Admittedly, OAPEC's shriveling supply in and after the October War had sparked the original steep rise in the price of crude oil in the fall of 1973, which in turn set off the critical reactions in the OECD. But the October War itself, it must be remembered, had aroused far more limited international concern than the energy crisis, affecting primarily the belligerents (Egypt, Israel, and Syria) and their active supporters (the members of the Arab League, the Soviet Union, the United States, and individual allies of the superpowers). The linkage of the Arab-Israel dispute and the energy crisis, which came to be known in the current idiom as the Middle East problem, launched the Arab-Israel dispute on its own earth-girding circuit, even before the UN Security Council stopped the war twenty days after its start.

In analyzing the abrupt globalization of the Arab-Israel dispute, one must bear in mind that the European allies of the United States (with the exception of Norway and potentially Britain, and the partial exception of the Netherlands) are energy-vulnerable, not to the same degree as Japan, but certainly much more so than Canada and the United States. The vulnerability goes a long way toward explaining their unfolding attitudes and policies. After October 1973, the West European countries and Japan did not recover from the trauma of the Middle East problem. As we have seen, they were forced to find an unstable and uncomfortable position between the demands of the Arab members of OPEC, which threatened the use of their oil power, and those of the United States, under whose umbrella the industrial allies still clustered.

The Arab oil states were using the oil weapon—the threatened or actual manipulation of supply and price—to isolate Israel. In the October War, it enabled them to go to the emergency aid of Egypt and Syria, which as marginal oil producers were not members of OPEC. The cutback of oil shipments to the OECD, especially the embargoes of the United States and the Netherlands, were designed among other purposes to put pressure on Washington to hew to the Arab line. After the war, oil power enabled the Arab oil governments to go to the longer-range aid of the Palestine Arabs and all frontline Arab states, by putting muscle into the attempted economic boycott of Israel, which the Arab states tried to shore up throughout the OECD.

This evoked from Israel and its American supporters defensive measures that focused on attempts, through legislative and administrative action, to enforce the US government's proclaimed opposition to the Arab boycott and the provisions against the discrimination already in the lawbooks. The federal government, and a number of large state governments, endorsed the warning against the intrusion into international economic transactions, above all into world commerce, of racism—in particular, discrimination against American citizens on grounds of religion. At the same time, spokesmen in Washington contended that the Arab boycott of Israel could best be resolved through a settlement of the Arab-Israel dispute.

Advocates of Israel addressed comparable appeals to the other OECD governments, with variable but generally less productive results. In any case, experience had shown that the boycott, as in the past, continued to be applied unevenly at best and with pragmatic flexibility. Major corporations, in the US and other industrial countries, did business openly with both Israel and the Arab states. Additionally, in awarding new contracts, Arab governments and businessmen were prone to take decisions largely on the basis of such traditional commercial criteria as quality, price, and prompt delivery rather than on the political stance of the exporting country.

In upholding the boycott, Arab spokesmen never tired of explaining that they had simply adopted a hallowed instrument of US foreign policy, commonly used in an international crisis or actual war. The war with Israel, they argued, had never ended, because a truce or an armistice represented no more than a cessation of hostilities, not a formal settlement. When pressed to move toward formal peace, the Arab states proved no less inflexible than Israel, as attested in the fall of 1975 by the inflamed reaction throughout the Arab world to Egypt's second interim agreement with Israel, which bound the parties, not to a full settlement, but merely to a temporary suspension of belligerency. The mutual suspicions, and the tensions they engendered, ran too deep on both sides to arouse realistic expectations of an early, durable, and general accord. The net effect of the new lease on life that the oil weapon gave to the Arab League's economic boycott office, was to project the Arab-Israel dispute into the national politics of many countries, rich and poor, that had been adversely affected by the energy crisis.

Confusion thus prevailed over the continuing relationship between the Arab-Israel dispute and the energy crisis. The two were not actually decoupled in March 1974 when Secretary Kissinger, with the support of Saudi Arabia, persuaded the Arab oil states to end the cutbacks and the embargoes. The Arab oil states, within the Arab League, simply shifted to a more subtle use of the oil weapon. They implied that a renewal of the war with Israel would yield an even more drastic reduction of oil sales than in 1973-74. With this warning, they hoped to bend the industrial states to a pro-Arab position. Arab League spokesmen also implied that a settlement of the Arab-Israel dispute, on Arab terms, would automatically settle the energy crisis. In fact, a general Arab-Israel agreement might remove one irritant. But the option in the application of oil power for other goals than isolating Israel would remain so long as the sellers' market lasted. Moreover, the energy crisis itself could not be resolved except through the development of long-range, cooperative policies among the industrial states and in consultation with the nonindustrial states.

The chapters in this book that assess the changing attitudes in the First World toward the Arab-Israel dispute underline the appreciable move from what had been an earlier pro-Israel neutrality to a pro-Arab neutrality. The most energy-vulnerable industrial states—Japan and much of Western Europe—tended in effect to appease the Arabs. These changes could be attributed to their perception of the security interest, which they believed required an early solution of the Arab-Israel dispute. The comparable change in official attitude in Canada derived largely from economic considerations, the hope of selling advanced technology and consumer goods to the oil states at competitive prices. Yet the governments of Japan, Western Europe, and Canada were at pains to publicize their endorsement of the principle of the continued existence of Israel. In mid-summer of 1975, the statement by the eleven heads of socialist governments in Europe, convening in Sweden, opposed any attempt to expel Israel from the United Nations. The Nine had already gone further in May by concluding with Israel a trade and cooperation agreement, which cut tariffs on Israel's industrial products by 60 percent as of 1 July 1975 and pledged to eliminate them altogether by 1977.

The political assurances of the industrial states, however, gave scant comfort to Israel, which questioned the firmness of their commitment to its secure existence. Israel's suspicions were not always put into words; its fixed, defensive policies on the Arab states and the Palestine Arabs often spoke more loudly. Many Israelis were persuaded that, in a crunch, their beleaguered state could not rely on ostensible friends whose record of response to the demands of the Arab oil states appeared, in the Israeli perspective, to derive more from expediency than from principle. They were angered by the engrossment of the industrial states with an early settlement of the dispute with the Arabs, giving primacy to time over terms. To put it differently, Israel's own preoccupation with security and military self-reliance reflected the nagging doubts of its government and public over the wisdom of leaning on others when political survival might be at stake. Western, including American, observers frequently described Israel's policies as intransigent. This criticism most Israelis felt was one-sided, in view of the inflexible ambiguity of the Palestine Liberation Organization (PLO) on the future of Israel, a deliberate vagueness to which all Arab governments subscribed. In addition, many Israelis and their foreign sympathizers harbored exaggerated fears about the petrodollars that the Arab oil states might pour without limit into the conflict with Israel, which would then potentially be placed at comparative disadvantage, despite the generous aid from the United States. Above all, the growing consensus in the industrial world on the need to bring the Palestine Arabs into any formal settlement, even if always tied to assurances for Israel's continued existence, made Israelis jumpy. They and their patrons, however, most deeply resented the spreading pressure on Israel by OECD countries to recognize the PLO without insisting on reciprocity.

Uppermost on the minds of the energy-vulnerable industrial governments lay anxiety about another Arab-Israel war. Many were convinced of its inevitability and its certain accompaniment by oil cutbacks and embargoes. Politicians, like generals, remain captives of the last crisis. War is not inevitable until it actually breaks out. In the event of another war with Israel, the Arab producers might reasonably be expected to slow or shut down the flow of crude oil to individual industrial countries, or perhaps even to the OECD area as a whole. Whatever the consequence, there was hardly likely to be a repeat performance of 1973-74. The major consumers had in the interval come together in the IEA and in its evolving cooperative program that aimed to assure rational and collective action, despite the divergent national energy conditions and interests. They were already exchanging information and attempting to coordinate guidelines, among them plans for emergency sharing of oil and the buildup of strategic stockpiles, pending agreement on comprehensive policies.

The Arab states, led by the oil producers, also used the newfound influence to bend the Fourth World toward an anti-Israel posture. The Arab League and the Organization for African Unity pledged mutual support for upgrading liberation movements. Through comparable combinations, the Arab League shepherded anti-Israel resolutions and actions through the UN General Assembly, and at times also the Security Council, despite US opposition. The league systematically politicized the UN specialized agencies such as UNESCO, WHO, and ILO, as well as UN and other international meetings, such as the Women's International Year World Conference in Mexico City in June 1975. The Arab states used these agencies and meetings as platforms for enlarging international support for the Palestine Arabs. In the Euro-Arab dialogue, which France had inspired, the EEC sought to explore economic issues of mutual interest (trade, investment, technology). The Arabs on their side never tired of attempting to commit the European powers to an unmistakable anti-Israel position; they also demanded far-reaching preferential trade agreements. The EEC resisted these pressures, and the dialogue moved, if at all, only sluggishly.

Since Japan and Western Europe, France excepted, recognized their inability to project mediatory influence into the Arabs' quarrel with Israel, they willingly allowed the United States to act as sole mediator for peace. Ever since the creation of Israel in 1948, the quest for "evenhandedness" had motivated US policy on the Arab-Israel conflict. That term conveys many meanings. It might connote nothing more than the search for neutrality in the Arab-Israel conflict, enabling the United States to judge each issue on its merits. After 1955, the Kremlin systematically endeavored to polarize the Arab-Israel zone, by proclaiming the Soviet Union as the faithful friend of the Arabs and the United States as the constant companion of Israel.

In reaction, the US pursued the diplomacy of antipolarization, in which it admitted its friendship with Israel, but simultaneously made ardent efforts to preserve the friendship of friendly Arab states. From the outset, for example, the US adamantly refused to recognize Jerusalem as the capital of Israel. The position on Jerusalem was not wholly motivated by the appeal for Arab friendship, as was, however, President Eisenhower's pressure on Israel in the 1956 Suez crisis to reverse its policy on the occupation of Sinai. President Kennedy instituted in the early 1960s a generous program of agricultural surplus aid to Egypt. Even President Nixon, who ordered the airlift to Israel in the October War, had four years earlier urged the substantial but conditional return of the occupied territories to the Arab states, the so-called Rogers Plan, a proposal that Israel strongly disliked. In other words, pro-Arab policies offset pro-Israel policies all along, regardless of the party in power. Evenhandedness, in this context, was a projection of the standard position taken by the United States in the postwar Middle East and North Africa. In these years, whenever Britain and France were negotiating for the surrender of their imperial holdings, the United States took a middle position between its allies and the emergent states struggling for national independence.

Under President Anwar al-Sadat, Egypt after the October War accepted US mediation as the most likely means of persuading Israel to evacuate Sinai. Sadat perceptibly believed that only the United States could move Israel out of the occupied territories. With prevailing attitudes in the OECD favoring a pro-Arab neutrality, Israel's major resource for vigorous survival was narrowed to the unquestioned support of the American government. If this were to take such shape, the continued strong pro-Israel policies in the US might be viewed as evenhanded, not in an American context, but in an OECD context. More than that, the United States for the first time accepted an openended commitment to peacekeeping as well as peacemaking in the Arab-Israel zone. This was suggested by the high cost of Kissinger's modest, if dramatic, peacemaking achievements and perhaps even more by the US obligation to peacekeeping, as the sole external electronic surveillant of the second Egyptian-Israel interim agreement of September 1975.

The energy crisis and the Arab-Israel dispute created new problems for allied security. On the surface, it appeared that Soviet influence in the Arab-Israel area had sharply declined after the October War. The Soviet Union in effect had opted out of the mediation effort, because of failure to establish its impartiality by restoring diplomatic relations with Israel. Still, the foreign policymakers in Moscow could, and indeed did, contribute to slowing the pace and reducing the scale of Kissinger's accomplishment, even though the USSR itself, given its continued strained relations with Israel, could not in the foreseeable future become a credible proponent of stability in the Arab-Israel zone.

* * * *

While anxiety about the general fossil-fuel condition has not vanished, there is nevertheless too much complacency—in attempts to solve the energy problem—over action that might or should be taken to restore stability to the international oil industry, over the future role of the US in international energy crisis management, over the spread of nationalism and the weakening of cooperative endeavor, over the politicization of the oil industry (less in management, which has always been politicized, than in marketing) because of its enmeshment with the Arab-Israel dispute, and finally over solving that dispute.

The days of the oil industry as such are numbered, its limits fixed by the coming exhaustion of its resource. It will be replaced before the disappearance of the natural supplies by an international energy industry, doubtless with many more participant national units than now prevail in the exploration, development, transportation, refining, and marketing of oil. It would be prudent if governments and businessmen and people at large tried to learn the lessons of their experience with oil and to benefit from past errors. Given the record of mankind, it would be a safe and sage bet that we shall repeat many of the same mistakes and commit many new ones. But the policymakers should at least be urged to give undivided attention to the technical, political, and economic problems of reshaping the international oil industry into an international energy industry, so that adequate safeguards might be instituted to satisfy national—among them, environmental—interests and to guarantee plentiful supplies for all states on uniform terms and at equitable prices.

The international leadership of the US, as noted, has been fitful at best. It has from time to time taken strong and, on balance, sound measures in the common interest. Most observers who have commented on the lack of sustained American leadership have attributed it to Watergate and to the national elections of 1976.

While these factors ought not to be ignored, much more serious has been the entrapment of the energy issue in the ongoing domestic controversy between the Congress and the President. While it is essential, for inspired and forceful US leadership in international energy affairs, to return the next president to the White House with an unquestioned public mandate, that in itself will not be adequate. As the first order of energy business, the post-election president should bend every effort to dissociate the energy-related problems from the constitutional struggle. Moreover, he will have to bear in mind that US leadership in the energy crisis after 1973 resulted from the personal diplomacy of a powerful and imaginative secretary of state. A strong president's ability to resuscitate US international energy leadership and to infuse new life into the unfolding international energy program might thus be enhanced by a strong secretary of state.

There is little point in our continuing to beat our breasts over the reasserting nationalism in the industrial states and the consequent undermining of the OECD partnership. Nationalism in energy affairs can be a benignant trend, since each industrial country has particular patterns of energy use and external dependence that differ from those of its partners. The problem in any international endeavor is not to suppress nationalism but to harness it. All states share an interest in a vibrant international energy industry that can become to some degree self-regulating while remaining fully accountable to the governments of the countries that it serves and sensitive to their demands. Besides, if nationalism has hampered effective cooperation on energy within the OECD, the industrial states might take some comfort in the multiplying signs of nationalism within the OPEC. So long as such comfort does not harden into passiveness, but is viewed as an opportunity for even larger constructive and cooperative action between the OECD and OPEC in their mutual interest, we may yet begin to experience less public and official anxiety over the future of energy.

The politicization of the oil industry by its entanglement with the Arab-Israel dispute and its wider implications may prove to pose the most stubborn difficulties. Among OECD members, it is clear, less alarm was aroused by the Middle East oil states' economic than by their political manipulation of oil. In the past, the Arab states have used oil power in their determined pursuit of justice for the Palestine Arabs. With that as precedent, what might prevent OPEC in the future from taking up other political causes? The industrial states were disquieted by having to pay an irrelevant political, as well as an oligopolistic economic, price for the oil they required for their economic health. This reinforced the lingering anxiety over the possibilities of another Arab-Israel war or the use of oil to extract still other political concessions. The fear, as the US understood from the start, could be laid to rest only by separating the Arab-Israel issues from those of the energy crisis.

That was one of the central goals of Kissinger's personal diplomacy. He proved unable in the end to separate the entwining controversies into their original components. Yet he dealt with each, as if the two had already been pulled apart. The next president and his secretary of state will have to work even harder to finish the job, so that the allies of the US may safely take the same stance. No one can deny that a formal Arab-Israel settlement would fulfill that purpose. But there are no easy routes to formal peace in the Middle East in the short term because the deep mutual suspicions betwen Arabs and Israelis and the tensions that they generate do not lend themselves to removal by simple formulas. There may not even be long-term peaceable solutions, only those which time itself might bring. But unless the Arab-Israel dispute and the energy crisis are cleanly decoupled, the industrial states are certain to be burdened by the continued intrusion of the quarrel into other issues and activities where it does not belong.

A moiety of mutual trust and good will, if the statesmanship can be found to evoke it, holds the primary hope for depoliticizing the energy crisis, overcoming the technological problems of discovering fresh supplies of fossil fuels and inventing new forms of energy, and reaching an agreed Arab-Israel accommodation.

Notes

2. US International Leadership

1. Henry R. Nau, "Diplomatic Uses of Technology in U.S. Energy Policy," Occasional Papers, no. 28 (February 1975) published by the Norman Patterson School of International Affairs, Carleton University, Ottawa, Canada; also L. Scheinman, "International Energy Research and Development: Problems and Prospects," in same.

3. Canada's Quest for Energy Autarky

1. The National Energy Board, created in 1959, regulates specific areas of the oil, gas, and electrical industries and advises the government on all matters concerned with the development and use of energy resources.

4. Western Europe: The Politics of Muddling Through

1. Kommission der Europäischen Gemeinschaft, *Notwendige Fortschritte auf dem Gebiet der gemeinschaftlichen Energiepolitik: Mitteilung der Kommission an den Rat,* 13 October 1972.
2. Op. cit., p. 16.
3. Cf. Louis Turner, "Europe: The Politics of the Energy Crisis," *International Affairs* (London) 50 (July 1974): 410.
4. Cf. Maull, "The Strategy of Avoidance," chapter 9.
5. Cf. Greenwood, "Canada's Quest for Energy Autarky," chapter 3, for a similar deal between western Canadian producer provinces and the eastern consumer provinces in 1961.

7. American Interest Groups after October 1973

1. For more details, see Trice, "Domestic Interest Groups and the Arab-Israeli Conflict, 1966-1974: A Behavioral Analysis," paper presented at the annual meeting of ISA, Toronto, Canada, February 1976.

2. See the following reports of the Anti-Defamation League, all issued in November 1973: *Negative Reactions to Israel's Plight; The Response of American Institutional Life to the Middle East Crisis;* and *American Press Reaction to the Mideast Conflict.*
3. A comparison of the 8 October, 22 October, and 10 December 1973 polls indicates that 47 percent, 48 percent, and 50 percent, respectively, of the informed public sided with Israel, while 6 percent, 6 percent, and 7 percent favored the Arab states. This distribution parallels that of a 1969 Gallup poll, when 50 percent and 5 percent of the informed public supported Israel and the Arab states, respectively.
4. Louis Harris, "Oil or Israel?" *The New York Times Magazine,* 6 April 1975, p. 21 ff.

8. Canada: Evenhanded Ambiguity

1. Address to the House of Commons, 16 October 1973, *Statements and Speeches* (Department of External Affairs, Information Division, Ottawa), pp. 1-2; hereafter referred to as *Statements and Speeches.*
2. "Canadian Participation in the United Nations Emergency Force for the Middle East," *Statements and Speeches,* 1973, no. 29, pp. 2-3.
3. Address to UN General Assembly, 29th Session, 25 September 1974, *Statements and Speeches,* 1974, p. 6.
4. "Canadian Participation in the United Nations Emergency Force for the Middle East," *Statements and Speeches,* 1973, no. 23, p. 8.
5. MacEachen, Statement to UN General Assembly, 20 November 1974, *Statements and Speeches,* 1974, no. 16.
6. Canadian Delegation to the UN, Statement on Resolutions 3236 and 3237 by Ambassador Saul F. Rae, press release no. 35, 22 November 1974.
7. Minutes of Proceedings and Evidence of the Standing Committee on External Affairs and National Defense, *House of Commons,* 22 October 1974, p. 16; reply to a question, House of Commons Debates, Hansard, 12 November 1974, p. 1260; and 26 November 1974, p. 1287.
8. In Riyadh, Prince Sa'ud ibn Faysal, the foreign minister, said he hoped that Canada would recognize the PLO because "this would be a major step toward bringing the whole issue into context. . . . But," he added, "representation is not the

crux of the issue, the real problem is how you resolve the problem between the Palestinians and Israel." King Husayn told Canadian reporters that insofar as Canadian recognition of the PLO is concerned, "I believe it is entirely up to them." See David MacDonald, "Arabs Don't Press Canada on PLO," *Winnipeg Free Press,* 20 January 1976.

9. *Montreal Star,* 19 January 1976.
10. Canadian Delegation to the UN, Statement on Resolutions 3236 and 3237, press release no. 35, 22 November 1974.
11. Canada opposed Resolution 3379, which declared Zionism to be racist, and two related resolutions on the implementation of the program against racism which were "tainted" by the reference to Zionism. One month later, however, Canada abstained on a resolution (3520) to implement the program of the Mexico City Conference on the Status of Women which included a declaration against Zionism.
12. Statement to the House of Commons, Hansard, 21 July 1975.
13. Statement to the press, 12 January 1976, Cairo, *Statements and Speeches.*
14. Ibid.; the Canadian International Development Agency (CIDA) would supervise Canadian bilateral aid. Egypt had not previously received CIDA project aid.
15. For a description of the repeated attempts to secure a statement of government policy on the boycott, see Frank Slover, "Arab Boycott of Israel a Topic to Avoid," *Montreal Gazette,* 15 January 1976. Slover argues that the subject of the boycott is deliberately avoided by officials of the Department of Industry, Trade, and Commerce and by the EDC.
16. Statement to the press, 12 January 1976, Cairo, *Statements and Speeches,* p. 5.

9. The Strategy of Avoidance: Europe's Middle East Policies after the October War

1. This might well be a more general aspect of decision-making in international bodies without a strong institutionalized, preprogrammed crisis-reflex reaction. It certainly appears confirmed by the failure to activate the OECD oil emergency scheme in 1973. If so, the crisis-reaction scheme of the IEA might be considered as inadequately mechanical to guarantee its success.
2. *Le Monde,* 10 October 1973.
3. *The Times* (London), 7 November 1973.

4. Full text in Keesing's Contemporary Archives 1973, p. 25.427.
5. Stanley Hoffman, "Franco-American Differences over the Arab-Israeli Conflict," *Public Policy,* no. 19 (Fall 1971), p. 541.
6. *Al-Nahar,* 4 December 1973.

10. Japan's Tilting Neutrality

1. Japan's other primary energy sources are coal, 16.3 percent; hydropower, 2.6 percent; natural gas, 1.1 percent; and nuclear power, 0.9 percent.

11. Petrodollars, Arms Trade, and the Pattern of Major Conflicts

1. Useful compilations of data on arms transfers are the annual issues by the International Institute for Strategic Studies of *The Military Balance,* and the Stockholm International Peace Research Institute's Yearbook, *World Armaments and Disarmament.*
2. See the interview in *The New York Times,* 13 November 1973.
3. For recent reports on Israeli planning along these lines see Zeev Schiff, "The New Balance of Power," *Midstream* (January 1976), pp. 7-15; William Tuohy, "Israeli Military Seen Stronger Than Ever," *The Los Angeles Times,* 9 February 1976.
4. On the technological breakthroughs in conventional weaponry represented by the new panoply of PGMs, see James Digby, "Precision-Guided Weapons," *Adelphi Papers* no. 118 (Summer 1975).
5. A February 1976 report by the General Accounting Office of the US Congress recommended eliminating most overseas military advisory groups because their main function has become the facilitation of arms sales to host countries.
6. Some prerequisites of viable arms control in the Middle East and the nuclear-arms problem are discussed in more detail in this author's article, "Not by War Alone: Curbing the Arab-Israeli Arms Race," *The Middle East Journal* 28 (Summer 1977): 233-47.

12. The Abiding Threat of War: Perspectives in Israel

1. See, for example, Thomas O. Enders, "OPEC and the Industrial Countries: the Next Ten Years," *Foreign Affairs* 53 (July 1975): 625-37.

2. See Ian Smart, "Uniqueness and Generality," *Daedalus* 104 (Fall 1975): 259-81.
3. Enders, op. cit., p. 628.
4. See Brian Beedham, "Survey: Out of the Fire: Oil, the Gulf and the West," *The Economist,* 17 May 1975, pp. 75-77.
5. See Jeremy Russell, *Energy as a Factor in Soviet Foreign Policy* (Lexington, Mass.: D. C. Heath & Company, 1976).

14. Mixing Oil and Money

1. For a concise and useful survey of the energy crisis and its economic implications, see Edward R. Fried and Charles L. Schultze, eds., *Higher Oil Prices and the World Economy: The Adjustment Problem* (Washington: The Brookings Institution, 1975).
2. US Treasury estimates, as quoted in *International Herald Tribune,* 20 January 1976 and 3 February 1976.
3. Idem.
4. C. Fred Bergsten, "Oil and the Cash Flow," *The New York Times,* 3 June 1974, reproduced in C. Fred Bergsten, *Toward a New International Economic Order: Selected Papers of C. Fred Bergsten, 1972-1974* (Lexington, Mass.: D.C. Heath & Company, 1975), chapter 8.
5. Cf. Benjamin J. Cohen, "The Political Economy of Monetary Reform Today," *Journal of International Affairs* (USA) 30 (Spring 1976).
6. See Robert Solomon, "The Allocation of 'Oil Deficits,' " *Brookings Papers on Economic Activity* 1 (1975): 61-79; and Andrew D. Crockett and Duncan Ripley, "Sharing the Oil Deficit," *International Monetary Fund Staff Papers* 22 (July 1975): 284-312.
7. See Erb and Low, "The Oil Crisis and Resource Transfers to the Developing World," chapter 15. Smaller countries have had to rely primarily on private international financial markets to finance current deficits. Only two multilateral recycling facilities have been established: the "oil facility" in the IMF and the Financial Support Fund in the OECD. The funds committed to the oil facility (now lapsed), however, were minuscule, and the Financial Support Fund was not yet ratified at the time of writing. To some observers, this suggests that the strong countries were deliberately trying to preserve their international status and influence at the expense of the weak. See Bruce Campbell and Lynn

K. Mytelka, "Petrodollar Flows, Foreign Aid, and International Stratification," *Journal of World Trade Law* 9 (November-December 1975): 597-621.

8. See Constantine Michalopoulos, "Financing Needs of Developing Countries: Proposals for International Action," *Essays in International Finance,* no. 110 (Princeton: International Finance Section, June 1975); and Gerald A. Pollack, "Are the Oil-Payments Deficits Manageable?" ibid., no. 111 (June 1975).
9. OECD, *Economic Outlook,* 17 (July 1975): 52, 58, and 117.
10. Ibid., p. 61; and IMF, *Annual Report 1975* (Washington, 1975), p. 13.
11. Idem.
12. A World Bank estimate, as quoted in *The Economist,* 16 August 1975, p. 60.
13. An estimate of the joint Development Committee of the IMF and World Bank, as quoted in *The Economist,* 10 January 1976, p. 73.
14. Idem.
15. Ibid., pp. 73-74.
16. See *IMF Survey,* 5 January 1976, p. 8.
17. Thomas D. Willett, "The Oil-Transfer Problem and International Economic Stability," *Essays in International Finance,* no. 113 (Princeton: International Finance Section, December 1975), p. 16.

15. Resource Transfers to the Developing World

1. *The Economist,* 21 February 1976, p. 84.

17. The International Energy Agency: The Political Context

1. For parts of the following discussion I draw on my "The United States, Western Europe, and the Energy Problem," *Journal of International Affairs* 30 (Spring 1976), to which the reader is referred for more detailed treatment.
2. Henri Simonet, "Energy and the Future of Europe," *Foreign Affairs* 53 (April 1975): 455.
3. Etienne Davignon, "The New International Energy Agency of OECD," *OECD Observer* 73 (January-February 1975): 20-25.
4. "The IEA Long-Term Cooperative Program," U.S. State Department Briefing Paper, 15 January 1976, and Department of State Press Release no. 43, 2 February 1976.

See also Clyde H. Farnsworth in *The New York Times,* 31 January 1976.

5. Some of the following is drawn from Kohl, "The United States, Western Europe, and the Energy Problem," cited.
6. David P. Calleo, "The European Coalition in a Fragmenting World," *Foreign Affairs* 54 (October 1975): 98-112.
7. Daniel Yergin, "European Energy: A Policy Evolves?" *European Community* 192 (January-February 1976): 31-36.

Contributors

BENJAMIN J. COHEN, associate professor of international economic relations at the Fletcher School of Law and Diplomacy; in 1975-76 visiting research associate at the Atlantic Institute for International Affairs (Paris); author of *The Question of Imperialism: The Political Economy of Dominance and Dependence* and other works.

MELVIN A. CONANT, international energy consultant; formerly assistant administrator for international energy affairs, Federal Energy Administration, Washington, D.C.

GUY F. ERB, senior fellow at the Overseas Development Council; former US Foreign Service officer and economic analyst in UN Conference on Trade and Development and UN Development Program; co-editor, *Beyond Dependency: The Developing World Speaks Out.*

YAIR EVRON, lecturer in international relations at the Hebrew University of Jerusalem and co-chairman of the Strategic Studies Section of its Davis Institute for International Relations; currently research fellow at the Program for Science and International Affairs, Harvard University; author of *The Middle East: Nations, Superpowers and Wars;* editor of *Strategic Issues: Terrorism, Surprise and Control of Violence* (forthcoming).

TED GREENWOOD, assistant professor of political science at the Massachusetts Institute of Technology and a research associate in the Program for Science and International Affairs, Harvard University; author of *Making the MIRV: A Study in Defense Decision-Making;* has also published papers on energy policy and politics.

WOLFGANG HAGER, a research fellow at the Research Institute of the German Society for Foreign Policy, has studied in Germany,

Sweden, and the US; author of *Western European Economic security;* coauthor with Max Kohnstamm of *A Nation Writ Large? Foreign Policy Problems before the European;* editor of *Erdol und Internationale Politik.*

KAZUSHIGE HIRASAWA, president of the Asia-Pacific Association of Japan; free-lance writer and lecturer on politics and political news commentator and interviewer for the Japan Broadcasting Corporation (NHK); former foreign service officer; editor-in-chief of Japan Times (1956-71).

J. C. HUREWITZ, professor of government and director of the Middle East Institute, Columbia University; author of *The Middle East and North Africa in World Politics* and other works.

PAUL JABBER, author of *Israel and Nuclear Weapons;* coauthor with William B. Quandt and Ann Mosely Lesch of *The Politics of Palestinian Nationalism;* assistant professor of political science at the University of California at Los Angeles.

WILFRID L. KOHL, associate professor of international affairs and director of the Johns Hopkins University Bologna Center; author of *French Nuclear Diplomacy;* editor of *Foreign Economic Policies of Industrial States* and *Comparative Foreign Policy Analysis: Theory and Cases* (both forthcoming).

HELEN C. LOW, a staff associate at the Overseas Development Council.

T. R. MCHALE, office of the president, ITT; service with Morgan Stanley (1946-76) and as an adviser on hydrocarbon sector planning in the Saudi Arab Central Planning Organization (1970-74.

HANS MAULL, research fellow at the Centre for Contemporary European Studies at the University of Sussex; former research associate at the International Institute for Strategic Studies in London; author of *Oil and Influence: The Oil Weapon Examined* and *Olmacht: Ursachen, Perspektiven, Grenzen.*

WILLIAM D. NORDHAUS, professor of economics at the Cowles Foundation for Research in Economics at Yale University.

KIICHI SAEKI, president of the Nomura Research Institute in Japan; former senior professor at the National Defense College (1953-61) and its president (1961-64); author of *Security of Japan;* coauthor of *Security of the Far East* and *Energy Crisis and Japanese Strategy.*

MASEO SAKISAKA, president of the National Institute for Research Advancement (Tokyo); chairman of the board of directors of Japan's Institute of Energy Economics and its former president (1966-76); a member of Prime Minister Miki's Economic Council.

LAWRENCE SCHEINMAN, professor of government and director of the Peace Studies Program at Cornell University; currently on leave to the Energy Research and Development Administration as senior policy analyst for international policy planning; author of studies on international organization, nuclear energy, and European integration.

IAN SMART, deputy director and director of studies, the Royal Institute of International Affairs (London); former member of the British Diplomatic Service and assistant director of the International Institute for Strategic Studies; author of papers on international security, arms control, Middle East politics, and international energy questions; coauthor with Martin Saeter of *The Political Implications of North Sea Oil and Gas.*

JANICE GROSS STEIN, associate professor of political science at McGill University; coauthor with Raymond Tanter of *International Crisis Management: Israeli Decision-Making, 1967 and 1973* (forthcoming).

ROBERT H. TRICE, assistant professor of political science at the Ohio State University; major research interests focus on the effects of interest groups, the mass media, and public opinion on American foreign policy.

Bibliography

I. National Responses to the Energy Crisis

Adelman, M. A. "Politics, Economics, and World Oil." *American Economic Review* 64 (May 1974): 58–67.

Amuzegar, Jahangir. "The North-South Dialogue: From Conflict to Compromise." *Foreign Affairs* 54 (April 1976): 547–62.

Bohi, Douglas, and Russell, Milton. *Policy Alternatives for Energy Security*. Baltimore: The Johns Hopkins University Press, 1975.

The Brookings Institution. "Cooperative Approaches to World Energy Problems." Tripartite report by fifteen experts from the European Community, Japan, and North America. Washington, D.C.: The Brookings Institution, 1974.

Campbell, John C., and Caruso, Helen. *The West and The Middle East*. New York: The Council on Foreign Relations, 1972.

Canada, Department of Energy, Mines, and Resources. *An Energy Policy for Canada: Phase 1*. Ottawa: Information Canada, 1973.

Chisholm, A. H. T. *The First Kuwait Oil Concession*. London: Frank Cass, 1975.

Erickson, Edward W., and Waverman, Leonard, eds. *The Energy Question: an International Failure of Policy*. 2 vols. Toronto: University of Toronto Press, 1974.

Ford Foundation. *A Time to Choose: America's Energy Future*. A Report of the Ford Foundation Energy Policy Project. Cambridge, Mass.: Ballinger Publishing Company, 1974.

Gasteyger, Curt, ed. *The Western World and Energy*. Atlantic paper. Farnborough: Saxon House, 1974.

Goldsborough, James. "France, the European Crisis, and the Alliance." *Foreign Affairs* 52 (April 1974) 538–54.

Greenwood, Ted. "Canadian-American Trade in Energy Resources." *International Organization* 28 (Autumn 1974): 689-710.

Grenon, Michel. *Ce Monde affamé d'energie*. Paris: Robert Laffont, 1973.

Hager, Wolfgang, ed. *Erdöl und internationale Politik*. Munich: Piper Verlag, 1975.

Hunter, Lawson A. W. *Energy Policies of the World: Canada.* Newark, Delaware: Center for the Study of Marine Policy, University of Delaware, 1975.

Kilbourn, William. *Pipeline.* Toronto: Clarke, Irwin & Company, 1970.

Krueger, Robert B. *The United States and International Oil: A Report for the Federal Energy Administration on U.S. Firms and Government Policy.* New York: Praeger Publishers, 1975.

Levy, Walter J. "World Oil Cooperation or International Chaos." *Foreign Affairs* 52 (July 1974): 690–713.

Maxwell, Judith. *Energy from the Arctic: Facts and Issues.* Washington: Canadian-American Committee, 1973.

Odell, Peter R. *Oil and World Power: Background to the Oil Crisis.* London: Penguin Books, 1974.

Otaiba, Mana Saeed al-. *OPEC and the Petroleum Industry.* New York: Halsted Press, 1975.

Plotnick, Alan R. *Petroleum: Canadian Markets and United States Foreign Trade Policy.* Seattle: University of Washington Press, 1964.

Saeter, Martin, and Smart, Ian, eds. *The Political Implications of North Sea Oil and Gas.* Guilford: IPC Science and Technology Press, 1975.

Sampson, Anthony. *The Seven Sisters: The Great Oil Companies and the World They Made.* New York: The Viking Press, 1975.

Shwadran, Benjamin. *The Middle East, Oil and the Great Powers.* 3d ed. New York: Halsted Press, 1973.

Stocking, George W. *Middle East Oil: A Study in Political and Economic Controversy.* Nashville, Tenn.: Vanderbilt University Press, 1970.

The Trilateral Commission. *OPEC, The Trilateral World, and The Developing Countries: New Arrangements for Cooperation.* New York: The Trilateral Commission, 1975.

Tsurumi, Yoshi. "Japanese Multinational Firms." *Journal of World Trade Law* 7 (January–February 1973): 74-90.

———"Japan." In *The Oil Crisis: In Perspective,* Raymond Vernon, ed. *Daedalus* 104 (Fall 1975): 113-28.

Turner, Louis. "Europe: The Politics of the Energy Crisis." *International Affairs* 50 (July 1974): 404–15.

Vernon, Raymond, ed. *The Oil Crisis: In Perspective.* Proceedings of the American Academy of Arts and Sciences. *Daedalus* 104 (Fall 1975).

Willrich, Mason. *Energy and World Politics.* New York: The Free Press, 1975.

———."Energy Independence for America." *International Affairs* 52 (January 1976) 53–66.

Yager, Joseph A., and Steinberg, Elinor B. *Energy and United States Foreign Policy.* Cambridge, Mass.: Ballinger Publishing Company, 1974.

II. Changing National Perspectives on the Arab-Israel Dispute

Aron, Raymond. *DeGaulle, Israel, and the Jews.* New York: Praeger Publishers, 1969.

Badeau, John S. *The American Approach to the Arab World.* New York: Harper & Row for the Council on Foreign Relations, 1968.

Balta, Paul, and Rulleau, Claudine. *La Politique arabe de la France de DeGaulle à Pompidou.* Paris: Sindbad, 1973.

Bell, Coral. "The October Middle East War: A Case Study of Crisis Management during Détente." *International Affairs* 50 (October 1974): 541–53.

Buren, Rainer. "Bemerkungen zum Stellenwert der arabischen Staaten in der aussenpolitischen Konzeption der Bundesrepublik Deutschland." *Beitrage zur Konfliktforschung* 4 (April 1974): 47–63.

Calleo, David P. "The European Coalition in a Fragmenting World." *Foreign Affairs* (October 1975): 98–112.

Crosbie, Sylvia Kowitt. *A Tacit Alliance: France and Israel from Suez to the Six Day War.* Princeton: Princeton University Press, 1974.

Davis, John. *The Evasive Peace: A Study of the Zionist-Arab Problem.* London: John Murray, 1968.

De la Serre, Françoise. "L'Europe des Neuf et le conflit Israelo-Arabe." *Revue Française de Science Politique* 24 (April 1974): 801–11.

Hager, Wolfgang, ed. *Erdöl und internationale Politik.* Munich: Piper Verlag, 1975.

Halperin, Samuel. *The Political World of American Zionism.* Detroit: Wayne State University Press, 1961.

Hammond, Paul Y., and Alexander, Sidney S., eds. *Political Dynamics in the Middle East.* New York: American Elsevier Publishing Co., 1972.

Hoffman, Stanley. "Franco-American Differences over the Arab-Israeli Conflict." *Public Policy,* no. 19 (Fall 1971): 539–66.

Hurewitz, J. C. *The Struggle for Palestine.* New York: Greenwood Press, 1968 (hardcover); Schocken Books, 1976 (paperback).

Isaacs, Stephen. *Jews and American Politics.* New York: Doubleday & Company, 1974.
Kolodziej, Edward A. *French International Policy under de Gaulle and Pompidou.* Ithaca, N.Y.: Cornell University Press, 1974.
Laqueur, Walter. *A History of Zionism.* New York: Holt, Rinehart and Winston, 1972.
Maull, Hans. "Oil and Influence: The Oil Weapon Examined." *Adelphi Papers,* no. 118. London: International Institute for Strategic Studies, 1975.
McPeak, Merrill A. "Israel: Borders and Security." *Foreign Affairs* 54 (April 1976): 426–43.
Mellah, F. "L'Attitude de l'Europe face à la crise pétrolière," *Chronique de Politique Etrangère* 27 (May 1974): 357–90.
Miller, L. B. *The Limits of Alliance: America, Europe, and the Middle East.* Jerusalem Papers on Peace Problems, no. 11. Jerusalem: Hebrew University of Jerusalem, 1974.
Pickles, Dorothy. "The Decline of Gaullist Foreign Policy." *International Affairs* 51 (April 1975): 220–35.
Quandt, William; Jabber, Fuad; and Lesch, Ann Mosely. *The Politics of Palestinian Nationalism.* Berkeley: University of California Press, 1973.
Rodinson, Maxime. *Israel: A Colonial Settler State?* New York: Pathfinder Press, 1974.
Sheehan, Edward R. F. "Step by Step in the Middle East." *Foreign Policy* 22 (Spring 1976): 3–70.
Silverberg, Robert. *If I Forget Thee O Jerusalem: American Jews and the State of Israel.* New York: William Morrow & Co., 1970.
Stookey, Robert W. *America and the Arab States: An Uneasy Encounter.* New York: John Wiley & Sons, 1975.
Sus, Ibrahim. "Western Europe and the October War." *Journal of Palestine Studies* 3 (Winter 1974): 65–83.
Ullman, Richard H. "After Rabat: Middle East Risks and American Roles." *Foreign Affairs* 53 (January 1975): 284–96.
———. "Alliance with Israel?" *Foreign Policy* 19 (Summer 1975): 18–33.
US Congress, Senate, Committee on Foreign Relations. *Activities of Nondiplomatic Representatives of Foreign Principals in the United States. Hearings.* Washington, D.C.: Government Printing Office, 1963.
Zeigler, Harmon. *Interest Groups in American Society.* Englewood Cliffs, N.J.: Prentice-Hall, 1964.

III. Oil and Politics in the Middle East

Abir, Mordechai. *Oil, Power and Politics: A Study in Contemporary International Relations.* London: Frank Cass, 1974.

Adelman, Irma, and Morris, Cynthia Taft. *Economic Growth and Social Equity in Developing Countries.* Stanford, Calif.: Stanford University Press, 1973.

Ajami, Fouad. "Between Cairo and Damascus: The Arab World and the New Stalemate," *Foreign Affairs* 54 (April 1976): 444–61.

Anthony, John Duke. *Arab States of the Lower Gulf: People, Politics, Petroleum.* New York: Middle East Institute, 1975.

———, ed. *The Middle East: Oil, Politics, and Development.* Washington: American Enterprise Institute for Public Policy, 1975.

Aruri, Naseer, ed. *Middle East Crucible: Studies on the Arab-Israeli War of October 1973.* Wilmette, Illinois: Medina University Press, 1975.

Becker, Abraham S.; Hansen, Bert; and Kerr, Malcolm. *The Economics and Politics of the Middle East.* New York: American Elsevier Publishing Co., 1975.

Bell, C. "The October Middle East War: A Case Study in Crisis Management during Detente." *International Affairs* 50 (October 1974): 531–43.

Bittar, S. al-. "The Implications of the October War for the Arab World." *Journal of Palestine Studies* 3 (1974): 34–45.

Chubin, Shahram, and Zabih, Sepehr. *The Foreign Relations of Iran.* Berkeley: University of California Press, 1974.

Evron, Yair. *The Demilitarization of Sinai.* Jerusalem Papers on Peace Problems, no. 11. Jerusalem: The Leonard Davis Institute for International Relations, 1975.

———. *The Middle East: Nations, Superpowers and Wars.* New York: Praeger Publishers, 1973.

Glassman, Jon. D. *Arms for the Arabs: The Soviet Union and War in the Middle East.* Baltimore: The Johns Hopkins University Press, 1976.

Gottheil, Fred M. "An Economic Assessment of the Military Burden in the Middle East: 1960–1980." *Journal of Conflict Resolution* 18 (September 1974): 502–13.

Halliday, Fred. *Arabia without Sultans: A Political Survey of Instability in the Arab World.* New York: Random House, 1975.

Handel, Michael I. *Israel's Political-Military Doctrine.* Cambridge,

Mass.: Harvard University Center for International Affairs, 1973.

Harkavy, Robert E. *The Arms Trade and International Systems.* Cambridge, Mass.: Ballinger Publishing Company, 1975.

Heikal, Mohamed. *The Road to Ramadan.* New York: Quadrangle/The New York Times Book Co., 1975.

Hershlag, Z. Y. *The Economic Structure of the Middle East.* Leiden: Brill, 1975.

Herzog, Chaim. *The War of Atonement.* Boston: Little, Brown and Company, 1975.

Horowitz, Dan. "The Israeli Concept of National Security." In *Dynamics of Conflict,* edited by Gabriel Sheffer. Atlantic Highlands, N.J.: Humanities Press, 1975.

Hurewitz, J. C. *Middle East Politics: The Military Dimension.* New York: Farrar, Straus & Giroux, 1974.

———. *The Persian Gulf: Prospects for Stability.* New York: The Foreign Policy Association Headline Series, 1974.

Iskandar, Marwan. *The Arab Oil Question.* Bayrut: Middle East Economic Consultants, 1974.

Itayim, Fuad. "Arab Oil: The Political Dimension." *Journal of Palestine Studies* 3 (Winter 1974): 59–73.

Jabber, Fuad. *Israel and Nuclear Weapons: Present Options and Future Strategies.* London: Chatto and Windus for the International Institute for Strategic Studies, 1971.

———. "Not by War Alone: Curbing the Arab-Israeli Arms Race." *The Middle East Journal* 28 (Summer 1974): 233–47.

Kennedy, Edward M. "The Persian Gulf: Arms Race or Arms Control?" *Foreign Affairs* 54 (October 1975): 14–35.

Kerr, Malcolm H., ed. *The Elusive Peace in the Middle East.* Albany: State University of New York Press, 1975.

Looney, Robert E. *The Economic Development of Iran: A Recent Survey with Projections to 1981.* New York: Praeger Publishers, 1973.

Luttwak, Edward, and Horowitz, Dan. *The Israeli Army.* New York: Harper & Row Publishers, 1975.

Mikdashi, Zuhayr. *The Community of Oil Exporting Countries: A Study in Governmental Cooperation.* Ithaca, N.Y.: Cornell University Press, 1972.

Park, Choan-ho, and Cohen, Jerome Alan. "The Politics of the Oil Weapon." *Foreign Policy* 20 (Fall 1975): 28–49.

Perlmutter, Amos. "Israel's Fourth War, October 1973: Political and Military Misperceptions." *Orbis* 19 (Summer 1975): 434–60.

Safran, Nadav. *From War to War.* Indianapolis: The Bobbs-Merrill Co., 1969.

Sayigh, Yusef A. "Arab Oil Policies: Self-Interest versus International Responsibility." *Journal of Palestine Studies* 4 (Spring 1975): 59–73.

Shihata, Ibrahim F. I. *The Case for the Arab Oil Embargo: A Legal Analysis of Arab Oil Measures.* Bayrut: Institute for Palestine Studies, 1975.

Tachau, Frank, ed. *Political Elites and Political Development in the Middle East.* Cambridge, Mass.: Schenkman Publishing Co., 1975.

Tahtinen, Dale R. *The Arab-Israeli Military Status in 1976.* Washington: American Enterprise Institute for Public Policy Research, 1976.

Tueni, G. "After October: Military Conflict and Political Change in the Middle East." *Journal of Palestine Studies* 3 (1974): 114–30.

US Government. *The International Transfer of Conventional Arms.* A Report to the Congress from the US Arms Control and Disarmament Agency. Washington, D.C.: Government Printing Office, 1974.

IV. Future Challenge

British-North America Committee. *Higher Oil Prices: Worldwide Financial Implications.* Washington and London, 1975.

Brzezinski, Zbigniew; Duchene, François; and Saeki, Kiichi. "Peace in an International Framework." *Foreign Policy* 19 (Summer 1975): 3–17.

Bundy, William P., ed. *The World Economic Crisis.* New York: W. W. Norton & Company for the Council on Foreign Relations, 1975.

Campbell, John C.; de Carmoy, Guy; and Kondo, Shinichi. *Energy: A Strategy for International Action.* New York: The Trilateral Commission, 1974.

Chenery, Hollis. "Restructuring the World Economy." *Foreign Affairs* 53 (January 1975): 242–63.

Clapp, Priscilla, and Halperin, Morton H., eds. *United States-Japanese Relations: The 1970s.* Cambridge, Mass.: Harvard University Press, 1974.

Committee for Economic Development. *International Economic Consequences of High-Priced Energy.* New York, 1975.

Connelly, Philip, and Perlman, Robert. *The Politics of Scarcity: Resource Conflicts in International Relations.* New York:

Oxford University Press for the Royal Institute of International Affairs, 1975.

Davignon, Etienne, "The New International Energy Agency of OECD." *OECD Observer,* no. 73 (January–February 1975): 20–25.

Development Assistance Committee. *Development Cooperation: 1975 Review.* A Report by the Chairman. Paris: *OECD,* 1975.

Elliot, Iain F. *The Soviet Energy Balance: Natural Gas, Other Fossil Fuels, and Alternative Power Sources.* New York: Praeger Publishers, 1974.

Enders, Thomas O. "OPEC and the Industrial Countries: The Next Ten Years." *Foreign Affairs* 53 (July 1975): 625–37.

Erb, Guy F., and Kallab, Valeriana, eds. *Beyond Dependency: The Developing World Speaks Out.* Washington, D.C.: Overseas Development Council, 1975.

Farman-Farmaian, K., et. al. "How Can the World Afford OPEC Oil?" *Foreign Affairs* 53 (January 1975): 201–22.

Freeman, S. David. *Energy: The New Era.* New York: Random House, 1974.

Fried, Edward R., and Schultze, Charles L., eds. *Higher Oil Prices and the World Economy: The Adjustment Problem.* Washington, D.C.: Brookings Institution, 1975.

Gardner, Richard N.; Ikita, Saburo; and Udink, B. J. *A Turning Point in North-South Economic Relations.* New York: The Trilateral Commission, 1974.

Hansen, Roger D., and the staff of the Overseas Development Council. *The U.S. and World Development: Agenda for Action, 1976.* New York: Praeger Publishers, 1976.

Hirasawa, Kazushige. "Japan's Emerging Foreign Policy." *Foreign Affairs* 54 (October 1975): 155–72.

Horelick, A. "The Soviet Union, the Middle East and the Evolving World Energy Situation." *Policy Science* 6 (March 1975): 41–48.

Issawi, Charles. *Oil, the Middle East and the World.* The Washington Papers, no. 4. New York: The Library Press for the Center for Strategic and International Studies, 1972.

Kaiser, Karl. "The Energy Problem and Alliance Systems: Europe." *Adelphi Papers,* no. 115. London: International Institute for Strategic Studies, 1975: 17-24.

Kohl, Wilfrid L. "The United States, Western Europe and the Energy Problem." *Journal of International Affairs* 30 (May 1976).

Lantzke, Ulf. "Die Internationale Energie-Agentur als Antwort auf die Energie-Krise," *Europa Archiv,* no. 10 (25 May 1974): 313-24.

Translated as "IEA: Answer to Energy Crisis." *The German Tribune: Economic Affairs Review,* no. 7 (1975): 1–6.

Low, Helen C., and Howe, James W. "Focus on the Fourth World." In *The U.S. and World Development: Agenda for Action, 1975.* New York: Praeger Publishers, 1975: 35–54.

Mabro, R., and Monroe, E. "Arab Wealth from Oil: Problems of Its Investment." *International Affairs* 50 (January 1974): 15-27.

MacKay, D. I., and MacKay, G. A. *The Political Economy of North Sea Oil.* London: Robertson, 1975.

Mazrui, Ali A. "Black Africa and the Arabs." *Foreign Affairs* 53 (July 1975): 725–42.

Morley, James William, ed. *Prologue to the Future: The United States and Japan in the Postindustrial Age.* Lexington, Mass.: D. C. Heath & Company for Japan Society, 1974.

Overholt, William H. "Japan's Emerging World Role." *Orbis* 19 (Summer 1975): 412–33.

Pfaltzgraff, Jr. Robert L. "The American-European-Japanese Relationship: Prospects for the Late 1970s." *Orbis* 19 (Fall 1975): 809–26.

Pollack, Gerald A. "Are the Oil-Payments Deficits Manageable?" *Essays in International Finance,* no. 111. Princeton: Princeton University International Finance Section, 1975.

Simonet, Henri. "Energy and the Future of Europe." *Foreign Affairs* 53 (April 1975): 450–63.

Tsunoda, Jun. "Japanese Security Problems and Perspectives in the Late 1970s," *Orbis* 19 (Fall 1975): 874–86.

Wakaizumi, Kei. "Japan's Dilemma: To Act or Not to Act." *Foreign Policy* 16 (Fall 1974): 30–47.

Waverman, Leonard. "Oil and the Distribution of International Power." *International Journal* 29 (1974): 619–35.

Willett, Thomas D. "The Oil-Transfer Problem and International Economic Stability," *Essays in International Finance,* no. 113. Princeton: Princeton University International Finance Section, 1975.

Williams, Maurice J. "The Aid Programs of the OPEC Countries." *Foreign Affairs* 54 (January 1976): 308-24.

Yergin, Daniel. "European Energy: A Policy Evolves." *European Community* no. 192 (January-February 1976): 30–36.

Index

For Product Safety Concerns and Information please contact our EU representative GPSR@taylorandfrancis.com Taylor & Francis Verlag GmbH, Kaufingerstraße 24, 80331 München, Germany

Batch number: 10726011

Printed by Printforce, the Netherlands